ROBERTA

ROBERTA

A MOST REMARKABLE FULBRIGHT

DOROTHY D. STUCK
NAN SNOW

The University of Arkansas Press

FAYETTEVILLE • 1997

01 00 99 98 97   5 4 3 2 1

Designed by Alice Gail Carter

♾ The paper used in this publication meets the minimum requirements
of the American National Standard for Permanence of Paper
for Printed Library Materials Z39.48-1984.

Frontispiece photograph courtesy of Suzanne Teasdale Zorn

*This project is supported in part by a grant from the Arkansas Humanities Council
and the National Endowment for the Humanities.*

LIBRARY OF CONGRESS
CATALOGING-IN-PUBLICATION DATA
Stuck, Dorothy D., 1921–
Roberta, a most remarkable Fulbright /
Dorothy D Stuck and Nan Snow.
p.   cm.
Includes bibliographical references and index.
ISBN 1-55728-460-1 (cloth : alk. paper)
1. Fulbright, Roberta Waugh, 1874–1953.
2. Women journalists—Arkansas—Biography.
I. Snow, Nan, 1936–   .   II. Title
PN4874.F76S78   1997
070'.92—dc20
[B]   96-31043
CIP

To the scores of Arkansas women

whose gifts of self and service have helped shape

Arkansas history

whose stories have never been told

ACKNOWLEDGMENTS

When we first undertook the project of writing about the life and work of Roberta Waugh Fulbright, some individuals expressed doubts that sufficient materials would be available to write her story in book form. After all, the contributions of women have largely been omitted from the records of Arkansas history.

We didn't feel that a lack of written records should deter us from the task. Ironically, we uncovered a treasure-trove of memories revealed through oral history interviews with family and friends. We also found a wealth of information in a first-person account of much of her life in Roberta's newspaper column, "As I See It," and a delightful recounting of the Fulbright ancestry and progeny, *A Fulbright Chronicle,* written by her grandson, Allan Gilbert. Gilbert's research of the Waugh, Stratton, and Fulbright families and his own personal experiences with his grandmother provided valuable insights and entertaining anecdotes.

For helping us uncover the details of the life of this truly remarkable woman, we are indebted to Roberta's son, the late Sen. J. William (Bill) Fulbright, who indulged us through several lengthy interview sessions, and to his wife, Harriet, who provided family photographs and other information. We are appreciative of the assistance the senator's former secretary, Mariam Southerland, provided in making interview arrangements and locating family members for us.

We also thank Roberta's grandchildren, Doug Douglas, Roberta Fulbright Foote, Allan Gilbert, Patty Fulbright Smith, Kenneth Teasdale, Betsey Fulbright Winnacker, and Suzanne Teasdale Zorn for sharing with us personal memories of their grandmother. Three other family members, nephew Richard Waugh, niece Margaret Waugh Crittenden, and cousin Martha Twichell, graciously provided recollections.

We are grateful to the late Ray Adams, Harry S. Ashmore, Judge Thomas Butt, Floyd Carl Jr., the late Morris Collier, Judge Maupin Cummings, Bill Dunklin, John Erickson, Lucy Freeman, Jean

Gordon, Sam Harris, Maude Gold Hawn, Marion Hays, Sam Hodges, Eloise King, Dr. Robert Leflar, Betty Lighton, Robert S. McCord, Cone Magie, Donald Murray, Willie Oates, the late Henryetta Peck, Bill Penix, Sam Schwieger, the late Connie Stuck, Ed and Liz Summers, Ruby Thomas, John M. Wallace, Bob Wimberly, and Jamie Jones Young, all of whom shared their memories of Fayetteville, Roberta Fulbright, and her family. While not all are quoted directly, the background and anecdotal material they provided has contributed much to our understanding of the character and personality of Roberta Fulbright and the surroundings in which she lived. We treasure the personal, and sometimes poignant, memories they shared.

We have devoted the better part of four years to researching and recording the life of Roberta Fulbright. Our search for authenticity often took us to Fayetteville, and we thank the residents there for their patient and helpful responses to our oft-repeated inquiries as to who knew Roberta and how they knew her. We owe a special thanks to Peg Anderson, who was diligent in locating people for us.

A debt of gratitude goes to the archivists and librarians who assisted us in hours of painstakingly slow research. We are particularly indebted to Betty Austin, Fulbright archivist in the Special Collections Division of the University of Arkansas Libraries in Fayetteville, who uncovered a wealth of original documents and published materials for us, often with little direction on our part.

For assisting us with research, we also thank Thomas (Pete) Jordan of the Washington County Historical Society; the staff members of the Arkansas History Commission; the genealogy staff of the Fayetteville Public Library; Sarah Weaver of the Friends of Keytesville (Missouri), Inc.; genealogist May (Bartee) Couch of Marceline, Missouri; staff members of the Missouri State Archives in the Office of the Secretary of State, Jefferson City, Missouri; Randy Roberts, senior manuscript specialist, Western Historical Manuscript Collection, Ellis Library, University of Missouri, Columbia; and staff members of the State Historical Society of Missouri, Columbia.

To the reviewers of our manuscript—Willard B. Gatewood, Mary Frances Hodges, Elizabeth Jacoway, Elly Peterson, Hoyt Purvis, and Katherine B. Rinehart—we express our gratitude. They uncovered errors we could no longer see, provided constructive criticism, and gave encouragement when it was needed. To Nan's husband, Ken Snow, we say thanks for photographic assistance and occasional chauffeuring, but most of all for his patience and understanding.

We wish to thank Miller Williams, director of the University of Arkansas Press, who expressed early interest in our manuscript and was the first to call us "authors." We are also indebted to the members of his staff, especially to managing editor Debbie Self for her keen eye, literary talent, and patient shepherding through the publication process; to marketing manager Beth Motherwell for her enthusiastic support and guidance; and to designer Alice Gail Carter for her perceptive artistic touch.

Despite our exhaustive research, there are, of course, some gaps in our knowledge about Roberta's ancestors and periods in her life, particularly her early years in Missouri. Rather than make assumptions, we have limited our narrative in those instances to events documented by archival materials or her own written recollections. Many of our favorite events and incidents come from her own words drawn from her columns.

We are convinced, after spending countless hours perusing her writing, that she could have told her own story better than anyone. Such was her considerable writing talent and her own astute observations about herself, including her strengths and weaknesses. Yet, she once wrote disparagingly of autobiographers: "The worst you can say about the autobiographers is that you frequently feel they have written about the wrong people." So perhaps it is best that her story be told by others, but wherever possible in her own words. And for those words, we are grateful.

It has been a rich and rewarding experience for us. Whatever insight into this remarkable woman's life emerges from these pages may be attributed in large part to her family and friends and the dedicated professionals who assisted us; whatever errors remain are strictly our own.

CONTENTS

PROLOGUE

Some memories fade like sepia prints. Others crystallize and their sharp edges cut through time with a clear image. My memory of the day Roberta Fulbright died is one of those.

It was Sunday. I was lost in thought as my husband, Howard, drove us across east Arkansas. We were on our way home from the 1953 midwinter Arkansas Press Association meeting. My mind was centered on the new duty I had taken on as president of the Arkansas Newspaper Women.

The radio news item shattered my reverie like a rock cracking glass: "Roberta Fulbright died at her home in Fayetteville today. She was the mother of Senator J. W. Fulbright and publisher of the *Northwest Arkansas Times* . . ."

The moment must have lodged itself in memory for several reasons. I had been thinking of this woman, with whom I had shared space and time only twice. The thoughts were in connection with my new duty, for I had felt the need to go to Fayetteville and visit with her; I wanted to get her ideas on how to strengthen the Arkansas Newspaper Women, which came into being because of her. I felt a great sense of loss, robbed of the chance for her ideas and support. As a fledgling editor and columnist, I wanted to know her better and now that could never be.

Next came the sobering thought that my first official responsibility would be to pay tribute to her in a communication to her senator son and other family members. It would not be an easy task for me because I did not know her well.

I met Roberta Fulbright in 1942. I was a student at the University of Arkansas and sat across from her at dinner. I was impressed by her wit and her warm personality, and I relished her keen interest in my opinions and those of my sister students about the war that had been declared recently. She saw the woman in every girl that night, and somehow we sensed it and grew in her presence.

Our only other contact came seven years later in June 1949. I was the wife of a newspaper publisher. His editor had quit. Until another could be hired, I was answering the phone and writing society news. For this reason, I received a letter from Roberta Fulbright. It invited me to a meeting to discuss founding a newspaper women's auxiliary to the Arkansas Press Association. I felt ineligible but was persuaded to attend as a show of support for the idea. Once again I was impressed by this woman's strong personality, her insight, and vision but especially her genuine interest in all of us. So, apparently, were the other twenty-four women who signed on that day as charter members of the Arkansas Newspaper Women. We wanted her to be our first president, but she declined. Our first official act after organizing was to make her honorary president for life. Now her life and her term had ended. I wrote our official condolence to Senator Fulbright. He answered and said he would stop by to see me the next time he was in east Arkansas. He did, and we became warm friends developing a mutual respect through shared causes.

But I did not get to know Roberta Fulbright until now. Bringing her to life, albeit literary life, has been a source of joy and fulfillment of a dream born the day she died.

—DOROTHY D. STUCK

ROBERTA

CHAPTER I

A Starting Place

Roberta Waugh Fulbright was a Virginian by heritage, a Missourian by birth, and an Arkansan by long tenure. This blending of three disparate cultures into a single personality would forever mark the character of this formidable woman through the passages of her life.

Yet it was her Missouri pioneer roots that left the strongest imprint upon her. The strength and perseverance shown by both of her grandmothers as they endured the hardships of the frontier made an indelible impression on Roberta.

At the peak of the great westward migration, in 1850, her paternal grandparents, Thomas Edward and Lucy Jones Waugh, a young couple of English ancestry, packed their belongings and left their farm home in Virginia in search of a new life in Missouri.

The hardest part of a long journey, it is often said, comes in the first few miles. For Lucy Waugh, the pain of leaving home was acute. As the heavily loaded wagons lumbered through the lush green valleys of Virginia, she looked longingly at the beauty of her native state, realizing, perhaps, that she would not see it again.

By the thousands, emigrants like Thomas Edward and Lucy Waugh left the routine of familiar surroundings for an uncharted and unpredictable future. By boat, wagon, and horseback, countless families trekked westward. Restlessly, relentlessly, they pushed this country's borders farther and farther west. News of gold in the Pacific west and promise of government land grants in the midwest lured easterners onto the frontier trails.

For many of these pioneers, Missouri was the jumping-off place for the long, dangerous trip to the Far West. For others, already weary from their journeys and anxious to settle down, Missouri became a stopping point, a place to stay and take root. The young Waughs had heard the news of unsettled farmland waiting for claim in Missouri. Under federal land-grant policies, a farmer could claim a piece of land, clear it, build a home, and then purchase his land at the minimum auction price after it was surveyed. This land-grant system, founded in the philosophy of absolute, individual property ownership, created the groundswell of westward movement.

For Thomas Edward Waugh the promise of his own land held a strong appeal. His forebears had settled in several counties in Virginia, yet he owned no land of his own. He left Virginia briefly to attend dental school in Baltimore. Upon his return he practiced dentistry and rented and farmed his mother's land. It was to his mother's farm at Waugh's Ferry that he took his bride, Lucy, to live following their marriage in 1848. A growing number of other Waugh family members had the same idea and also crowded into the old farmhouse. This provided the impetus for Thomas Edward and Lucy to make the risky decision to head west.

Like her husband, Lucy's father, M. L. Jones, a Baptist preacher, had never owned his own land. He rented a farm near Richmond from the time he was married until he died when Lucy was fourteen. His widow, Sophia Snead Jones, was the daughter of Robert Snead, a soldier who fought at Yorktown in the Revolutionary War. After her husband's death, she and her family lived for a time with relatives until she was able to buy a farm in Bedford County near Waugh's Ferry. In Bedford County, at an old-fashioned tent meeting, Lucy and Thomas Edward met.

Their desire for their own start in life and for their own land led them to begin the arduous trek to Missouri. Although Lucy and Thomas Edward made their decision to leave in the spring of 1850, their departure was delayed when Lucy's mother, Sophia, decided to join them, and it was necessary to sell her farm. When they finally departed by wagon several months later, the traveling party included the Waughs and their infant son, Sophia and her three other daughters, her sister Martha, the family slaves, and Thomas Edward's cousins, Tom and Mary Williams and their family.

Lucy left her native state with a deep feeling of sadness. "Not alone for the rocks and hills of my native land do I sigh, but for its noble, generous, kind-hearted, Christian men and women," she lamented later in her memoirs, *Twilight Memories*.

With wistfulness, the traveling party rode for one last time beneath the Natural Bridge of Virginia. When they reached the Ohio River, they switched from wagons to a steamer for the trip to St. Louis. There they boarded another steamer on the Missouri River, getting only as far as St. Charles before ice obstructed navigation.

While the group waited in St. Charles, Thomas Edward decided to go ahead in search of a new home. Traveling first by wagon and then by horseback, he found land at government price on the north side of the Missouri River in Chariton County in north central Missouri.

Thomas Edward Waugh did not choose this particular county by happenstance. Many Virginians who made their way across the continent to Missouri had already congregated in Howard and Chariton counties. "It was almost," said historian Ralph R. Rea, "as though a chunk of Virginia had been carved out and transported to a new western land." In fact, many of the new communities bore the names of Virginia towns and counties. This included Chariton County, although it was spelled Cheriton in Virginia.

After looking over the area, Thomas Edward returned to St. Charles for his family, but the trip to Chariton County was delayed for two weeks when he became ill with a cold. Finally, in the dead of winter, they started their journey in three wagons. "We had a rough, cold trip," said Lucy. They reached their new home on February 22, 1851.

Four days later another son, James Gilliam, was born to Thomas Edward and Lucy. Surely the wagon trip in raw winter weather must have been an ordeal for Lucy. As was characteristic of the women moving westward, she made no mention of her pregnancy in her memoirs. She simply announced the birth.

A few years after the Waughs made their move to Missouri, another Virginia couple, John and Julia Allen Stratton, arrived in Chariton County. The threat of Civil War, the promise of reasonably priced land, and the prospect of a new Virginia enclave had drawn them, too, to Missouri in 1856.

Also of English extraction, John Stratton traced his family to Wiltshire, England. His forebear, Edward Stratton, settled in Bermuda Hundred, Virginia, around 1640. His father, Maj. Peter Baugh Stratton—nicknamed "Fighting Peter"—served under Gen. George Washington in the Revolutionary War and later became a prosperous Virginia farmer, establishing a plantation called Red Oak. John and Julia Stratton were married in 1840 in Virginia and moved in 1856 to Missouri, where they settled outside Rothville on a farm which eventually encompassed four hundred acres.

For the genteel Virginians, their arrival in Missouri must have provoked images of the rough-and-tumble frontier. In the mid-1800s, Missouri was, in fact, part of the western frontier, a place in transition with literally thousands of travelers crossing its borders on their long journeys west. The Chariton County officials were trying to negotiate with the railroad to obtain tracks through the county to help alleviate the transportation problems.

Those who chose to stop in Missouri farmed the fertile land, built their houses, and raised their families. They relied on tobacco as their primary crop, as they had done in Virginia, but also planted wheat, oats, corn, and vegetable gardens and raised cattle, pigs, and chickens. Although nearby Brookfield had one store where provisions could be purchased, the farms provided almost everything these settlers needed.

Missouri's new settlers battled long, hard winters when cold north winds brought blowing snowstorms, followed by spring mud seasons filled with too much rain. In the summers they endured heat, hot winds, and drought—sometimes broken by torrential rains, dried fields, the scourge of grasshoppers, and crops so poor that they occasionally brought less than they cost to grow. While autumn brought cooler, more colorful days of harvest, the tinge of frost in the mornings brought the first signs that yet another bitter winter was about to begin.

All too often these hardy settlers fell prey to such illnesses as typhoid and malaria, treated only with calomel, castor oil, and quinine. "If that won't do, repeat the dose," was the only direction the doctor had to give.

Still they persevered, and each Sunday they paused to give thanks for what they had. The church became the place for solace, spiritual sustenance, and socializing. Two years after their arrival, the Waughs, along with Lucy's mother, sisters, and aunt, were among the founding members of the Yellow Creek Baptist Church in the town of Rothville. The church disbanded in 1862 as Civil War hostilities intensified, but it was reorganized as the Rothville Baptist Church in 1865.

Because the area was so sparsely settled, it was some time before local schools were established. Then, the nearest school "was two miles off and across two creeks," according to Lucy.

The Waughs and the Strattons took up government land on adjoining farms a mile north of Rothville. While northern Missouri bore little resemblance to the gentle hills and green foliage of Virginia, it did offer the untamed beauty of the wilderness and open country with gentle rolling plains which rose and fell in unending patterns. Most of the township was prairie land, with only about a third in timber. For the most part, the timber was concentrated in small groves and along the creek banks. In its own different way, it was breathtakingly beautiful with large horizons and unending skies. Just south of Rothville was a large lake inhabited by wild ducks, geese, and swans. Indeed, it was the government's aim, in providing land for claim, to bring this wilderness under cultivation.

"Like all new settlers, we found it hard to make any money for several years," Lucy Waugh wrote in her memoirs. Just as they began to get their farms in shape, the Civil War erupted, bringing upheaval to their lives. If they had come to Missouri in hopes of escaping the war, as many settlers had, they were soon to be tragically mistaken.

Missouri entered the Union in 1821, the second state following Louisiana to be carved out of the vast expanse of land acquired in the Louisiana Purchase. Under the terms worked out by the Missouri Compromise, the admission of Missouri as a slave state was balanced by the admission of a northern state, Maine, as a free state.

Despite its admission as a slave state, Missouri's settlers came from disparate backgrounds and regions, finding themselves with conflicting loyalties in their new communities. The state was home to both Union and Confederate sympathizers. Many of Missouri's new settlers, including the Virginians, brought their slaves with them; abolitionists expressed their outrage. The abolitionists and pro-slavery forces in Kansas and Missouri had been spilling blood for years. This volatility and Missouri's location as a border state made its residents especially susceptible to marauding Union troops and southern bands of bushwhackers. Historian Ralph R. Rea put it in perspective when he wrote of "this great forgotten class."

> Volumes have been written about the Civil War, dealing either with the Union or Confederate viewpoint, but little has been told of the countless thousands who stood between the opposing factions, with some very definite convictions on both sides. The majority of the inhabitants of Missouri and the Ozarks section of Arkansas were in this category. There were few Secessionists and still fewer Abolitionists in either place. In both, the preponderant sentiment was in favor of remaining in the Union; however, their opposition to what they considered coercion of the South was just as strong. The background of these people was southern, they having migrated west from Virginia, Tennessee or Kentucky; yet, few of them were slaveholders—practically none on a major scale. Their first reaction to the War was one of neutrality, which is a position they conscientiously sought to maintain. Circumstances soon forced them to take one side or the other in a war they did not want.

Lucy Waugh's vivid account of her own experiences during this period supports this thesis.

While no major Civil War battles were fought in Chariton County, it was the scene of a peculiar kind of guerrilla warfare. Former Missouri governor Sterling Price, who came from Keytesville, the county seat, wanted Missouri to maintain armed neutrality; the Union declared him a traitor. Later he led a group of southern settlers in joining the Confederate army. In 1864, bushwhackers burned the county courthouse and murdered the sheriff. This was the atmosphere of uncertainty and fear in which the Waughs and the Strattons tried to go about their daily lives.

Not far from Rothville, units of the Union army were quartered at Brookfield. Hostilities between army troops and bushwhackers soon involved the Waughs and Strattons, despite their best efforts to stay out of the fray. Both the Union troops and the roving outlaw bands appeared periodically to demand meals and supplies. As these encounters intensified, visits by the Union troops turned to harassment for these transplanted, slave-holding Virginians.

The frontier warfare was not the only problem. In March 1864, one of the Waughs' sons, Thomas Edward Jr., age nine, died of spinal meningitis. His death came with devastating swiftness. On the morning of March 23 he ate his breakfast as usual. Then later in the morning he complained of feeling ill. A doctor was summoned, but by two o'clock the following morning the boy was dead.

The family had little time to grieve. One evening four months later, more than forty Union troops came to the household to feed their horses and order supper, planning to spend the night. Bushwhackers fired over the head of their sentinel stationed by the front gate, while the Waughs could only stand by helplessly.

Frightened by the possibility of attack, the Union troops decided to return to Brookfield, taking Thomas Edward Waugh with them, forcing him to ride behind the soldier with the slowest horse. He was held prisoner in the Brookfield quarters.

One night several weeks later, Lucy Waugh and her children were awakened by loud knocking at their door.

"Who is there?" she called out, fearing the worst.

"Friends," came the reply.

When she opened the door, she found herself facing the muzzles of three guns. Reacting with a loud scream, she slammed the door and bolted it. Despite the threats of the intruders, she refused to open the door again until she was dressed.

When she did open the door to the three intruders, she saw many more men in the yard. The spokesman of the group asked if her name was Waugh, telling her the group was a body of Confederates from the northwest part of the state trying to join a company of Confederate troops. They had been told, he claimed, to come to her for directions to the encampment.

Already suspicious of this claim, and ever cautious, Lucy replied, "I can't be the person you were directed to for information, for I know nothing in the world about it."

"Are you a widow?" the man inquired. When she responded that her husband was a prisoner in Brookfield, the man cursed the Brookfield troops. Still, she remained cautious, professing no allegiance to either side.

Leaving her relieved but frightened by the experience, they moved on to the neighboring Stratton farm. There John Stratton, who took their word that they were Confederates, expressed sympathy for the southern cause. Summarily, he was taken a short distance from his home and shot to death.

Before they left, the marauders set fire to the Stratton home as the horrified family—including a young Martha (Pattie) Stratton—watched it burn. She and her sisters attempted to enter the house to retrieve some belongings but were turned away by the marauders. The identity of the marauding band was never established, although Lucy Waugh always believed they were Union troops from Brookfield.

This was not the only tragedy of the war for the Strattons. Two of the older sons, Peter and William, had joined the Confederate army. Peter was wounded during the battle at Corinth, Mississippi, and later died from the wounds. William was injured during the battle at Vicksburg, Mississippi, but survived. A third son, Archie, was charged, when he was fifteen, with bushwhacking a Union officer. His mother, Julia, smuggled tools to him while he was jailed at Brookfield, and he managed to escape and join the Confederate army. He, too, survived the war. With the pluck and courage characteristic of frontier women, Julia Stratton gathered the remainder of her family around her and kept them going.

Although Thomas Edward Waugh was released from Brookfield, he knew he was no longer safe. He fled to Texas. His family remained for a time on the farm but, realizing they, too, were in jeopardy, fled to the home of relatives in Illinois, where young James Gilliam Waugh, barely into his teens, and his brothers worked to help support the uprooted family. As soon as he could make his way safely, Thomas Edward joined them.

The family remained in Illinois until 1867, when they returned home to their Rothville farm. There they found that the railroad reached nearby Keytesville the same year. While Rothville had long been a farming settlement, the first business structure was not built until 1868. Other businesses soon followed, including a drugstore, general merchandise store, harness shop, blacksmith shop, wagon maker, and flouring mills. Officials filed the town plat in 1883. Thankful to be alive and back in Missouri, although the war had robbed them of most of their material goods, the Waughs worked hard to restore their farm, producing successful crops and acquiring livestock. Depression gripped much of the country following the Civil War, and money was in short supply. They borrowed money, at a high rate of interest, to get their new start, and that, said Lucy Waugh, was "injudicious."

In a letter addressed to the Honorable Louis Benecke, a politician, attorney, and bank director in Brunswick, Missouri, Thomas Edward wrote:

> Have you heard anything recently from our application for money. I would like to know more deffinitely [sic] about the matter. I would still like to get the money. You will please write to them and know something certain about it. Please attend to it and let me know positively whether the money can be had or not.

It is not known from whom Thomas Edward was seeking a loan nor whether or not he ever received the money. The likelihood is that he did not, for Lucy wrote later, "Pay-day came for us," and in 1876 the Waughs gave up their farm for property in Rothville. Thomas Edward ran for Chariton County clerk in 1878 on the local Greenbacker ticket, but lost.

Another family—whose name would be immortalized in children's literature—arrived in Chariton County in the summer of 1868. Charles and Caroline Ingalls, with young daughters Mary and Laura, came by covered wagon from Wisconsin. Charles Ingalls had bought land, sight unseen, two miles from Rothville on a tributary of Yellow Creek.

The Ingalls family arrived in August, too late in the year to plant crops; it was necessary to wait until the following spring. After only a year, they moved on to Kansas, making another home on the prairie. Laura Ingalls Wilder, who was only two years old when the family left, was too young to remember her time in Chariton County, but her books about her succeeding years on the frontier, including *The Little House on the Prairie,* provide a graphic account of this period's challenges and privations.

Records do not reflect whether the Ingalls family became acquainted with the Waughs and Strattons during their brief time in Chariton County. Donald Zochert, in his biography *Laura,* points out there were no roads, no houses, and no neighbors when the Ingalls family built their house. While the Ingalls moved on, the Strattons and Waughs remained. Despite the tragedy, turmoil, and aftereffects of the war, Rothville was now home to these pioneering families.

The Waughs were the parents of ten children; the Strattons, eleven. They were bound together by the boundaries of their adjoining farms, their Virginia heritage, and their shared experiences in Missouri. The families were united by the marriage of James Gilliam Waugh to Pattie Stratton in October 1871. Like their parents before them, they made their home on a farm.

James Waugh was a taciturn man, well accustomed to the rigors of farm life. His bride, Pattie, was born in 1849 in Virginia, shortly before her parents made the move to Missouri. She was a lovely young woman, regal in bearing, but not afraid to tackle the hard work of a farm home.

The Waughs' first child was a daughter, Roberta, born on Valentine's Day, February 14, 1874, in Rothville—the small, rural "sort of place," she would say many years later, "where the real aristocrats of America come from." She was named for her great-aunt Berta, a sister of Lucy Jones Waugh, one of those hardy pioneers in the group that made its way from Virginia. At the time of her birth, Roberta later recalled, her family "had a good many of the faults and virtues of the class who have good blood in their veins and no money in their bank account and a few nagging debts."

Life on the farm was hard, dictated by the vagaries of the weather. Her ancestors, Roberta said, "had been poor in Virginia and remained fairly so for years in Missouri." Her family used to refer often, she said, to the fact that they "came from Virginia" until a sort of unspoken slur was implied: "'Huh, they came because they got so poor, they could not stay.'" Still, she mused, she and her family had red plush furniture and marble-top tables in the front room, which was reserved for special occasions.

The Waughs continued to raise tobacco as their primary crop, but the corn they grew and the hogs they raised were sent on the main line to Chicago. The harsher weather in Missouri was not as favorable for growing tobacco as had been the more moderate Virginia climate, and as Roberta remembered, "altogether they did not get very rich." In addition to farming, Roberta's father, James, worked as a carpenter and builder.

"We used to, in private, take many a fling at the few richer persons among us. We would ridicule their thrift, their industry, and their stinginess," Roberta said in looking back on those early days. Mother Pattie, though, counseled Roberta early on that it wasn't only the rich who loved money; in fairness, she felt, the poor loved it, too, and sometimes only a lack of industry and a failure of frugality were all that separated the two. Whenever Roberta found herself criticizing those who surpassed her, she was often reminded of Pattie's words. "It seems to me," Roberta reminisced, "one of the good things she left me—just try to be fair. It's true, one never achieves it, but it's one of the things worth working for as long as one lives."

Roberta was soon joined in the fledgling family by brothers William Thomas, James Gilliam, and Charles Merriweather. A sister, Lucy, died in infancy, December 29, 1881, when Roberta was seven. Unfortunately, the death of an infant or child was still all too common in the 1880s. The January editions of the *Chariton Courier,* which reported the death of Lucy Waugh, also told of the death of another infant, as well as a fifteen-year-old boy; the accidental shooting deaths of two other children; and the drowning of one or two young people who were ice skating at nearby Columbia. If anyone doubted the perils of growing up on the frontier, the grim stories told a different tale.

Many daily tasks faced the Waugh household. During the cold, gray winter months, father James was up early splitting kindling and making fires in the kitchen and front-room stoves, while Pattie was breaking ice in the water bucket and chopping cold lard with a butcher knife or hammer to make hot biscuits for breakfast. The sounds of her parents' voices as they chatted while going about their chores remained throughout Roberta's lifetime as "the pleasantest of sounds."

Hog-killing time came in the winter, Roberta said. "We waited until it was good and cold, usually January." While she could describe in detail the steps taken, she hastened to add, "I never did it."

Coffee was ground in a mill on the wall. Bacon or ham—available from the most recent hog killing—and eggs, biscuits, and sorghum rounded out breakfast. "It was considered a necessary accomplishment for a young lady to know how to roast coffee in that day, and to let it burn was fatal," Roberta recalled. She and her mother baked pies, cakes, and bread for Saturday mealtimes. Then they cleaned and dressed some of the chickens they raised for Sunday dinner. "By the time we took a bite we had earned it," Roberta maintained. Quite simply, the farm provided what there was to eat.

As was the case with farm families of those days, six days of the week had clearly designated chores. Monday was washday; Tuesday, ironing; Wednesday, darning; Thursday, sewing; Friday, cleaning; and Saturday, baking. Household linens and clothing were "manufactured at home," as Roberta put it. "A bought pattern was a luxury."

The boys in the family—Tom, Jim, and Charles—handled the daily chore of milking the cows. After they poured the milk in barrels, it became Roberta's responsibility. "One of my vivid memories was when I let cream escape with the top off. Cream invaded the sacred precincts of kitchen and dining room." It also fell her lot to clean it up. Her after-school task was cleaning the smoked-up lamp chimneys for the seven or eight kerosene lamps in the household and filling them with fuel. Despite the chore, she said, "that was a step ahead of the tallow candle era of my grandparents." She regarded washing the dishes as a prize job because it seemed needed. "Washing the dishes had its fine points," she insisted.

Looking back at this way of life, Roberta mused that the value of hard work was lost when such chores became obsolete. On the coldest days of winter the men went outdoors to cut ice and packed it in sawdust in a little ice house on the side of a hill. "What a scarcity a chunk of ice was in August," Roberta said. "We at our house had a home-made refrigerator, no G.E. My father made it, it was good, and was two or three layers thick with a tin-lined box for ice."

"Summer," she said, brought "heat, flies, mosquitoes, malaria interspersed with typhoid fever." This was when the refrigerator became needed, "So we attempted to use our ice for the ill and special company." Although a nearby lake provided a lovely view from the family's front yard, it did contribute to the outbreaks of malaria and had to be drained.

While Roberta later lamented the loss of values that early farm life taught, she admitted she would not trade the days of the past for more modern luxuries like electricity and plumbing to which she had grown accustomed. When she was growing up, a bath on Saturday night was one of the real "outings" of the week. "The hard coal base-burner which gave us class in the upper 10 was aglow on Saturday night, preparatory to Sunday, and the wash tub brought in. A shawl draped over the chair behind the tub and ablutions were off to a start."

On Sunday, the family went to the Missionary Baptist Church, housed in a barn-shaped building with the town cemetery behind it. While the property belonged to the Baptists, they shared it with three other congregations—Methodist, Presbyterian, and Christian (Disciples of Christ)—each congregation holding services one Sunday each month. They did have a combined Sunday School and Christmas celebration. "We usually had four really A-One preachers instead of one mediocre," is the way Roberta saw it.

In addition to providing spiritual support, the church was the social center of the small community. "We went to church to sing, to get some conversation, and to visit our friends and to hear a sermon," Roberta said. At the same time, she pointed out, "the precepts laid down remain the basis of all character." "My mother," she once wrote, "qualifies in my memory as a real saint; my father as a more-than-average Christian."

Social life was limited to a few parties—taffy pulls, spelling bees, or cornhuskings. On special occasions there were games such as "charades" or "consequences." She admitted not being very adept at playing "follow the leader," perhaps an early indication that she felt leadership was her role in life.

Roberta always lamented how very scarce music was. But there were simple daily pleasures such as "gates to hang on, stile blocks to be mounted, or lanes to walk along," she remembered years later. "Altogether, with very little spending, we lived romantically and pleasantly."

Roberta's first recollection of people getting from place to place was on horseback. Children rode behind their parents, just as they slept in a trundle bed at the foot of the big bed and ate at the second table. "Children came in second in those days," she wrote.

While Roberta's parents were settled happily in Missouri, other family members still felt the pioneer longing to move farther on the frontier. "My earliest memory," she recalled, "was seeing my uncles set out for the West in two-horse covered wagons, beds and all camping equipment." The beds were made of straw tick; the food for the long, arduous journey was limited to potatoes, apples, flour, sugar, and perhaps a slab of home-cured bacon. These supplies would last about a month; after that the travelers were on their own. For Roberta and the others who remained behind, one letter a month could be expected. It all seemed romantic to her at the time, "but I do not seem to have any later record of a ranch or farm in the far west as a result," she acknowledged.

The lumber wagon was also a means of family transportation, and the better ones had a spring-seat in front. There was also the spring wagon deluxe—Roberta called it a luxury liner—a light, two-seated, two-horse rig. Then came one-horse and two-horse buggies, much favored by all, though few in the community could afford one.

"Since I was a child," Roberta wrote much later, "the dirt roads, dust and bumps in summer, ice and clods in winter and mud and slush the rest of the time are vivid memories." She spoke often about the clime and conditions. "We grew fine grains, grasses, fruits and men, but I'll tell you when you've struggled with Missouri mud and climate it puts fight and win in your blood."

The sole doctor for the community was Pattie Waugh's brother, Dr. Charles Stratton. He rode horseback on his rounds and carried a miniature drugstore in his saddlebags. Often he found himself sicker than those he visited. When he returned home, he sent a bill and hoped for the best.

Following the Civil War, Missouri fell prey to the robberies of the notorious outlaw gangs led by Cole Younger and Jesse and Frank James. In 1866, in Liberty, Missouri, just over eighty miles from Rothville, the James gang committed the first daylight bank robbery. Some sixteen years later, when Roberta was eight years old, her father went into business for a time with his brother William in Brookfield. It was there that Roberta witnessed the escape on horseback of bandits who had committed a daring daytime robbery. Standing outside in the yard, she heard a frantic neighbor call out, "robbers," and she watched as six of them went dashing by, shooting at random, right and left. As she stood frozen, watching in horror and fascination, one of the shots hit a house near her. After that day, she often stopped and checked the bullet hole. Fifty-seven years later she wrote, "I bet I could find it now." From that day on, whenever she saw men on horseback, her blood ran cold.

The robbery that she recounted came on the heels of the heyday of the James and Younger gangs. Near the time that Roberta witnessed the Brookfield robbery, Jesse James was killed by a member of his own gang who sought to collect a ten-thousand-dollar reward. While she did not attribute the Brookfield robbery to these infamous gangs, Missourians of that time were acutely aware of the dangers of those bold, daylight robberies.

Weddings brought joy and celebration to the harsh realities of farm life. One of Roberta's earliest recollections was of going to a double wedding where her father held her up over the crowd so she could see the couples as the vows were said. But food more than romance caught her youthful attention. She remembered vividly the wedding table laden with tiered wedding cakes and butter molded in the form of a cow. She could not recall ever getting a taste of those delicacies, saying later, "Somehow I think we must have gone home before my turn came. That is, I think if I had ever eaten that cake I would remember it."

The wedding of her uncle, Dr. Charles Stratton, and his bride, Mattie Hutcheson, also made quite an impression on the young Roberta because she and her family arrived in style in a hired, double-seated barouche. As she described it, "This vehicle had two seats, a top, fenders, and a low step which impressed me as most elegant."

Roberta's father rented the barouche and team of horses from the livery stable for the twenty-mile round trip at a cost of $3.50, a large-sized dent in the family budget. The trip took two hours each way, but was well worth it for the grandeur. Roberta, herself, felt grand in a peacock blue dress and a straw hat with blue ribbons on it. The arrival of the barouche did not cause the only stir. The groom—delayed by his medical rounds—arrived late for the cere-mony, creating additional excitement in the crowd.

Roberta often said that her mother bequeathed to her the finest memories of her life. "I grew up in about the most peaceful era this country has seen," Roberta said. "My mother, who suffered endlessly during the Civil War (misnamed)[,] often said to me, 'My dear, so long as we can have peace nothing else matters.'" Still, Roberta admired the beauty her mother saw in everything, her willingness to share meager resources, and her sense of fairness, as well as her sense of the proper values in life.

Pattie Stratton Waugh "had the Englishman's self-respect," her daughter recalled, "but not a trace of vanity or conceit." She had delicate features, fine soft hair, and fair skin. "Her eyes," Roberta marveled, "were the blue of heaven's azure." While Roberta thought her beautiful, it was her mind and heart that made the larger impression. "She was gentle, soft-voiced, very pleasing to know, but unassuming." Life was hard for Pattie—the farm work was difficult, with never-ending chores—but her daughter "never caught a gleam from her that life was not gloriously worth living."

Roberta's fascination with Christmas began as a child when, she said, "I used to hold my breath . . . to see if papa went to town on Christmas Eve. He usually did. Christmas in those days was simple, but just as thrilling." "Gifts were small," she added, "but they made Christmas." Her mother, Roberta said, "had the passion for it and bequeathed it to me."

While the family had very little money, "We did have 'time' and appetite," she pronounced. Despite the meager resources, it was a happy childhood for Roberta. She enjoyed living among her many kinfolks and the local townspeople. Years later she would still remember pleasant Saturdays visiting the local general store run by the "nicest Virginia gentleman who taught me to wrap a package." She had other memories, too:

> I remember picking wild greens at the corner of the rail fence on the main and only street in the village where I grew up . . . I remember my grandmother and her flowers and how I got my first love of gardens . . . I remember riding behind my mother on horseback to see her mother and she let me slide down and pick wild strawberries and then climb back up from the rail fence . . . I remember the tobacco hanging in the open tobacco barns at my grandmother's . . . I remember how as youngsters we were forever chewing gum from the cherry trees and peach trees and even the resin weed and sometimes harness wax.

As the eldest of the Waugh children, Roberta was called "Sis" by all in the family. She was endowed with a sense of self-confidence, instilled in her by her mother, and as she grew into young womanhood, she gained a reputation for being talented and bright. "I loved to stand up and spell down," she said. "Geometry and evolution were not my fields." Like so many students of her time she remembered fondly the "Blue Back Speller which holds a place in our education system second to Webster's Dictionary."

The young Roberta enjoyed what social life there was: "We played tennis, rode horseback and in carriages. We hugged our beaus and went to church. Protracted meetings were the rule in

August after the corn was laid by, and the dust was good and deep. We went far and near (two or three miles)."

She learned to play the piano and the organ. With the arrival of a new organ at the community church, she became the organist for the four congregations sharing the church. This necessitated displacing the tuning fork man who had given the congregations the proper pitch for singing hymns when no accompaniment was available. While Roberta realized the man's disappointment at being replaced, she nevertheless was not hesitant in accepting the new job that the acquisition of the church organ brought. "I also recall the tuning fork operator getting up and leaving the auditorium when I played 'All Hail the Power of Jesus Name' but it does not seem to have been too serious," she said. "I was at best mediocre," she admitted, "but the best they had."

When she was sixteen, Roberta got her first teaching job. "I went to be examined for a county certificate to teach in Chariton County . . . I made my best grade in Civil Government . . ." She was rated as qualified to teach. As she remembered it: "I tried my prowess at a summer school of two months about three miles from home. I furnished my own car and gas in the form of an old black nag, and saddled her myself and swept out the school house to boot. For this distinguished service I received $30 per month for two months." Roberta was particularly apprehensive about the school director's sons, whom she described as big bullies. "I was really scared," she admitted, "but got through okay." Her take-charge personality had its effect.

Even though times were hard, the education of their children was important to Pattie and James Waugh. At some financial sacrifice, they sent Roberta away to high school, an event which would always stand out in Roberta's mind as a sacrifice for her, too. "I remember freezing my ears still when I drove with my father to high school in Kansas City and when I got in they hurt unbelievably. I bawled and they went out and got snow and put on them and they swelled up; got double in size and purple."

Pattie saw to it that Roberta spent two years at the nearby University of Missouri in Columbia, a rarity for young women in those days. The two years of college study, required for a teaching certificate in Missouri, would always be in her mind one of the most exciting times of her life. "Always, in the recesses of my mind I wished for more," she said. "I had never seen anything so ideal as the University and its environs appeared to this little country girl from North Missouri when she landed in Columbia," she marveled. "I was charmed." "I was from the country, and full of self-confidence (not a bad heritage) as I look back," she said years later. "All of the experiences of the campus were almost atomic to me." She was a good student who took advantage of the social and cultural activities that college life afforded.

Already outgoing and gregarious, she came to the attention of Kappa Kappa Gamma sorority, the only national women's sorority on campus at the time.

> It was small and inexpensive but the material taken was good (if I may say).
> . . . The Kappas had a room for meeting and their snob-bishness seemed rather stupendous and ludicrous to me and I said no. Before Christmas they asked me if I would ask my mother during holidays and see about the money which I am not sure if it were $5 or $10—five I think.

She did join Kappa Kappa Gamma, and it was an affiliation which remained important to her throughout her lifetime. More than fifty years later she would write, "I've never done them any good, but they boosted my ego for a half-century and more—and it's worth a lot."

She had another life-shaping experience while in college. Like most students, she was suffering a bout of homesickness when she decided to attend an evening meeting of the Athenian Society to hear journalist Walter Williams speak. Williams was a journalist of international stature, president of the Missouri Press Association when he was twenty-one, founder of Missouri's school of journalism, and a significant influence on Missouri politics, education, and journalism throughout a long career.

When Roberta heard him speak, he was on the staff of the *Columbia Herald*. A fine orator as well as journalist, he instilled in the young woman a lifelong love of journalism.

Little did Roberta know, as she sat captivated by the lecture (all homesickness forgotten), that the impression of a single evening would play a telling role in her life.

Following her two years at Columbia, she taught again in a country school. This time the school was farther from home, and she again rode horseback. Young women of that day, in order to be "ritzy" she said, rode side-saddle, dressed in a long skirt and habit, which, she acknowledged, "made it almost impossible to get off in style." So, for her trips back and forth to school she dispensed with style and dressed warmly and comfortably.

"The same old nag," from her previous teaching stint, "furnished transportation, but that was all okay and I got $35 per month for three months. I often wonder if I was worth the money. In this job it was winter term and I managed the fires also. At least I can't recall anybody else doing it, so I must have been janitor as well as teacher."

Now she had taught school, as she said later, "in two of the smallest and poorest paying districts in Missouri." She was a country schoolteacher with no thought of making journalism her career. But she would not put aside the inspiration Walter Williams provided.

CHAPTER II

The Farmer Takes a Wife

William Fulbright eagerly anticipated the journey into Brookfield as he hitched his favorite horse to a two-wheeled cart. A Rothville farmer and stockman, Old Bill, as he was known to family and friends, fancied himself quite a horseman. On this fine day he would take his wife, Ida, on a twenty-mile round trip so she could do some shopping, and he might just find some time to visit his favorite saloon. No doubt the thought of it spurred him on, and he set out in a gallop, with Ida holding on to the cart as best she could. They arrived in a rush, their trail of dust catching up with them as they came to a stop in town.

As Ida began her shopping, Old Bill made his way to the saloon, a favorite spot for the local farmers to gather awhile and talk about the condition of their crops, the latest tobacco prices, and the muddy roads. Naturally this conversation called for lunch and a little beer to go with it. Old Bill enjoyed these occasional forays into town to swap stories with his friends and to share with pride his latest accomplishments as a horseman. On this particular day, his mind preoccupied with the stories he had heard and the ones he had told, Old Bill left the saloon, retrieved his horse and cart, and headed home. When he arrived at the farm, anxious to relay the day's news to Ida, he realized she was not at home. He had left her back in town. There was nothing to do but turn around and head back immediately. He couldn't take time to change horses or he would suffer the embarrassment of his wife knowing she had been forgotten.

Back in Brookfield, with great aplomb, he gathered up Ida and her purchases and once again, with his horse in a gallop, headed back home. When the horse, cart, and two riders reached the side yard by the house, the horse stopped for a moment, as if to consider the ignominy of it all, and promptly fell dead. What Old Bill told Ida about this turn of events was never recorded for posterity. Neither is it known how this event may have affected his reputation as a fine horseman. This story, whether true or apocryphal, remained for years a favorite of Roberta Waugh's family who lived in the same community.

Old Bill and Ida Fulbright, like the Waughs and the Strattons, came to Missouri to farm the land. But, unlike their neighbors, they came not from Virginia, but from Green County, Indiana, and they came at the close of the Civil War.

Old Bill traced his ancestry to his great-grandfather, Johan Vilhelm Volbrect, who came to America in the mid-1700s from an area near Berlin, Germany. In America, the family name became Fulbright, perhaps because of an error by officials admitting them to the country or as the result of a decision by family members, themselves, who believed they needed a name more easily spelled and pronounced in their adopted homeland.

While Johan settled in Dutch Cove, Pennsylvania, and other early family members also settled in the east, each succeeding generation of farmers moved gradually westward. Grateful for their new start in America, their patriotism was evident in the naming of male offsprings who were assigned such names as George Washington Fulbright and Andrew Jackson Fulbright.

Old Bill's patriotism was manifested in the two tours he served as a cavalryman in the Union army during the Civil War. In 1861, he served three months with the Indiana Volunteers and was discharged as scheduled. As the war dragged on, he again served with the volunteers and was discharged following the war's end in the summer of 1865. A carpenter at the time the war broke out, he later turned to farming.

A son, Jay, was born to Bill and Ida Fulbright a year after the end of the Civil War, on September 11, 1866, in Rothville. A daughter, Zoe, followed. Some family charts show that Jay and Zoe were the only children in the family. Other charts indicate that two other children were born to Bill and Ida. If so, they did not live to maturity.

Like Roberta Waugh, Jay Fulbright knew the hardships of farm life. His father, a stern, impatient taskmaster, schooled him in the rigors of farm chores. Young Jay decided that while farming might be necessary to give him a start, he would not make it his life's work. Business would be his forte. A year's study at the academy in Chillicothe, Missouri, gave him the jump start he needed to make good on that promise to himself. He also had an ally in his mother. Just as Pattie Waugh made sure that Roberta went to college, Ida Fulbright saw to it that her son spent a year at the University of Missouri.

As a young man, Jay, along with most of the community, found pleasure in attending the Friday night gatherings at the town hall at Rothville. There an old-fashioned debating society debated issues of the day. This was followed by poetry recitations and a tableau. One Friday night Jay, who participated in theater productions at the University of Missouri, selected Roberta to be in a tableau with him. Although the two had not met, he obviously was impressed by the bright, confident young woman who unabashedly participated in the evening debates. "He sent into the audience for me to come to the stage," she recalled. "In this scene the woman was chopping wood and the man was sitting by in ease . . . that was humor in those days." Thus, a courtship began.

In those days Christmas was the true test of a courtship. "If you did not receive a gift from your friend, you could guess that there was nothing to it," Roberta declared. Her courtship with Jay passed the test when he gave her a book, a "proper gift." Surely Jay—eight years Roberta's senior—saw in the young Roberta the sparks of intelligence and ambition which she had displayed early on. He also saw in her a kindred spirit and an ideal helpmate for the kind of life he sought.

One of Roberta's girlhood memories was of accompanying her aunt to see the trousseau of a young bride. "She and her love had been sweethearts from childhood and it fired my imagination and kindled romantic thoughts in my brain," Roberta confessed. And Jay Fulbright, full of self-confidence and daring, rekindled these thoughts as their courtship began from that evening's meeting.

Like the example of her parents and the young lovers she admired, the courtship of Roberta Waugh and Jay Fulbright was a small-town romance. Jay was employed for a time in construction work for the Atchison, Topeka, and Santa Fe Railroad, but he was already on the lookout for business opportunities. His determination to make something of himself and to rise above the probable poverty a farm life would bring appealed to a young woman of Roberta's intellect.

College educated and talented, Roberta was well regarded in Rothville and, as such, was seen as a good catch for Jay. A perky, pleasant-looking young woman, she had a direct and confident manner. She learned, however, that despite his obvious interest in her, Jay would hold his own in their relationship. Once, during a buggy ride, the young couple got into an argument. Exasperated by Roberta's willingness to argue with him, Jay stopped the buggy and insisted she get out and walk.

"One thing he was thorough about was work," she said. "He knew its worth, its meaning, and how it was done and no teensy-weensy job would pass with him for work," she wrote. "His mind worked in as straight a line as anyone I've ever known."

Their marriage, October 30, 1894, again united local families just as the marriage of Roberta's parents had done. Despite her recollections of the lovely wedding dresses worn by the brides of her childhood memories, and her own early ideas of having a similar wedding dress, Roberta was married "in a tweed traveling suit with stiff white collar and cuffs—and the collar almost cut my throat." Practicality already ruled the day for the young Fulbrights. Roberta's uncle Richard Stratton, a local minister, performed the ceremony.

Looking back on life with Jay, Roberta said, "He always expected the limit of me. He even gave me Milton's *Paradise Lost* as a Christmas gift before we were married and the Bible as a wedding gift. He knew little of either one, but it seemed fitting to him that I should know." Her husband, she pointed out, "had the old-fashioned idea that the woman should be religious." Even in their early years he called her "Old Woman" or "Old Lady," terms of endearment to his way of thinking.

He was a mild-mannered, yet exacting, man with occasional bursts of fiery temper usually punctuated with fierce expressions of "gol-durn-it," "gad," or "dad-swipe-it," his idea of profanity. He possessed an athletic build, a winning smile, a calm self-assurance, and a countenance which reflected his singular determination to succeed.

Roberta, too, possessed an air of self-assurance. Of average height, solidly built, with fine, dark hair usually worn pinned up on her head, her open face and direct gaze revealed even then the intensity with which she would live her life. Her face followed closely the almost square shape of her father's face, and she habitually tilted it to the left. She had a prominent nose, and the thin lines of her mouth seemed always about to smile.

"The biggest pick anyone ever makes is in a mate and upon selecting the best depends one's fate in life," she declared, and she never regretted the pick she made.

"While Jay expected much of me, almost beyond measure, I never had cause to doubt for one minute his loyalty and devotion, and knew always I was wanted," Roberta would write later. He sold a weekly newspaper, which he owned and operated in Blairstown, Missouri, to come home and get married.

Despite their dreams and ambition, the young couple began married life on a thousand-acre farm near the towns of Rothville and Sumner. Old Bill and Ida Fulbright gave the young couple the farm—with a mortgage on it. At the time they married, Roberta was teaching school but she returned to farm work gladly. She enjoyed the challenges and rewards of farm life, remembering with fondness her years of growing up on a farm.

However, she would muse later, she gained an appreciation of what it took just to get butter on the table. "When I first married I was afraid the milking, skimming, souring, churning and so forth were going to be my Waterloo," to say nothing of the hog killing, smoking of the meat, soap making, and putting up ice. Jay, she said, "was a farmer par excellence, and to my mind that is the occupation of all occupations."

Through hard work the young couple soon paid off the mortgage. "We didn't even drink coffee for the first few years, but later gave in on that," she admitted. "We had no cocktails, no toddies, although the elders sometimes indulged. But we were blazing a trail—our trail."

Their first child, a daughter whom they named Frances Lucile (and called Lucile), was born September 26, 1895. Two years after moving to the farm, Jay had accumulated enough capital to buy the Sumner Exchange Bank of Chariton County in the small town of Sumner, a bank on the verge of failure. "Old Woman," he told Roberta, "I bought the bank." He also acquired part interest in a small general store. This necessitated that they move to town, a move Roberta viewed with regret.

"I cried over it and over the farm," she said, "but very soon we had moved to the little town in the coldest, roughest road season you could imagine."

These roads were a rough buggy ride for a young mother. Jay read with interest of the development of the horseless carriage and vowed he would have one. This was about the same time the first telephones were being installed in town. As Roberta recalled, "Jay said, 'I won't have one of those things; they're no good.' Well, with his progressive mind it took about three months to prove to him that they were a convenience and we soon had one."

They continued to get about in a horse and buggy for several more years. Then, as Roberta told it, "At last an Oldsmobile came to Brookfield, Mo., owned by a banker friend of ours. It was steered with a lever, had high wheels like a buggy, was cranked with a crank, and Jay went up to inspect it. It did not quite measure up to his ideas so we did not get one until some time later."

When they moved to Sumner, Jay and Roberta rented a small two-story house only a few blocks from the bank. For the most part now they were town dwellers, although they kept the farm for several more years.

The family grew quickly. A second child, Anna Waugh, was born March 17, 1898. Despite the demands of motherhood, Roberta was soon "working as a regular hand in the bank. I nursed the baby until 10 [o'clock] and went down and stayed until noon, went home, nursed the baby and stayed about an hour and back to the bank. The bank prospered, the babies also."

The bank did, indeed, prosper, and it attained a rating as one of the strongest banks in the area. Surely her work schedule was not conventional behavior for women of the late 1800s, but to Roberta, who never shied away from hard work, and to Jay, who was anxious to provide the best for his growing family, it was the only way to get ahead.

Roberta did take one break from the routine when she and several friends decided to make the trip to Columbia for home-coming at the university. According to their well-laid plans, the group would catch an evening excursion train on the Wabash, arrive in time to spend the day at the university, and return home, all for a two-dollar round-trip ticket.

Jay did not favor the trip, according to Roberta, but she and her friends were determined. The plans did not go well:

> (We) sat up all night in a dingy old railroad station by a coal stove, waiting for that dinky little train which was eight hours late. We even had plenty of time to go home for breakfast, but I was afraid my husband would jostle me and talk me out of the trip. So, sometime in the forenoon we boarded that train and arrived in Columbia shortly after noon supposedly for the day.

By that time some of her exuberance for the event had cooled, and she saw herself as disheveled and dowdy. The group found that the campus and faces had changed from their memories of it:

> We finally found one family we had known there, and when they had sorted us out, they were glad to see us. By that time the train was leaving for home.

She did return again for happy times on the campus, but for the immediate future she turned her attention to family. And the family did continue to grow. Now two sons were added: Jay Jr. (called Jack), born September 2, 1899, and James William (called Bill), born April 9, 1905. To accommodate the growing family, Jay and Roberta made two more moves in Sumner before settling in a house on the town's main street.

Jay did not limit his business activities to the bank and store. He acquired and sold land in Kansas and the Oklahoma territory; he sold wood to meat packers, including Armour, Swift, and

Cudahy. His father-in-law, James Waugh, in addition to his farming, became an officer in the Sumner bank and loaned money to Jay for the purchase of the Kansas land.

By 1906, Jay was looking for other business ventures. Concerned about educational opportunities for his children in the small community and weary of the harsh northern Missouri winters when roads were frequently impassable, he decided that the best opportunities lay in the fertile Mississippi River delta. He thought that Memphis, Tennessee, situated in the heart of the delta, would have a key role to play in the economic development of the area. He decided to look into it. From the sale of the bank and the ranch land in western Kansas, Roberta said later, "we mustered cash enough" to make the move.

Jay's parents, Bill and Ida, had already left Missouri ahead of the younger Fulbright family, following their retirement from farming. They settled near Fayetteville, Arkansas, where the winters were not as severe. After their first winter in Arkansas, the elder Fulbrights, Roberta said, "bought a little place by spring. They just had to touch the soil again."

Separation from her family, especially her beloved mother, was painful for Roberta. She had spoken in favor of another location in Missouri.

> I had put up a big plea to move to Columbia, Mo., where both Jay and I had been to school, just long enough to tell it, and I was bewitched with it, but "no"—A new field was to be sought—A place to do Business, in which role Jay did not consider Boone County, Missouri and Columbia qualified. Without aim we came, without aim we remained tho in our sub-conscious we had aimed for Memphis, Tenn.

The younger Fulbrights went first to Fayetteville. Situated near the borders of Missouri and the Oklahoma territory, Fayetteville occupied a strategic spot in the Ozarks, a mountain range highlighted by its rocky fault-topped hills and knobs, its lush green cover, and meandering creeks rising from abundant springs.

The land that was cleared, although rocky and hard, yielded timber and stone, as well as good farm and pasture lands. The soil, derived from the weathering of the rocky hills, provided the county's agricultural crops: fruit, grains, and truck vegetables. There was also an abundance of poultry and dairy and beef cattle.

Apples were the most successful crop at the turn of the century, and Washington County, where Fayetteville was situated, was home to a thriving apple industry. Grapes, peaches, and strawberries provided secondary crops. Three train lines dispatched these products to markets beyond the local area. Canning factories processed tomatoes and beans, and cold storage facilities were built to store the produce for shipping.

When the young Fulbright family arrived in Fayetteville, 80 percent of the county's population lived on farms, and county schools didn't open each year until the crops were laid-by. Fayetteville was the center of this thriving economy, also capitalizing on its surrounding natural resources, including clay, timber, stone, wool, and hides.

As with many southern towns, the town square served as the heart of retail activity. A new courthouse, built in 1904 on College Avenue just off the square, provided a striking symbol of civic progress. The railroad depot, which was a beehive of comings and goings, was the town's social center. It was not uncommon for the town's citizenry to visit the depot just to see who was coming and going. The year the Fulbrights came to town the grand, new Washington Hotel was built at the corner of Block Avenue and West Mountain Street on the square. Roberta also took note of the livery stables; there were no cars. At the Washington County Fairgrounds a race track was being graded.

"In truth, College Avenue was where quality resided in those days," Roberta later noted. "Their horses, carriages, housing and attire were quite impressive to a girl who had just come from the Truman state where the mule was our insignia and where style was mostly in the minds of the natives who knew they were well born and high type and from Virginia and all that, but were not much to look at."

As the county seat, Fayetteville was the political and business center of a 958-square-mile agricultural area. The town was also home to the University of Arkansas, a land-grant college. The presence of the university was a source of pride to area residents who raised funds for its location in Fayetteville through a one-hundred-thousand-dollar county bond issue, a thirty-thousand-dollar city contribution, and some individual donations of land. Founded in 1871, the school enrolled its first students in January 1872. By 1910, the town had a population of almost five thousand, of which nine hundred were University of Arkansas students and teachers. To the Fulbrights, having come from the small town of Sumner, Missouri, Fayetteville must have seemed a large and bustling place.

"It was in strawberry time when we came and lettuce time and greens and everything good," Roberta remembered, "so in a few days we just from the cold of north Missouri winter had to purchase a plot of ground and a house."

Because Jay thought the summer weather in Fayetteville would be more hospitable for his young family than the delta region, he bought at auction a two-story house outside of town, west of the university. It would be a comfortable place for them to stay while he went on to Memphis to check out opportunities there.

While the younger Fulbrights were settling in, Bill and Ida soon returned to Missouri. Old Bill not only fancied himself a good horseman, but a good trader as well. "My father-in-law," Roberta related years later, "a trader of note in the old days in Missouri[,] said—'I could hold my own in Missouri, but I'll be damned if I can in Arkansas.'"

The house, known as the Haskell Place, which Jay bought, was built around 1900 as a "summer place" by Oklahoma's first governor, Charles N. Haskell of Muskogee. "I think a political seed must have fallen round abouts," Roberta said. The house, with its double living room and abundance of porches, suited the needs of the family and soon became a social center for friends and extended family. In fact, the home became a gathering place for any and all who dropped by, a pattern which continued throughout Roberta's life. Possessed with an easy charm and ebullient nature, she naturally drew people to her.

Seeing his family well settled, Jay went on to Memphis and invested in real estate there, but he remained only temporarily. The attractions of family and opportunity in Fayetteville drew him back to the Arkansas town.

Just as he did in Missouri, Jay bought into a bank in Fayetteville. It was to be the beginning of a new life for the Fulbrights.

CHAPTER III

The Mountaintop

Roberta thrived on her new life in Fayetteville. Although Jay set his sights on business, the family was not completely divorced from the farm life she loved so much. The Haskell Place, with its eighty acres, was located on a hill above the fairgrounds. No sooner had they moved in than the dust from the grading of the race track "whirled and swirled upon our front porch," complained Roberta. She must have thought she had simply exchanged Missouri mud for Arkansas dust.

Still, the new homeplace provided ample land for growing a large garden and raising cows, horses, pigs, and chickens and was a good place for Lucile, Anna, Jack, and Bill to combine outdoor amusements with farm chores.

The family especially enjoyed picnics at nearby Cato Springs; occasionally they would ride in a carriage to the White River to camp for the weekend. At night they would lay a baited line across the river, and the next morning they would take the fish they caught from these lines and cook them for breakfast. It was the kind of self-sufficient family activity which reminded Roberta of her early years in Missouri.

Just as Roberta was thriving in this atmosphere, so was Jay. A forceful, resolute man, he projected a calm and dignified demeanor, accentuated by his business suit, starched white shirt, bow tie, and jaunty hat. To his children, and increasingly to his new community, he created an image as a no-nonsense father figure.

He continued to speculate in real estate and profited from his purchase of a section of land in Kansas. He also had holdings in Oklahoma, Texas, Missouri, and Tennessee. Still, he used banking as his base. He became a major stockholder in two Fayetteville banks, Citizens and Arkansas National, and served as president of the latter. He also acquired stock in several banks in small communities surrounding Fayetteville, including the banks of Winslow, Elkins, St. Paul, and Citizens Bank of Pettigrew.

Because of his farm background, he was especially astute in judging the merit of farm loans. Once, however, he personally made good on a bad loan he had recommended, although he had no legal obligation to do so.

In addition to banking, real estate, and timberland, he continued to expand his business interests. Gradually, his holdings came to include Fulbright Wholesale Grocery Company, Ozark Poultry and Egg Company, Crystal Ice Company, Fayetteville Mercantile Company, Phipps Lumber Company, the Washington Hotel, and the Democrat Publishing and Printing Company. For a brief time, he invested in a real estate and insurance business, J. C. Mitchell and Company. He also held stock in the Fayetteville Lumber and Cement Company and the H. C. Bone Stave Company of Stilwell, Oklahoma. Another of his purchases, in 1916, was a small railway line, the Combs, Cass, and Eastern Railroad. Built in 1915 as the Black Mountain and Eastern Railroad over twenty-nine curving, mountainous miles from the Frisco branch at Combs in Madison County to Cass in Franklin County, the railroad moved hardwood timber harvested from land which Jay owned in the Cass area.

Always ambitious, self-reliant, and never afraid to take a risk, Jay possessed a knack for figures and an innate business shrewdness. He was adept at identifying firms with financial or management difficulties, taking them over, and restoring them to financial soundness, just as he had done with the bank in Sumner.

While he was often unfamiliar with the nature of the businesses he acquired, he never considered that a drawback. A good judge of character and talent, he developed a pattern of selecting invest-ment partners or managers who were knowledgeable in the areas needed. After giving early attention to the details of the business and setting it on a successful course, he would turn daily opera-tional responsibilities over to them. It was a pattern which proved to work well.

One of his managers was Roberta's brother, Tom, who managed the Crystal Ice Company, an ice delivery company. Tom, five years younger than Roberta, moved to Fayetteville after meeting and marrying Josephine Droke, Jay and Roberta's neighbor. Jay sold Tom an interest in the ice company, and Tom was soon encouraging him to purchase a local Coca-Cola franchise for the princely sum of fifty-five hundred dollars. It turned out to be one of the family's most successful ventures, although few had a vision then of Coca-Cola's coming popularity.

The ice company also produced Fulbright's Ice Cream. An advertisement in the local newspaper, the *Daily Democrat*, promoted the ice cream's "delicacy of flavor" by stressing the "absolute cleanliness" of the ice cream factory. "Scarcely any woman's kitchen receives the scrupulous care and eternal vigilance we give to our factory," proclaimed the Fulbright ad.

Not all of Jay's ventures were as profitable as the ice and bottling company. An investment in a zinc mine near Joplin, Missouri, lost money, and Phipps Lumber, though it remained in the family for many years, was never a big moneymaker. Jay bought the controlling interest in Phipps in 1920. Located on the periphery of the University of Arkansas, Phipps produced fine-textured hardwood wagon parts, primarily for the Springfield Wagon Company. It was the largest plant of its kind west of the Mississippi River and one of the largest hardwood operations in the country. Reflecting later on the company, Roberta said, ". . . we have struggled with making money from Phipps Lumber Co., but we got it after nearly everybody in the territory had cars and did not care for wagons."

Jay did not linger over losses, always looking ahead to new projects, an entrepreneur in the truest sense. Where others saw possible loss, he saw potential opportunities. His boldness "pushed the Fulbrights' fortunes to an estimable point," one observer said.

He was one of five men who formed a partnership to develop the poultry industry in northwest Arkansas. M. L. Price had come to Fayetteville representing Aaron Poultry and Egg Company, a subsidiary of Armour and Company. He set up shop in the old mill building next to the wholesale grocery company operated by Jay Fulbright and Frank Gray. When the Aaron Company left in 1915, the new partnership organized its own company with Jay

Fulbright as president. Price, who remained in Fayetteville, became vice president.

"My husband built the first big poultry barn," remembered Roberta, ". . . he had the vision of this area as a big locality for poultry." Once again he proved prophetic as the northwest Arkansas area would later become a leading poultry producer.

Jay did not involve himself in politics; instead, he exerted his increasing influence on Fayetteville and Washington County through his powerful and expanding business interests. He was involved, however, in civic activities. He was an organizer of the chamber of commerce, charter member of the Rotary Club, and served as president of the Washington County Fair Association for thirteen years. Roberta remembered that the first appearance of an airplane in Fayetteville was at the County Fair in October 1911. Jay, she said, "paid a huge sum (for the day and time) for a 15-minute flight." The Pusher biplane, piloted by Glen Martin, was shipped in by railroad and assembled at the fairgrounds.

Jay also worked to locate the five-state Western Methodist Assembly on Mount Sequoyah in Fayetteville. When Roberta later looked back on that action, she observed:

> We were in on the founding. My husband, in fact, the heads of the three banks at that time—J. R. Harris, J. H. McIlroy and Jay Fulbright—had the vision and headed the project, as I recall. W. S. Campbell tells me we presented $35,000 cash, purchased all [of the] top of East Mountain, 80 acres, and Happy Hollow Farm, 320 acres.
>
> We owned the top of that mountain [Mount Sequoyah] when the Assembly was put across. My husband was committed to the idea that if we launched the Methodist[s] up here in Northwest Arkansas, we would have the University. In those days we had a fight each Legislature to keep the University. I have often wondered why he did not salvage a place for a cabin for himself. The same could be said for West Mountain or Haskell Hill, but building the town and anchoring the University were prime objects in his mind.

Jay Fulbright "had a hand in all manner of things," Judge Thomas Butt would remember years later. He helped obtain the land for the Veterans Administration Hospital and served as the president of a group that encouraged the development of the first golf course in northwest Arkansas.

He promoted the benefits of both aviation and tourism to the area and chaired the city sewer and water commission, always promoting a city water treatment and distribution system, something which did not come to fruition until after his death. He made available to the city the land where the water plant was later located and, wrote family chronicler Allan Gilbert, "he reaped public criticism, as a profit-hungry banker for his vision in the matter."

A proponent of a series of small dams on the nearby river, he continually promoted the need for an ample water supply. To Roberta he would say, in his characteristically straightforward way, "I tell you, old woman, I want everybody to have plenty of water in Fayetteville." He also believed that water revenue would help to finance the city.

Looking back on his efforts, years later, Roberta would say:

> The City water system and the streets claimed his attention in the same degree. I hope I am pardoned when I call to mind his excellences for he really had them. I suspected it always, but at this vantage point I know it and am more convinced each year.

He helped the University of Arkansas acquire its first gymnasium. When Francis A. Schmidt became the director of athletics in 1922, he wanted to organize a basketball team for the 1923 season. But the university had no gymnasium. Working with Schmidt, Jay led a group of businessmen in arranging for a wooden structure which had served as an automobile showroom and garage to be moved to the campus to serve as the gymnasium. It was located just north of the site where the university's Fine Arts Center was later built.

Described charitably by some as an old garage, it housed—in addition to a basketball floor—an office, an equipment room, and a dressing room. This makeshift gymnasium was used until a field house was built in 1937. By this time called "Schmidt's barn," the structure was sold and moved to the grounds of Fayetteville High

School. (Today it still stands as a cabin retreat for the Thurlby family on Big Piney Creek near Russellville, Arkansas.) During these busy years for Jay, Roberta was not involved in the businesses on a daily basis as she had been when she worked at the bank in Sumner. However, she did like to keep up with Jay's ever-expanding business interests. She was fully occupied with her growing family and church, club, and social activities.

She was an active member of the Christian Church (Disciples of Christ), an association which she maintained throughout her years in Fayetteville. "I was brought up to the close [*sic*] communion and immersion of the Missionary Baptist Church," she said, "but I married a member of the Christian Church and that shattered me a bit."

"To him," she observed, "close [*sic*] communion was the unpardonable sin. Well, I combatted the idea about 10 years, and then to please my husband whom I really thought too wonderful, when we moved to Arkansas I went with him to the Christian Church and was content. Nothing was said, I just moved in." It was Roberta, then, who became the ever-active churchgoer, teaching a Sunday School class for many years. Jay, she wryly remarked, "used to often say, regarding church, 'I'll send a hand.'" That hand was Roberta.

For Roberta and Jay, the move to Fayetteville had given them a contented, comfortable life, and with the four children—Lucile, Anna, Jack, and Bill—they settled into a familiar routine. This routine was soon to be altered. Thinking their family was complete, Jay and Roberta were about to be doubly surprised.

On April 2, 1911, Roberta gave birth to twin daughters—Helen Stratton and Roberta (Bo) Epperson. She was thirty-seven years old and now the mother of six children. At the time of the births, Roberta was also suffering from abscesses of both knees. Jay, sympathetic to his wife's ordeal, said he had never felt so sorry for anybody in his life. Family members, including Jay's mother, Ida, and one of Roberta's cousins, came from Missouri for a time to help out the burgeoning family. Those who expected Roberta's comings and goings to be curtailed were soon mistaken. "Roberta's pattern of social and civic activities were scarcely disturbed by the advent of the twins," wrote Allan Gilbert. "Jay, for his part, was tolerant of Roberta's interests."

The now larger family moved in 1912 to a house on Hill Street in an area just south of the University of Arkansas campus, known variously as Putnam Heights and Professor's Hill, since several university professors resided there.

As the prospect of world war appeared on the horizon, it cast a pall on life in Fayetteville as it did elsewhere. As World War I approached, Roberta got a lesson in grabbing your chance while you can. Jay sent away to a jewelry company for an assortment of lapel pins so that Roberta could select one she wanted. Trying to be economical and not knowing what was ahead with the war closing in, Roberta said righteously, "I don't want one, [I] don't think it right to buy pins when there is a war." Abiding by his wife's wishes, Jay sent the pins back with this report. The amazed jewelers said to him, "You should have your wife's sanity looked into."

"I think they were right," she was forced to acknowledge years later. "I never got the chance again, and it was a plain error from every angle."

The war did bring sacrifice to life in Fayetteville. Citizens busied themselves with Red Cross drives and sales of war stamps, while the *Daily Democrat's* bulletin board was changed hourly to reflect the casualty reports from the battles in France and Belgium. By 1918, troops were quartered and trained at the university. For young Bill Fulbright the memories of those days remained vivid:

> At the university, a student training corps was organized and the students began training with rifles and bayonets. Banners and posters urging us on to victory were all over the campus and there were frequent meetings and demonstrations. I, of course, was too young to understand the war. All I could understand was that war involved the entire nation and had a great effect even on the lives of the ordinary people.

As if the war were not enough, the influenza epidemic which was sweeping the country took seven thousand lives in Arkansas, more than three times the number of Arkansans killed in the war.

The epidemic struck Fayetteville with full force in October 1918, closing schools and other public facilities and suspending classes at the university. It subsided in early November, but in a brief time, it claimed the lives of local residents, students, and soldiers alike. So, it was with great rejoicing that Fayetteville celebrated Armistice Day, November 11, 1918, when the citizenry, the student training corps, and army personnel gathered on the square for a patriotic celebration. They were confident that good times lay ahead.

The Fulbright family had moved again at the outbreak of World War I, this time to 5 Mont Nord. The name Mont Nord, the French equivalent of North Mountain where the house was located, had been given to the street to assign it the appropriate elegance. Located on a wooded hillside north of the town square, this short street was the site of some of the most impressive residences in northwest Arkansas, among them the house that Jay Fulbright bought.

Built shortly after the turn of the century by J. E. Mock, the house was a stately, two-story red brick Classical Revival home with a façade of six white Greek columns, an impressive mountaintop view of downtown Fayetteville, the university campus, and the surrounding Boston Mountain range of the Ozarks, and blessedly for summer, a good breeze. With the lot's upward slope, rising from Mont Nord street to the front entryway, the house was an impressive and imposing sight. Over the years, it became the gathering place for local dignitaries, including university professors and their wives. "It was kind of a social club," Bill Fulbright mused.

Roberta was in her element. She savored the give and take of brisk discussion and the forays into philosophy. Jay, too, enjoyed "good literature, good lectures, and good living." But, of the two, Roberta was the sociable one. As for Jay, she was all he needed.

The house, with its study and formal living and dining rooms, was well suited for entertaining. Dark walnut paneling and a symmetrical double staircase to the second floor, illuminated by a spectacular peacock etched in a stained-glass window on the landing wall, added to a feeling of elegance for these gatherings.

Upstairs there were four bedrooms and a large sleeping porch.

The impressive front entrance, with its stately columns, veranda, and upstairs balcony, was used only by visitors and then only occasionally. Family members came and went by the side door and spent their family time together in the study or in the sunroom which Jay added. With its casual wicker furniture, the sunroom lent itself to informal gatherings and conversation. Family members regularly ate their meals in the combination kitchen-breakfast room, saving the large dining room, with its impressive Austrian dining table, for parties and special dinners. Roberta's piano was housed in the living room.★

Roberta had little time for domestic duties. Although she was regarded as a good cook, she was seen as "slap-dash" in the kitchen, always in a hurry to move on to something else. Thus, the family employed a cook, Omy Buchanon, to prepare the meals. The Fulbrights' oldest daughter, Lucile, often assumed the role of mother hen, assigning kitchen duties to the other siblings. The preparation of duty lists and assignment of errands was sometimes a point of contention between Lucile and brother Jack, occasions which sister Anna referred to as "tough times in the kitchen."

While Roberta was not a stern disciplinarian and was tolerant of the whims of the children, Jay took a sterner view. Once when Roberta's extended family joined them for dinner, two of her young nephews decided they did not want to eat the cream gravy served with the meal. This drew a reprimand from their Uncle Jay.

Everyone took a turn at entertaining the young twins, Helen and Bo. Once Anna and cousin Margaret Waugh Crittenden decided that the best way to keep the lively twins quiet was to "play church." They designated Helen and Bo to be the choir members, thinking this would bring some discipline to their behavior. Undaunted, the two youngsters whispered and talked their way through the "services."

It was at Mont Nord that Roberta's passion for gardening

★ The house later featured an Italian marble mantelpiece, originally given to J. H. Stirman, a Fayetteville retail merchant, by the well-known merchant prince of America—A. T. Stewart of Alexander-Turney-Stewart and Company. The mantelpiece came to Fayetteville by way of ocean, the Gulf of Mexico, river to Van Buren, Arkansas, and then overland on the final leg of the journey. After the deaths of the Stirman family, the mantelpiece was purchased by Phil McGuire and installed in his house on West Dickson Street. It was later purchased by the Fulbright family.

gained fruition. She was always happiest when working or strolling in her backyard garden, which she described as "a lovesome thing." Others described it as the most beautiful garden in northwest Arkansas. "Plant a tree, an iris, or a hollyhock, it will return you more interest than anything I know of," she once said. While the backyard garden claimed much of her time, the front lawn, with its upward slope from the street, garnered little of her attention.

To Roberta, family, friends, and gardens made life complete, but her idyllic existence was marred by the death on January 8, 1918, of her beloved mother, Pattie, who suffered from heart problems. Her mother had been a strong, positive force in her life, and Roberta deeply felt the loss. Pattie Stratton Waugh, who had suffered the indignities of the Civil War, saw her father taken away and murdered, lost a young child, and endured the hardships of pioneer life, was a model of strength and dignity to her daughter.

Her mother, Roberta wrote years later, "bequeathed to me the finest memories of my life . . . She possessed a love of beauty, though she had little. She would always say something like this on my birthday after I had left her. 'My child, I wish I had something beautiful to send you.' She always had the beautiful wishes . . . To me, she fulfilled the role of mother to the utmost. Never while she lived did I not crave a conversation with her. Never did I tire of being with her. Her memory is enshrined in my heart today and every day."

For a long time the family had two pale yellow horses called Tom and Bird who were teamed to the carriage when the family went to Sunday School. There was frequent debate between Lucile and Jack as to who would drive the buggy. Finally, Jay kept the promise he had made to himself in Missouri. He purchased a two-cylinder, chain-driven Reo, with a crank on the side. At the time, the Fulbrights were one of only a handful of families in Fayetteville who owned a car; they were the first to have a five-passenger car. (Three Ford coupes preceded it, according to Roberta.) "Our biggest escapade," she said, "was when we came to town with visitors and left the crank out on the hill. We had to call Jack and he caught a horse and brought us the crank."

The roads didn't keep pace with the car. While the Reo was described as a touring car, its tours were brief. Roberta wrote: "We used to struggle down the hill to the Federal cemetery to run up and down a block or two of good road there, then to the fairground to go round and round the track, but we have been car addicts ever since. They have absorbed much of our income."

Once Lucile took the family car out for a drive. The car, which had an air starter, stalled. To restart it, the car had to be cranked, a task Lucile was not prepared to perform. So she left the car where it stopped. The result: a frozen engine and ruined blocks.

The children were growing up and beginning to go their own ways. The four older children—Lucile, Anna, Jack, and Bill—had known the hard, early years in Missouri, and were now enjoying the more prosperous times, although Jay was insistent that the boys, particularly, learn the value of hard work—which they did in the various family businesses. The young twins came along too late to know the more difficult early days, and they reveled in the good times at Mont Nord.

Lucile attended the University of Missouri and the University of Arkansas where she pledged Zeta Tau Alpha sorority. She was the oldest child and the first to marry. On June 5, 1920, she married Dr. Allan A. Gilbert, a physician who received his medical training at Washington University in St. Louis. The wedding was held at the First Christian Church in Fayetteville with the groom's father, Rev. H. M. Gilbert, officiating.

Anna was her sister's maid of honor and also designed the floral arrangements, featuring a succession of floral arches along the aisle. (Surely this talent for flowers, now passed on to her daughter, pleased gardener Roberta.) "It was," according to the *Daily Democrat,* "one of the most beautiful and impressive weddings ever occurring in Fayetteville." Jay and Roberta hosted the wedding reception at Mont Nord.

The newlyweds soon built a home across from the Fulbrights. When it came time to decorate it, Lucile ventured across the street to her mother's house and helped herself to some of Roberta's pictures. If she ever missed them, Roberta didn't let on. She was pleased to have the young couple living so close to her. In addition to "sharing" pictures, Lucile also shared her mother's love of gardening, and the two could continue to indulge themselves in that hobby together.

Anna enrolled at the University of Missouri where, like her mother, she pledged Kappa Kappa Gamma sorority. After finishing college, she taught in Fayetteville and then went to Morehead, Kentucky, where she taught in a high school operated by the Christian Church for children of Appalachian miners.

On June 25, 1921, Anna married Kenneth Teasdale, a St. Louis attorney, whom she met while both were students at Missouri. The wedding was performed at Mont Nord under the stairway arch. The bride's ten-year-old twin sisters, Helen and Bo, were the only attendants, coming down the double stairway sprinkling flower blossoms in the bride's path. About one hundred and fifty guests, invited informally, witnessed the ceremony and joined in the reception and buffet.

The Teasdales made their home in St. Louis. Anna, like her mother, was a well-read, well-informed lover of discussions and a delightful storyteller. She was interested in everything and everybody.

Helen and Bo were now the two girls left at home, still enjoying their status as the youngest and fending off the teasing of their brother Bill, who, also still at home, thought they were bedeviling him.

At Anna's wedding reception, the two girls were given the assignment of tending the youngsters at the wedding whom they took upstairs to the third-floor attic to get them out from underfoot of the grownups. There, young cousin Richard Campbell (Dick) Waugh discovered—stored away and long-forgotten—a candied apple, which he promptly ate, followed by some rich, dark chocolate. Not surprisingly, he became violently ill. It was, he remembered years later, his only unpleasant visit to Mont Nord.

Jay and Roberta's older son Jack, a good athlete, wanted to play college football. He enrolled first at the University of Arkansas, then at the University of Missouri, and finally at Harvard, where he found "his teammates didn't like people who weren't

Harvard-bred, especially wild men from the west," his brother Bill later said. Jack was incorrigible, his sister Anna once declared.

Bill, in the meantime, began elementary school at the Laboratory School in Peabody Hall on the University of Arkansas campus and continued through high school on the campus, a fifteen-minute walk from home. Parents Jay and Roberta, perhaps because of their own educational experiences, were much in favor of education for their children. During his high school years, they gave Bill a choice. He could attend summer school or help out with the family businesses. Mindful of the hot, dirty work at the feed company, lumber company, or ice plant, he always decided on summer school.

These summer school credits enabled him to enter the University of Arkansas at age sixteen. There he played tennis and football, becoming as a seventeen-year-old sophomore, a campus hero in the 1922 homecoming game when he was responsible for the game's only points—a touchdown and a field goal—to clinch a victory over conference rival Southern Methodist University.

These busy and fruitful years for the Fulbright family did not portend events to come.

CHAPTER IV

"Me and Men"

"We came in with apples, cider, dirt roads, grapes," Roberta once said when describing the Fulbright family's arrival in Fayetteville. "While the apples, cider and grapes remained staples in the area for many years, the dirt roads finally gave way to paving."

By the decade of the 1920s, Fayetteville boasted several miles of paved roads, a welcome addition for the Fulbrights and their automobile. The streets around the square were paved, an event celebrated with bands and street dancing.

Jay Fulbright's timber interests, along with Phipps Lumber Company and his other businesses, were providing employment opportunities in the community. Despite the new paved roads, the family ice company was hiring workers to deliver ice by mule team. Agriculture continued to dominate the local economy. Washington County was the leading wheat producer in the state and boasted the largest acreage of strawberries. The canning and poultry plants in the area were doing well.

Two of Roberta's brothers—Tom and Jim Waugh—had joined the Fulbright family in Fayetteville and were working in the family business enterprises. Her youngest brother, Charles, who attended the University of Arkansas for a year, had returned to Rothville to follow the family farming tradition.

It was in this decade that Roberta made her first, but short-lived venture into politics. In 1919, Congress passed the Nineteenth Amendment giving women the right to vote, and in June of that year Arkansas became the twelfth state in the union to ratify it. In 1920, the amendment was adopted. After eighty-four years of statehood, Arkansas women were granted the right to vote, even though they had first been permitted to vote in the state's party primaries in 1917. On the heels of this landmark event, Roberta ran for the local school board as a candidate backed by the League of Women Voters. She was defeated 298-174 by Art Lewis, president of the First National Bank. Roberta attributed her defeat to the fact that few women had yet paid the poll tax required for voting in Arkansas. If she were disappointed by her defeat, she gave no indication of it.

When the University of Arkansas celebrated its fiftieth anniversary in 1922, the Fulbright home was chosen as the place for Gov. T. C. McRae to stay while in Fayetteville for the celebration, undoubtedly providing official recognition of the standing of Jay and Roberta Fulbright in the community. Perhaps it was hoped, too, that the Fulbrights would exercise their powers of persuasion on Governor McRae, who, that same year, proposed that the state purchase Camp Pike near North Little Rock from the U.S. Department of War and establish an agricultural and mechanical college. Needless to say, such a proposal did not meet with favor by the Fulbrights or Fayetteville.

The selection of the Fulbrights to host the governor was somewhat ironic in light of the distrust University of Arkansas president John C. Futrall felt for the press in general and, in particular, the *Fayetteville Daily Democrat,* partly owned by Jay Fulbright. However, this small business matter never affected the close friendship of the Fulbrights and the Futralls.

The university assigned no overall, coordinated public relations responsibility on campus for the semicentennial event, recalled Robert Leflar, later the distinguished dean of the Law School. The *Daily Democrat,* which planned a special edition for the occasion, wrote to several university department heads seeking material. Futrall, concerned about what the individual responses might bring, then asked the department heads to clear everything with the publicity office before its release. Leflar, at that time a student assistant in the public relations office, prepared news releases for the event. The *Daily Democrat* got the material for its special edition.

While the decade of the 1920s offered a promising start in Fayetteville, it brought an abrupt change of fortune for the Fulbright family. In 1922, Roberta's brother Tom died suddenly of coronary thrombosis. He was forty-three years old. Tom had purchased a share of the successful Coca-Cola franchise, and he managed the ice company of which the bottling company was a part. He was also a stockholder in the Fayetteville Mercantile Company. As such, he was a vital part of Jay's business enterprises. He and his wife, Josephine, had two sons, Richard Campbell and Thomas Droke. His death was a severe blow to the entire family.

Then, in July 1923, Roberta and Jay, who was suffering the effects of a lingering infection, traveled to Keytesville, Missouri, to be at the bedside of his ailing mother, Ida. (His father, Bill, died several years earlier in California.) When they returned home from the trip, Jay went to bed suffering from a high fever. Shortly after their return to Fayetteville, his eighty-two-year-old mother died. He was unable to return to Missouri for her funeral.

While Jay had never been seriously ill, he had for the previous year been experiencing some medical problems, including high blood pressure and bad teeth. He made trips to medical facilities in Battle Creek, Michigan, and to Barnes Hospital in St. Louis seeking treatment, but had not benefited.

Morris Collier recalled one earlier occasion in 1921 when Jay Fulbright was ill—suffering from a cold and congestion. Young Collier, who made deliveries for his father's Red Cross Drugstore, was sent to Mont Nord to deliver a liquid compound. It was dark when he left the drugstore and, unable to see well, he wrecked his bicycle, spilling the aromatic compound all over himself. Because of the strong aroma which then engulfed Collier, another delivery person had to be sent to deliver the needed medicine to the Fulbright home.

The illness Jay suffered on his return home from Missouri was much more serious than his 1921 illness and worsened rapidly. Two physicians—a neurologist and an internist—came by train from St. Louis to treat him. On Saturday, July 21, he lost consciousness, and on Sunday, his condition reached a crisis. The attending physicians held out little hope for his recovery. But later that same evening there was a slight change for the better; Roberta could at least hope.

However, this respite was brief. On Monday, July 23, Jay died quietly at 11:55 A.M. at Mont Nord. He had been critically ill fifty-six hours and confined to his home less than a week. He had visited town for the last time on the previous Tuesday.

His physicians attributed the high blood pressure and internal complications as direct causes of his death. Roberta would always believe that perhaps infection, caused by his bad teeth, was a contributing factor. He was fifty-six years old; Roberta was a widow at age forty-nine. She was—suddenly and shockingly—without the husband who had been not only her love, but also her anchor and guide. Since her late teens he had been her hero. Now she was bereft of his companionship and counsel. It was a loss which would remain with her for the rest of her life, and she never ceased to sing his praises.

Jay Fulbright's funeral was scheduled for 5 P.M. the following day, July 24, at Mont Nord. While Roberta and her family suffered from the shock of his death, so did the city of Fayetteville. The bank which Jay served as president—Arkansas National—closed at noon Monday immediately after learning of his death; the city's other banks closed the next day at noon. All businesses with which he was associated were closed throughout the day of his funeral. Many other businesses closed during the funeral hours, and the courthouse offices closed in tribute. Jay's *Daily Democrat,* an evening newspaper, went to press early, at midday.

A meeting of the city council scheduled for that night was postponed in an act of respect for its chairman of the city water commission. The Rotary Club, of which Jay was a charter member, canceled its weekly meeting. The Lions Club passed resolutions expressing appreciation for his work and sorrow at his passing. At least one social gathering—a meeting of the young matrons' card club—scheduled for the following Thursday was postponed out of respect for the Fulbright family.

Former Arkansas governor Charles Brough, who was visiting his former home in Fayetteville, said:

> In Mr. Fulbright's death Fayetteville and Arkansas are losing
> a man they can ill afford to lose and one whose patriotism
> and sound business judgment have helped to build up
> Fayetteville, Washington County and Arkansas. During the
> war I was intimately associated with Mr. Fulbright in many

patriotic endeavors and from personal knowledge I know
the community has never had a more valuable citizen.

Members of the Fulbright family gathered for the funeral.
Roberta's father, James Waugh, came from Rothville. But Jay's
sister, Zoe, who had buried her mother in Missouri the week
before, was unable to attend.

There was no way that Mont Nord could accommodate all of
the mourners. The *Daily Democrat* reported that the funeral "was
one of the largest ever occurring in this community." The newspaper also took note that: "Throughout the day a stream of
sorrowing business associates and other friends wended their way
to the family home on the hill and even the spacious lawn was
thronged almost to standing room during the service which
opened at five o'clock. Practically all of the employees of every
business with which he was connected were among those present."

Rev. N. M. Ragland, pastor emeritus of the First Christian
Church where Jay and Roberta were members, conducted the
service, assisted by Rev. M. L. Gillespie.

To compound Roberta's grief, the burial procession to Evergreen Cemetery at the edge of the University of Arkansas campus
was delayed briefly because of rock encountered in preparing the
grave. When word was relayed at 6:15 P.M. that the grave was
ready, a large procession followed the pallbearers carrying the
casket to the cemetery. A simple interment ceremony was held at
the graveside. The Fulbright family was now without its patriarch.

"I recall very poignantly coming home from Evergreen
Cemetery," Roberta would say later, "and when I entered the little
library, with the chair, the fireplace and the scenes where my
husband and I loved and lived, I said, 'Jay is here for me, not there,'
and never again has my mind sought out the cemetery for comfort
or sentiment . . ."

On the day of Jay's death the *Daily Democrat* ran a front-page
"In Memoriam" listing the businesses in which Jay Fulbright held
an interest: Arkansas National Bank, Citizens Bank, Democrat
Publishing and Printing Company (publishers of the *Daily
Democrat*), Ozark Wholesale Grocery Company, Fayetteville

Lumber and Cement Company, Phipps Lumber Company, Ozark Poultry and Egg Company, Fayetteville Ice Company, the Washington Hotel, Fulbright Wholesale Grocery Company, Fayetteville Mercantile Company, H. C. Bone Stave Company in Stilwell, Oklahoma, Citizens Bank of Pettigrew, and the banks of Winslow, Elkins, and St. Paul. Additionally he had significant holdings in timberlands, business houses, and apartment property.

On the day of his funeral, *Democrat* editor Lessie Read wrote this tribute:

> The *Democrat* is sad today. Many other business firms whose doors are also closed in memory are sad today, for the master-mind that built them has gone to his last long rest.
>
> In the prime of life, Death called, and none there is who may say him nay. Thus, Fayetteville's most dominant figure in finance and the world of business passes, and many a day must also pass before another such shall come to take his place.
>
> "Jay Fulbright, genius," was the way his name was once written by one who knew and loved him well. Farm-born, country-reared, and college-bred, a lover of good literature, good lectures, and good living, Mr. Fulbright's especial genius ran to figures, and to him business was a game, the most fascinating game in the world and in comparison with which all other sports were tame. His aim in life was not merely to leave his family well provided for, but to build wherever he could a substantial business that employed and provided for many others.
>
> To play to win when he could, to lose with good sportsmanship when lose he must, to keep something always in reserve, to teach team-work, and to play the game fair and never whine—rules he learned on the athletic field at college—were the rules he applied to life.
>
> A good judge of character, his chief concern when he had built up a business, was to put in charge someone whom he could trust, and then to trust him. "Never employ a person whom you suspect, never suspect one whom you employ" was with him a business axiom. Another was: "Demand results, but leave the details to the one in charge."

Thus in building his own fortune, he also built fortunes for many another and just how many owe their business to Jay Fulbright, they alone know, but many a local business firm that does not bear his name will miss his steadying hand and his sound advice.

To the little company on the hill where he lived and among whom he was king, abiding sorrow has come. For in the old-time sense Jay Fulbright was head of his own household. There his slightest wish, his merest word was law, not because he required that it should be so, but because of the abiding faith of his family in his unerring judgment, the respect he inspired, the love lavished upon him. To them, the loss is irreparable. To the community at large the loss must be scarcely less.

Lessie Read's was not the only tribute to Jay Fulbright. In his one-hundred-year history of Fayetteville, author William S. Campbell said:

Jay Fulbright was a power. Whatever that means to you, it meant progress and development to Fayetteville. You might strenuously oppose something he proposed; but you liked him. He drove hard—he drove far. But he liked men and lived with them. He attained such success that he could have asked no man odds; but he wanted and loved friends. Such men are sinews to life. He is sorely missed.

Two decades later, Roberta wrote of her husband:

He had little time for the man or woman who eternally leaned on someone else, blamed someone else—the government, his employees or his parents. He was a stalwart, not afraid to take a chance and never whined when he lost. His mind worked in as straight a line as anyone I've ever known.

Roberta had little time to recover from the shock and to deal with her grief before she was swamped by business problems. In spite of all his business genius, Jay died without leaving a will. The partners in his many business enterprises, anxious about their own well-being, moved quickly to solidify their positions. Competitors, some convinced that Roberta was vulnerable and unsuspecting, sought to gain an advantage. Some were "silky smooth," Roberta's grandson Allan Gilbert later recalled. "They would pat her on the back and tell her, 'we'll take care of it for you.'"

"She got burned," stressed Gilbert, in some cases of misplaced trust. These businessmen knew that Jay was shrewd; now they wanted a piece of the business empire that he had built.

The turmoil came as a surprise to Roberta. She had assumed that Jay's longtime friends, business partners, and managers could be counted on to continue management of the companies as they were until she could review her situation and determine a course of action. Instead, she found herself suddenly and surprisingly under siege. If she were to salvage Jay's business interests and provide security for herself and her children, she would have to draw on her early-developed self-confidence and innate intelligence. These qualities would have to substitute for entrepreneurial experience.

Perhaps mindful of Jay's credo that he had little use for the man or woman who leaned on someone else, Roberta set about to unravel the intricate business problems left by his sudden death. She was named executrix of Jay's estate. J. L. Swafford of Fort Smith, who did the tax work for Jay and Roberta, was "the first encouraging, reassuring voice I heard after my own husband's going," Roberta remembered, and for years after she found him to be someone to trust and depend on.

Family members rallied around to help as best they could. Jack, now twenty-four, returned home from Harvard to manage Phipps Lumber Company and the ice company. Bill, who was eighteen, took a semester off from college, his duties ranging from washing bottles by hand at the Coca-Cola plant to serving as a director of the lumber company and the small railroad.

The only instruction Jay left Roberta was a word of advice he gave her shortly before his death when he told her, "Old Lady, if anything ever happens to me, you can trust Frank Gray to help you." Gray, one of the original incorporators of the ice company, also was involved in the Fulbright banking and wholesale grocery interests and served as an adviser for Jay's other businesses. His wife and Roberta were friends.

Although Jay was right about Frank Gray's willingness and ability to help, he did not anticipate the treatment that Roberta encountered from many other men in the local business community. Apparently they had convinced themselves either that Roberta would surely not attempt to manage Jay's business interests or, even if she did, a woman had no place in such endeavors.

Lawsuits abounded, some strategic, some intended to intimidate. These ran the gamut, some demanding divestment and payment, others seeking forfeiture, and others contesting titles. Above all, they were a frightening test of Roberta's determination. As Bill Fulbright pictured it, "I thought we were all going to the poorhouse."

One of the lawsuits came not from outside the family but from within. Tom Waugh's widow, Josephine, concerned about protecting Tom's investment in the ice company and worried about Jack Fulbright's plans for expansion, filed suit for settlement. Josephine had married Roberta's brother Jim following Tom's death. Jim's first wife, Artie Smart, had died sometime around 1920, leaving four children: Margaret, Lucy Frances, Thomas Edward, and Earl. Another child, Roberta, died in childhood. Jim farmed in Rothville until his wife's death when he decided to follow his sister and brother to Fayetteville. He was the secretary-treasurer and a stockholder of Phipps Lumber Company. After Jay's death, Jim and nephew Jack disagreed over management policies; Jim left the company.

Josephine Waugh's lawsuit resulted in the auction of the ice company, where young Bill Fulbright outbid Jim, who was bidding on behalf of Jim McIlroy of McIlroy Bank, Jay's banking rival. Interestingly enough, while the lawsuit and subsequent auction caused a rift of some years between Roberta and her brother Jim, it did not interfere with the family relationship which Roberta and Josephine enjoyed. Following the auction Jim accepted McIlroy's offer to manage a wood-working company in nearby Eureka Springs.

Those who expected to take on the widow Fulbright and win easily were in for some surprises, not the least of whom was Tom Hart, cashier at Arkansas National Bank, the bank Jay had served as president. Upon Jay's death, Roberta became a member of the bank's board of directors. Hart had doubts about the propriety of women in business. In turn, Roberta had doubts about Hart. It was an uneasy relationship at best.

Roberta soon sold the Arkansas National Bank stock and obtained sole ownership of the Washington Hotel where the bank was located. Through this astute move, she went from tenant to owner. It was not surprising that the bank later moved from the hotel lobby. Some years later, during the depression, the bank was absorbed by the First National Bank. It was early proof of her sound business instincts.

Some Fulbright assets had to be liquidated following Jay's death, but the family fears of bankruptcy were unfounded. One business, the poultry and egg company, did fail later when a plant manager absconded with funds.

Gradually, Roberta worked her way through the maze of business entanglements to place the Fulbright holdings on firm footing. In doing so, she had the assistance of Frank Gray, who served as president of Citizens Bank, Fayetteville Mercantile Company, and the Fayetteville Ice Company, and John Clark, a Citizens Bank cashier.

If other men in the Fayetteville business community thought that a woman had no place in business, they now knew that Roberta Fulbright was at least their equal in business acumen. She had earned their grudging respect. Shaped by her mother's wise counsel, her husband's no-nonsense business example, and her own ample endowment of self-confidence, she learned quickly to project an image of being in charge, able to handle anything that came her way. It was a persona unusual for a woman of that period, with the result that some of the men in the community regarded her as aggressive and domineering. But it was a persona which served her well in the immediate aftermath of Jay's death and in business battles in the years to come. According to William S. Campbell, in his history of Fayetteville, ". . . Mrs. Fulbright has carried on as becomes one who had long consorted with such a leader (Jay Fulbright)."

"Everyone in town assumed Jay Fulbright was the power," observed Floyd Carl Jr., who later joined the Fulbright-owned newspaper staff. "The sharks thought they would take it over. They were wrong; Mrs. Fulbright was the head shark."

"Although menfolk down around the square didn't know it, Roberta never considered 'giving up' as a viable option," said family biographer Allan Gilbert. "She set her hat, with what was to prove characteristic gumption, to carry on; if not in the exact footsteps, at least after the fashion of her late husband. If she expected a grudging admiration (and surely she must have) from those with whom she carried on her business affairs, she was to be disappointed. Downtown, her grit was generally interpreted as either a nuisance or a threat."

"Setting her hat," in Roberta's case, could be taken quite literally, for she was seldom seen in public without it. A solidly built fireplug of a woman, her full, square face and the determined set of her jaw accented by simple glasses and the ever-present hat, gave her an authoritarian countenance which served her well in difficult encounters. She walked with a purposeful, stately carriage in sturdy, sensible shoes, announcing through her appearance that here was someone to be reckoned with. Her resonant voice sometimes cracked as she spoke, but never did it interfere with her gift of gab or her ability to dominate a conversation.

Of Roberta's troubles during this period, *Democrat* editor Lessie Read wrote:

> Considering her a gullible widow, competitors and others acted accordingly, only to find her quite capable of taking care of herself, thank you! She held her own with the best of them (and the worst). She won every lawsuit against her or they were thrown out of court for lack of merit. Businessmen began to respect her as one of them. As a leading banker said to me, "Mrs. Fulbright is the best business man I know."

Still, obtaining credit, she learned, was a male prerogative. She was rewarded with sympathy, but not capital. "This was designed to encourage the widow to come to her senses and leave the business to its rightful masculine domain," pointed out Allan Gilbert. "It was, instead, a lesson in sexual prejudice she never forgot."

Some years later, in her newspaper column, under the heading "Me and Men," she recalled this experience.

> Men take it so hard and so poorly when women enter what they call "their field," that it's either too bad or it's ludicrous.
>
> I agree that politics and business are not a woman's field—not because she hasn't sense enough, but because she is so handicapped by the prejudice of the centuries, and because she has more important things to do.
>
> So long as a woman does poorly and the lords of creation can say, "Oh, it's nothing but a fool woman," they are fairly content, for they must, every mother's son of them, have a woman to do much of the work.
>
> But let a woman do WELL and she is all but burned at the stake. I will say for the benefit of those who may be interested, I did not choose business as a career, it was thrust upon me. I did choose it in preference to going broke or dissipating my heritage and that of my children.
>
> Right here, if there is a man who will agree to take my job, who can qualify and give bond, I'll give him a try-out. I need a rest. I am not a feminist in the accepted sense of the word. I have spent nearly all of my life loving a man and his children, protecting his fireside, fighting with him and for him. I am possessed of either an imaginary or real sense of honesty in public affairs and private. I don't know which. It's very difficult to see ourselves as others see us, but I just see it that way.
>
> Sometimes I'm a bit sorry for men. We women know so many things they will never know. I like them though.

With the estate's business interests now moving toward stability, the family formed the Fulbright Investment Company, a holding company, to manage the business and real estate holdings, including commercial and residential rental property. Son Bill returned to school at the University of Arkansas where he was president of Associated Students, a member of the student senate, an all-Southwest Conference halfback for the football team, and captain of the tennis team. In mid-December 1924, one month before his graduation in January 1925, at age nineteen, he was awarded a prestigious Rhodes scholarship for study at Oxford, England.

Despite her business entanglements, Roberta, too, found time to return to school, taking a course at the university in English composition.

On the heels of these positive events, tragedy again struck the family. On April 8, 1925, daughter Lucile, a director of the ice company and now the mother of young son Allan, died with even more suddenness than her father.

Since childhood Lucile had suffered brief bouts of illness that came quickly and disappeared with the same swiftness, possessing the characteristics of allergy attacks. Her illness was described in the *Daily Democrat* as a peculiar gland trouble that caused swelling in her throat.

Always vivacious, Lucile seldom let her attacks of illness interfere with her many activities. Only two weeks before her death, she had attended a picnic with friends and family at the country club. The day before she was fatally stricken, she had been to town. When she awoke the next morning, she complained of feeling ill. Doctors advised her to remain in bed.

At 1:30 that afternoon Lucile complained of swelling in her throat and sudden suffocation. Although doctors were summoned, she died almost immediately. She had lived in her new home less than a year.

Lucile's death, at age twenty-nine, brought fresh grief to a family still reeling from Jay's death and its aftermath. The April 8 evening edition of the *Daily Democrat* reported that, "The family were too prostrated this afternoon to give any information or announce funeral plans." Once again, Roberta and her family had been dealt a swift, cruel blow.

The funeral was held Friday, April 10. Originally scheduled for the Gilbert home, it was moved to Mont Nord to accommodate a large crowd. Less than two years following her father's death, Lucile was buried next to him in Fayetteville's Evergreen Cemetery.

Lucile's sister, Anna, was away on a European trip and was unable to return home in time for the funeral, but made a sad pilgrimage home the following Monday.

Years later, writing to eulogize a young Fayetteville man, Roberta perhaps had in mind the premature loss of her daughter when she wrote: "It takes a heap of loving and thought and work to get a young man or woman reared and educated and it is a great loss to the world to have them go so early." On another occasion she said the ". . . going of an older daughter leaves an ever-aching void and never-filled vacancy."

After Lucile's death, her physician husband, Allan Gilbert Sr., remained close to the family. For many years he served as physician and trainer for the University of Arkansas athletic teams. Their son Allan grew up in Fayetteville, spending a lot of time with his grandmother Roberta: ". . . it is he around whom my heart clusters," she said later, "and not . . . the spot she [Lucile] lies," reaffirming her belief in not seeking out the cemetery for comfort.

Bill Fulbright was to begin his studies at Oxford in the fall of 1925. Roberta accompanied him by train to New York City where twenty-five Rhodes scholars gathered to board their ship for England. Neither Roberta nor Bill had been to New York, so they spent several days sightseeing, visiting museums, and attending the opera. It was for both of them an idyllic time, the beginning of a grand educational adventure for Bill and the first of other such trips to come for Roberta. For a brief time they had been able to put aside the tragedies and setbacks of the 1920s and look ahead to what the future might hold.

The family mood was further brightened with the birth of Roberta's second grandchild and first granddaughter, Suzanne Fulbright Teasdale, to parents Anna and Kenneth Teasdale in St. Louis. The joys of two grandchildren brightened her days. She was also cheered for a time by a tour of Europe in 1926, led by Prof. Antonio Marinoni. Bill, still studying at Oxford, joined the tour in Vienna. The group traveled by limousine, visiting Rome, Venice, Naples, Florence, Bologna, Pompei, Vesuvius, and the Blue Grotto.

Fayetteville, too, was looking to a bright future. Celebrating its one hundredth birthday in 1928, the town boasted seven thousand residents and a thriving economy. The Fulbright businesses were on firm footing. As the time approached for Bill's graduation from Oxford, Roberta decided to go to England to spend some time with him and attend the graduation ceremony. She sailed for England, April 13, on the *Pennland,* enjoyed a leisurely crossing, and arrived at Plymouth, England, a week later. She would remain for several months. The twins were away at boarding school, and during the summer vacation months Anna Teasdale and young daughter, Suzanne, came from St. Louis to stay with them.

"This to me was almost a sacred pilgrimage and Oxford, with my boy, my Mecca," Roberta said. "I find great content from being near him, which I can scarcely explain; he seems much like his father and is very easy for me to live with; I lean on him intuitively."

While Bill completed his studies, Roberta busied herself with seeing the sights. When he had free time, they toured together and took in social events. She was captivated by Oxford and the prolific English gardens. She marveled at the beauty of the flowers: "The hawthorne is in blossom, with the odor that brings to mind when I was a child in woods back of our house," she wrote. Her only complaints were about the cool, damp weather, and she lamented, "I hear no good music here."

She became a convert to the English practice of taking afternoon tea. ". . . I am beginning to think I am a Tea-totaler, considering the large number of teas, in various and sundry places I have attended." However, a few days later her tea-totaling habits were broken when she reported that she went to a restaurant for dinner "and had cocktails, wine and everything." She also confessed to becoming an "addict of the book-shops."

After Bill's graduation, August 6, 1928, he and Roberta left for Switzerland and then went on to Paris. Following their extended tour of Europe, she returned home while Bill continued his travels.

Son Jack, who had returned home as first-born son to assume the role as new head of the family, encountered management problems at Phipps Lumber Company, as evidenced by his disagreement with his uncle Jim Waugh. Jack also formed plans to move and expand the ice company, an action which worried those who felt it was premature in the face of the early legal battles for control of Jay's businesses.

In the winter following Jay's death, Jack married Madeline MacKeckney, a native of Texas. Jack was serving as president of Phipps, but he was not suited to the work. Although a hard worker himself, the managing of others did not come naturally to him. He decided to seek opportunity elsewhere. In the late 1920s, he and Madeline moved to New Mexico where he entered the cattle business.

When Roberta returned to Fayetteville in October 1928, she had been gone more than five months. She was now confident in herself and her abilities. She had met family tragedy and business adversity head on, displaying a public assertiveness uncommon for women of her day. Her determination to secure and manage her husband's business interests and to secure a safe financial future for her children despite fierce opposition was viewed by some in the community as pure stubbornness.

"I thought when I began being active in business," she said, "that the men with whom my husband had labored would extend a welcoming hand to me. Not so. Resentment and distrust were ever present. It hurt then. Now I know it was only a natural reaction. What is termed as 'human nature.' They were jealous of their place, I of mine; so it was inevitable that some clashes occurred."

Now, with early battles won, her competence in business demonstrated, and her spirits renewed by her European odyssey, she turned her attention to solidifying her position in the community. "I always had to fight envy," she once told daughter Anna. Whether she meant she was resented by the old-line aristocratic families or by the businessmen she had bested—or both—is not known. But she would become a force to be reckoned with in the days to come.

For the most part, it was her practice to follow Jay's pattern of selecting competent managers—including family members—to oversee the daily affairs of business. As Lessie Read saw it, Roberta shared Jay's ability to pick the right people to do a job and the knack for acquiring and divesting holdings:

> While keeping in touch with her interests, she chooses good executives. So long as things run smoothly and well, she leaves most decisions up to them. Knowing this, naturally they are kept "on their toes" and do their darndest. If she finds an enterprise slipping, she either changes managers or sells out while prices are right. That she seldom sells is a compliment both to her and those she employs.

She did assume some company titles. She became president of Phipps Lumber Company and the Bank of Elkins, a member of the board of the Bank of Winslow, vice president of Fayetteville Mercantile, and publisher of the *Daily Democrat*. When Frank Gray, on whom she had relied so strongly, succumbed to pneumonia in 1932, she assumed the presidency of Fayetteville Ice Company and of Citizens Bank. Jay had been one of the original stockholders of Citizens when it was formed in 1907. Located on Dickson Street in Fayetteville near the Frisco Railway Depot and only a few blocks from the University of Arkansas, the formation of Citizens was intended to serve the university and the businesses in the Dickson Street area.

At Citizens, Roberta was joined on the board by another woman, Jobelle Holcombe, a highly regarded university faculty member. Roberta loved the atmosphere of the bank, perhaps recalling fondly the early days of her marriage when she worked alongside Jay at the little bank in Sumner. In 1936, she was one of only three women bank presidents among the 230 banks in Arkansas.

She briefly took a fling in radio, purchasing radio station KUOA in 1933 from the Southwestern Hotels Company, which had only owned it briefly after buying it from the University of Arkansas. The studios were moved to the family-owned Washington Hotel. Shareholders in the newly formed company, in addition to Roberta, were daughters Helen and Bo and John Clark. The purchase of the station was a preemptory move, designed to discourage others from entering the radio market, which she regarded as a competitor for advertising business with her news-paper. She later sold the station to John Brown, founder of John Brown University in nearby Siloam Springs.

Roberta Fulbright then turned her interest to her newspaper. It would become her love for many years and the base of her political power.

The Rothville Baptist Church, where Roberta served as organist in the late 1800s, still serves the small Missouri farming community.

Sumner, Missouri, where Jay and Roberta Fulbright lived and owned their first bank, remains today much as it was in those days. The Fulbright Museum, which depicts life in pioneer Missouri, is in the foreground.

Roberta Fulbright stands behind her first-born daughter, Lucile, who is between her grandfather, James Gilliam Waugh, and great-grandmother, Lucy Frances Waugh.

COURTESY OF HARRIET
MAYOR FULBRIGHT

Roberta's paternal grandfather, Thomas Edward Waugh.

COURTESY OF HARRIET
MAYOR FULBRIGHT

Ida Fulbright and grandson J. William (Bill) Fulbright.

Roberta's husband, Jay Fulbright, was a Fayetteville banker, businessman, and civic leader.

*Roberta and Jay with their
six children.* Left to right,
front row, *Anna, Bo, Helen;*
back row, *Bill, Lucile, Jack.*

Jay with twins Bo (left) *and Helen.*

Roberta at age forty-four.

*Roberta is in the center of family and friends
at a picnic on the White River.*

From left, *Jay, Roberta, Bill, Bo, Helen, and unidentified friend.*
COURTESY OF HARRIET MAYOR FULBRIGHT

*Roberta and
brother Tom.*
COURTESY OF HARRIET
MAYOR FULBRIGHT

Roberta and son Bill, front row, third and fourth from left, *at luncheon party for the Teasel Club, Pembroke College, Oxford, June 1928.*

COURTESY OF HARRIET MAYOR FULBRIGHT

Mont Nord, circa 1940.

COURTESY OF THE SPECIAL COLLECTIONS DIVISION,
UNIVERSITY OF ARKANSAS LIBRARIES, FAYETTEVILLE

Roberta, third from right, at a University of Arkansas function on the campus lawn.

Roberta loved the comfort of her sitting room at Mont Nord.

Roberta in her usual dark business attire with her trademark choker.

"...I am ensconced in a new office over the Democrat,"
Roberta wrote in 1935. Here, she is joined by son Bill.

Roberta with Bill and his wife, Betty, in Washington, D.C.,
in January 1945 when Bill was sworn into the Senate.

Roberta was the proprietor of her newspaper, in the old-fashioned sense, taking an interest in all of its operations. Here, she and son Bill check a press run.

Fayetteville's well-known College Avenue as it looked in the early years of Jay and Roberta Fulbright's residency.

*Roberta used the power of her newspaper to support
what and who she thought was best for the political
well-being of Fayetteville and Washington County.*

Simple stones mark the graves of Jay and Roberta
Fulbright in Fayetteville's Evergreen Cemetery.

*Roberta's influence on the life and progress of the
University of Arkansas was evidenced by the dedication in
1959 of Roberta Fulbright Hall, a women's residence hall.*

*The Roberta Fulbright Library Building
houses the Fayetteville Public Library.*

CHAPTER V

As I See It

In her bid for influence and acceptance, Roberta possessed a clear advantage: the power of the press. The newspaper which Jay Fulbright purchased in 1913, the *Fayetteville Daily Democrat,* held a particular appeal for her, for it rekindled an interest in journalism first discovered when she heard Walter Williams speak at the University of Missouri.

Jay purchased the newspaper at auction for eleven thousand dollars. It was, at the time, a small daily with a circulation of about fifteen hundred. Jay invested in the newspaper because, as Bill Fulbright said, "the fellow who owned it was in failing health and didn't have anyone else to run it." In other words, it was a typical Jay Fulbright acquisition.

Founded August 10, 1860, as the weekly *Fayetteville Democrat,* it was not the town's first newspaper. Several forerunners had already made their entries and exits. The *Democrat's* first editor and publisher was W. W. Moore. The Moore family published the paper throughout the first years of the Civil War, although Moore joined the Confederate army and served until the end of the war. Ironically, publication of the newspaper was interrupted when much of Fayetteville was burned and the newspaper's equipment was destroyed in 1862 by Confederate forces retreating from the nearby Pea Ridge battle.

Sons W. B. and E. B. Moore resumed publication of their father's newspaper on July 4, 1868. At least four other newspapers sprouted and died in Fayetteville in the mid-1800s. The *Democrat* survived despite its brief hiatus.

In 1884, Moore's two sons sold the paper to Sam Marrs and John Tillman (who later became president of the University of Arkansas). In 1893, Louise Payne, who believed there was a need for a daily paper in Fayetteville, convinced Marrs to let her publish a daily from the same plant which printed the weekly, although the news and advertising of the two papers remained separate. When Jay Fulbright purchased his interest, both newspapers and the printing plant were included in the sale. The *Democrat* occupied space on the top floor of a two-story brick building next to the Chic Shop just off the town square on the south side of Center Street.

After Louise Payne left the paper, John L. Stafford assumed the editorship, followed later by John Neely. When Jay sold an interest to Allen Gates of Little Rock, Gates became the paper's editor and J. Davis Hurst became associate editor. Gates later sold his interest to Dr. Charles Richardson, a Fayetteville dentist, and Hurst became editor and manager.

Dr. Richardson died in 1924, the year following Jay Fulbright's death. Despite her legal entanglements, Roberta acquired full interest in the newspaper from Dr. Richardson's heirs and became in 1926 the full owner and publisher.

The *Democrat* prided itself on its active role in the community. Its bulletin board kept residents informed of daily events in World War I, and when a crowd gathered in front of the office one momentous night in 1927, it kept them updated on the progress of the Dempsey-Tunney heavyweight prize fight.

Lessie Stringfellow Read, who joined the newspaper in 1911 as a reporter, became city editor during World War I while J. Davis Hurst was away in the military. When he returned, Lessie offered to give up the position in his favor, but he declined and became business manager. She became the managing editor in 1924.

A native of Temple, Texas, Lessie attended Leland Stanford University and the University of Arkansas. In addition to her work at the newspaper, she authored articles for national magazines and served as national press chairman of the General Federation of Women's Clubs. A tall, angular woman with prominent cheekbones, large, dark eyes, and short hair worn close about her face, her open countenance and eccentric dress belied her strong will and courage under fire.

Her journalistic fervor was not always matched by organizational skills, with the result that stories and headlines were sometimes dictated or dashed off on a sheet of paper as press time neared. She was fond of trivia, local lore, and stories about the famous who may (or may not) have passed through Fayetteville. She also fancied herself a poet. But beneath it all, she possessed a good journalistic sense of right and wrong, and she—like Roberta—was not hesitant about expressing her opinions in print. When the chips were down, Lessie stood tall.

During the years that Lessie and Roberta worked together, Lessie generally wrote the newspaper's editorials. This caused no problem since the two women almost always held the same view and became fast friends. Although Roberta said later, "Mrs. Read and I are not exactly 'two souls with but a single thought, two pens that write as one,'" they were friends and business associates for many years, and together they set the newspaper on a new course.

When describing their method of operation, Roberta wrote:

> I can only use those persons who see by their own head-lights and who are capable of running themselves. We do both strive to uphold the best interests of the community. We do both believe and practice integrity and sobriety and make sacrifices to that end. I'm pretty dry, but Mrs. Read is a little drier than I am. She crackles when she walks in the mud in wet weather. Also, she's a bit more mystical than I. She believes in Santa Claus a little more implicitly than I. But she is a person of wide sympathies and fine capabilities.

As a young woman in Missouri, Roberta had served as a country correspondent for a local newspaper, earning the princely sum of twenty cents per week for the personal items she submitted. Now, with her direct involvement in the *Daily Democrat,* her love for writing was once again stirred. When she went to England for her son Bill's graduation, her letters back home found their way into the newspaper. "The letters," the *Democrat* said, "were not written for publication but contain so much of general interest that the *Democrat* believed readers would enjoy them." Published under the heading "Letters from Oxford," seven letters appeared on a periodic basis and were well received by readers.

Still, Roberta did not begin writing a column upon her return from Europe. But the success of the letters did ultimately serve as the genesis for her recurring column, "As I See It," which she began in 1933 and continued for almost twenty years. Editor Read expressed it this way:

> It was just after having tried to read a McIntyre [referring to O. O. McIntyre] column in the morning newspaper that the *Democrat* editor said to the owner and publisher: "I can't read this stuff but I would like to read something you could write. Why don't you write us a column for the edit page?" Our Lady always being obliging acceded to this request. So the *Democrat* proudly is exhibiting a new column "As I See It" by Mrs. Roberta Fulbright that promises to be much better than most of those sold by syndicates.

Although the column did not appear every day, and not even on a regular schedule, it did appear frequently. Sometimes it was published on several successive days, and at other times, several days or weeks would elapse before it would appear again. In a compilation of Roberta's columns in 1952, University of Arkansas journalism professor W. J. (Walt) Lemke estimated that during those twenty years she wrote two million words for her column, in his estimation, "an astonishing figure."

Once, expressing her wonder at the ability of writers to produce book-length works, she proclaimed:

> It's just plain work to write even an effusion like "As I See It." Someone will say "Then why do it?" and I answer "I must." It is fraught with anxiety and to really produce books it would appear to me one would need to go into exile and confinement and wear sackcloth and ashes.

The column was always written in longhand, in pencil, on a ruled, legal-size tablet. Most often Roberta wrote it at home, at night; it was ready to be set in type early the following morning. Sometimes, depending upon her nocturnal notions, she sent several columns to the paper at the same time. By all accounts her bold, handwritten scrawl was difficult, if not impossible, to read.

When she first began writing the column, only one staff member—reporter Maude Gold Hawn—could readily decipher the handwritten columns and was assigned that task in addition to her reporting duties. Roberta appreciated the talent. "Maude," she said in a play on words, "is pure 'Gold.'"

"I knew pretty well how she thought," said Hawn in explaining her unique talent for translation. Hawn was schooled in journalism since her father, Julian E. Gold, was the publisher of the *Washington Telegraph* at historic Washington, Arkansas. (The *Telegraph*, according to Hawn, published continuously during the Civil War.)

After Hawn left the paper, each succeeding new reporter was assigned the transcription task. "That's how you started," recalled Floyd Carl Jr., who joined the staff in 1943, "writing obituaries and transcribing Mrs. Fulbright's column." Carl would sometimes have to tell her: "I can't make this out." Most of the time she would say, "Neither can I."

Roberta didn't limit herself to column writing. Throughout her ownership of the paper, she took seriously her role as publisher. In 1925, to broaden its scope of coverage, she added a column on Washington, D.C., affairs, "The Daily Washington Letter" by Charles F. Steward, described as a straight-from-the-shoulder column on Washington events. Over the years, other respected syndicated columnists followed.

By 1928, the paper's circulation reached twenty-two hundred. In 1929, Homer H. (Scotty) Taylor, who had made money in the oil business, offered to buy the paper for twenty-five thousand dollars. Never averse to a good business offer, Roberta countered with a price of thirty-five thousand dollars. Instead, Taylor opted to begin his own newspaper, the *Fayetteville Daily Leader*. A former sports editor for the *Democrat*, "he considered himself to be more of a journalist than Mrs. Fulbright," said author Allan Gilbert. He wasn't, however, as astute at business as his adversary.

With the gauntlet thrown, the competition soon followed. Roberta moved to a six-day publishing schedule, adding to her five weekday evening editions a Sunday edition with four-color comics (there was no Saturday edition). She leased wire services from both the Associated Press (AP) and United Press (UP). Although Taylor put in a modern plant and published six to eight pages daily, he could not compete with these moves. Also, while the editorial side of his paper fared well enough, the advertising side did not. With the competition dwindling, the *Democrat* discontinued its Sunday edition and went to a Monday through Saturday schedule. The *Leader* ceased publication in January 1931.

It was also in 1931 that the Arkansas Press Association magazine, the *Arkansas Publisher,* reported, "The *Fayetteville Daily Democrat* is one of the best dailies in the state outside larger cities. It is the *only* paper in the state with automatic printer service, carrying full leased wire of AP as well as UP."

From 1934 to 1937, Roberta's paper again faced serious competition, this time from the *Progressive Star,* which succeeded the *Arkansas Countryman,* published from 1921 to 1934. The *Star* was owned first by E. M. Scuggs, then by H. D. Phillips, and finally in 1937 by longtime *Democrat* staffer Davis Hurst. This time the editorial competition between the two newspapers focused on the battle over local governmental corruption and reform, with the papers taking opposite sides. Again Roberta prevailed in the newspaper war. After her purchase of the *Star* in 1937, it was discontinued.

On July 8, 1937, Roberta changed the name of her paper to the *Northwest Arkansas Times* not only to reflect its rapidly increasing circulation through expanded delivery routes, but also because the new name was more representative of its widening sphere of influence. Reports of the search for missing aviator Amelia Earhart provided the lead news for the first page of the newly named newspaper.

In "As I See It," Roberta wrote, "Northwest Arkansas is our own precinct. Our taxes, our crops, our battles, our celebrations, our resorts and our interests are one and the same. . . . change is constant and business institutions must grow or die. We specialize in growing." The paper's further growth was reflected by its move in 1940 to a new plant on North East Street.

Because it represented a significant investment, Roberta kept a close eye on her newspaper's membership in the wire services. She instructed the staff to notify the Associated Press each Monday as to the kind of stories they would need for succeeding editions. She expected these stories to be dispatched promptly, thus providing a lead time of several days. She exercised her publisher's prerogative to get her editors what they wanted.

She set her own 11:45 A.M. deadline for the AP to send over the wire the news stories they had indicated early each morning that they would provide during the course of the day. If the AP failed to make the deadline, she called them to find out why. In this, she brooked no opposition.

On Mondays, when the Arkansas Supreme Court handed down its decisions in Little Rock, she made it clear to the AP that she wanted the court's opinions to come over the wire in time for the 11:45 A.M. deadline for her Monday afternoon editions. Sam Harris, an AP wire editor in Little Rock at the time, covered the Arkansas Supreme Court for the wire service. Years later, he would remember that on Mondays he arose very early, barely taking time to shave before leaving home, and rushed to the Supreme Court offices to get the decisions as soon as they were handed down. He then telephoned his stories to the AP office in Little Rock so that they could be dispatched quickly on the wire. It was a tight deadline at best.

University historian Robert Leflar worked for the university during his student years writing press releases. Roberta was fond of describing him as her university reporter, a reference to the fact that the prolific release of news items from Leflar enabled her to report University of Arkansas news without having to hire a reporter for that beat.

"I have been thrust, fairly hurled, into the thick of business," she said. "I must take the blame and abuse and meet competition, and these are experiences which sometimes rub the fine bloom off the peach, and the dew from the rose." Partly for this reason, partly because of her natural love of journalism, she continued to keep a watchful eye on the paper's operation.

"What with the black clouds of damage suits always on the horizon, the ever-present spectre of taxes, more taxes and different taxes, with competition and abuse at one's throat at all times, one becomes almost hard. The urge to endure is present in most of us, and verily it is with me," she intoned.

While she valued the journalistic side of the paper and had a keen sense of its community responsibilities, she never lost sight of the bottom line. Her vigilance made the newspaper a profitable venture.

Occasionally she liked to hold court at the newspaper, sitting in her favorite chair near the news desk and indulging her life-long passion for conversation with any or all who stopped by from their businesses around the town square to talk business or politics. She did have some difficulty in catching a person's name upon introduction. This bothered her, but did not make her bashful. On one such occasion, reporter Floyd Carl Jr. introduced his father, a colonel in the military, to her. They talked at length. Later she asked Carl, "Who was the handsome colonel?" When Carl told her again that it was his father, she recovered quickly: "You don't take after him much, do you?" she adroitly replied.

Once she came to the office entreating the staff to give her something to do so she could be useful. They put her to work filing the mats used in reproducing pictures and advertisements. This tedious task soon convinced her to remain more at Mont Nord, coming to the newspaper office only when the occasion demanded.

It is surely surprising to those who found the name Roberta Fulbright synonymous with that of her newspaper to learn that the outspoken publisher was not always present at the daily workings of the newspaper. Many years later Maude Hawn still remembered that the telephone number at Mont Nord was 209 because the line between home and newspaper was kept quite busy. Whether telephoning instructions from Mont Nord or holding court in the newspaper office, there was never any doubt about the influence she wielded over the newspaper's operation and editorial policies.

"She wasn't all sweetness and sunshine," wrote Prof. Walt Lemke in introducing his compilation of her columns. "As I See It" was carried, for the most part, on the editorial page. She was a woman of firm convictions, and she was never shy in her columns about expressing her opinions about her hometown and its citizens, local and national politics and government, world affairs, an equal role for women in public life, religion, philosophy, travel, gardening, and her family. As *Time* magazine once put it, she wrote "on any topic that popped into her head."

What Roberta lacked in journalism training, she more than made up for with her natural writing ability. She could be folksy, sweet, amusing, straightforward, satirical, tart, even angry, but always the writing style was adapted to what the topic or occasion demanded.

She wrote nostalgically about her early days in Missouri, and she spoke enthusiastically about the advantages of Fayetteville as a place to live and work. She was equally enthusiastic about the small, rural communities surrounding Fayetteville, for they reminded her of Rothville where she grew up. "The heartstrings of the world are tuned to these rural centers . . ." she said.

Her column became an influential voice in the northwest Arkansas region, and in a one-time poll it was voted the most popular and widely read column in the paper. As Roberta Fulbright saw it was often the way Fayetteville saw it, too.

She unabashedly promoted civic projects in which she had a special interest—better roads, flowers planted along the roadways, a new library, a boys' club, and restrooms for women farm workers. While she was quick to praise progress, she was not shy about criticizing. She was a reformer, and if others in the community failed to do what she regarded as their civic duty, she took it upon herself to serve as the civic conscience, saying:

> A town should build upon the rock of honesty, fair dealing, not eternal bickering and jealousies.
>
> There is a type of person who cannot see beyond his own pocketbook. There is another who would oppose a visit from the Angel Gabriel and hosts if his name did not appear on the reception committee.

Still, she added: "We think Fayetteville pretty long on the constructive sort." Reflecting on her own audacity to criticize, she observed: ". . . even a cat may look at a queen, you know."

She memorialized the citizens she knew upon their passing. Years later, florist Ray Adams would still remember that when his first wife died, Roberta, the gardener, awarded her the ultimate praise: "She's not here anymore—her roses are blooming on the other side of the wall." In time, the community came to depend on Roberta to be the one to eulogize its citizens—to pen the appropriate memorial—and she did.

It bothered her when her stand on controversial questions drew criticism or when it conflicted with the interests of her newspaper. "But the word 'expediency' is not in her vocabulary," said Walt Lemke. Her outspokenness led some to believe she was arrogant or self-righteous. But, said one of her editors, Sam Schwieger, on looking back at her tenure, "She was pretty sincere in everything she said." She was, he believed, sometimes misunderstood by some in the community because they didn't have the same freedom to speak out. "It would be a better town if they had followed her advice," is the way Floyd Carl Jr. later put it.

While Roberta Fulbright was frank in her opinions, she once said, "I never write about anything that I'm not possessed of a lurking fear that perhaps I don't know what I'm talking about." Her consciousness of this journalistic responsibility remained with her throughout her days as a columnist. Once she wrote, "You cannot imagine how many hours I spend, how many obsessions I get worked out onto paper. Many is the time I have written my pet peeve down in black on white only to discover it was too trivial for publication. Or too mean, or just plain stupid." But she was never reluctant to vent her outrage in her columns. Hers was a passionate anger, and the objects of her wrath—most often politicians—were never in doubt about how she felt about them.

Disagreements with staff sometimes made their way into her column. "I wrote an article recently and in an unguarded moment I let the staff in on it. Well, they proceeded to perform a large dental job upon it and extracted all the teeth until it was so power-less as the 'canners code.' So my column has to make time for a day or so. I'm busy picknicking."

On another occasion, under the heading "Whose Fault?" Roberta wrote, "In my story of Williamsburg, I very arrogantly attempted to use a new word for my readers, but my proofreaders would have none of it. I attempted to say that Williamsburg had 'pleached' arbors (I had looked it up) but it came out 'bleached' arbors. Now, I'll let you look it up if you are interested."

Sometimes typographical errors caused her embarrassment. "In my going-on regarding the candidates for mayor I wrote 'No doubt they will find their niches later.' It got printed 'riches.' I apologize. (Handwriting is hard to read. Hope Santa Claus brings a typewriter for Christmas.)" At other times she was bothered by her own omissions, particularly when she failed to recognize someone by name as she tried to do each time she visited local clubs and schools. "I'm liable to report a wedding and forget the bridegroom," she chastised herself. According to Roberta's grandson Allan Gilbert, who worked on the newspaper staff, "She used grammatical construction no one ever heard of, but she was always right. Grandmother had no tolerance for incompetence."

Before he bought his own newspaper, Davis Hurst became the *Democrat* business manager. Of him, Roberta once said, "Although we sometimes differ, when it's a question of honesty we always agree. So we are able to work together, not always in peace and harmony but always in the desire to give the community a square deal, a good paper, a useful and efficient medium of advertising, a reliable source of news and enlightened opinion."

Roberta sometimes shared with her readers the inner workings of the staff:

> The other night I attended a dinner for the men who put
> out the Northwest Arkansas Times, who really set the type,
> make the mats, roll the Press, write the editorials and even
> gently—Brother—gently—Boss. . . . After a fried chicken
> dinner and several hours conversation we adjourned.

The big question of the evening, she acknowledged, was if the holiday editions could come out early, why couldn't the daily editions do the same? No doubt it was her question. The next day Sam Gearhart—at that time, vice president and general manager—called her. "We made it today at 2:37 o'clock," he said. "Bravo," was Roberta's response, "we knew it could and would be done."

It became a tradition for the paper to host an annual dinner for employees and their spouses, giving gifts to those with long tenure. Employees often provided the entertainment. When the dinner was scheduled near Roberta's Valentine's Day birthday, the staff gave her a bouquet of roses. In turn, she presented them with a Bible for the *Times* library. Of the attention she always received on her birthday, she wrote, ". . . I believe I am the only one connected with the *Northwest Arkansas Times* . . . who was thoughtful enough, farsighted enough, if you please, to have a birthday on St. Valentine's Day and it was about the swellest idea I ever had. I had it in a log cabin, too, that helps."

When it came to supporting her newspaper staff against outside pressure, she held firm. "If she thought you were right, she'd back you up all the way," reflected reporter Floyd Carl Jr.

Bob Wimberly, a Little Rock advertising and public relations executive, served as the paper's sports editor in 1942–43, while still a University of Arkansas journalism student. While covering his beat, Wimberly learned that the university board of trustees did not plan to pay Razorback football coach Fred C. Thomsen for the balance of his contract. Thomsen had weathered a threatened removal in December 1941 and shortly thereafter volunteered for military service. While he had not expected to enter the service until after the 1942 football season, he was called to active duty just prior to the season's start and later served in China.

In the 1941 confrontation with the university, Thomsen had reportedly demanded full pay for the duration of his contract. When he left for the service and the university replaced him with assistant coach George Cole, the university trustees decided that the contract did not have to be honored. Wimberly went to press with the story.

The chairman of the university board of trustees called Roberta to protest the publication of the article. Soon after, Wimberly was invited to tell the publisher his side of the story.

With Wimberly fearing the worst, Roberta sat down at his desk. Then to Wimberly's relief, she said, "Before we get started, I want you to know I support you. The university is wrong." With the *Northwest Arkansas Times* publisher backing her young sports editor and the paper sticking to its story, the university settled with Thomsen.

"She was nobody's fool," said Wimberly. "She was firm about the need for the university to be open and truthful and the responsibility of the newspaper to do the same." There would be no censorship of what Wimberly wrote.

"She had the kind of personality you'd develop if you had to fight to save those businesses," Wimberly emphasized. Floyd Carl Jr. agreed. "She was her own man," said Carl in a deliberate contradiction in terms. "They never scared her."

At the newspaper—as in all of her businesses—Roberta demanded a lot of her employees, but she gave a lot in return. Because she did not want to affect the employees adversely, she kept some businesses open which she actually would have preferred to close. In appreciation for their loyalty, she gave a parcel of land near Phipps Lumber Company to a group of employees seeking to build a church. As a result, the First Assembly of God church was built.

Sam Schwieger, who edited the paper briefly before accepting a better business opportunity, found Roberta Fulbright to be "forthright and honest. There was never a question of where she stood. She told you what she thought." Conversely, she could accept the same treatment from others. On one occasion when she came to the paper to check on her column, she asked Schwieger what he thought of it. Schwieger told her he didn't plan to run it. He got no argument.

No subject was too mundane for inclusion in her column. Once she wrote about zippers: "I wish Nelly Don and the other smart women who design women's dresses would adopt zippers for the underarm openings instead of snaps. Of all places the underarm is the worst place for snaps. Down you sit. Open you come."

The subject of marriage, and what she believed it took to make one successful, sometimes found its way into her columns. She concluded: "Marriage, we'll say, is a very complicated machine with heavy wheels and light bearings."

When needed, she could speak with tongue-in-cheek: "You have often heard the importance of 'timing.' Well, I'm good at it," she wrote. "On the very day when I attend a Lions' annual party, I come forth in my column with a big boost for Kiwanis. How was I to know that I would be invited to the Lions' party?"

Professor Lemke said, "There's a naiveté about her earlier columns on politics, but she learned fast." Writing of a local Jackson Day dinner, she commented, "I've either heard or read somewhere that the first thing a debutante should learn is to avoid

saying anything with sense in it. That also may be a rule of politics
. . . the speeches were mostly characterized by saying nothing of
importance."

On one occasion after attending a political rally at nearby
Bentonville, her penchant for verse came to the fore. She
described two candidates this way:

> I went to the animal fair
>   The big and the little were there
> The Big Baboon by the
>   light of the moon
> Was ranting and pulling his hair.
>
> The monkey he had spunk,
>   And said what he thought
>   and kerplunk,
> The people sneezed and fell
>   on their knees
> And are voting I think for
>   the monkey-monk.

Another time she summed up her feelings about politics this
way:

> Our politics remind me of the pies the mountain girl had.
> She asked the guest, "Will you have kivered, unkivered or
> crossbar?" All apple. Now that's what we have: kivered,
> unkivered and crossbar politics—all Democrats.

When commenting on a U.S. Supreme Court decision with
which she did not agree, she observed of Justice Owen Roberts,
who delivered the majority opinion, "A Republican," she said. "I
guess it's no sin to be a Republican, but it's hard on the country."

What she did see for the country and its democratic form of
government was best expressed in a 1938 column:

> The democratic mode of government is that it must be
> maintained by those governed, not the other way round. Our
> duty to our government is akin to our duty to our family.
>   I am often astounded at the way responsible persons feel
> toward their government. They rather take the view that any

and all devices arranged for those who really need them should be appropriated by themselves even though they may be living off the public funds already or be amply able to take care of themselves. Integrity in the individual members is the only possible way to have integrity in the whole body. Treat your government as you would have it treat you. Remember, it's the only one you have and changing is painful.

No one really loves to pay taxes, yet we know they are the life blood of governments everywhere. Time was when there were no public roads, no public schools, no post offices. All machinery of government was simple. But as our civilization becomes more and more complex taxes get higher, and we can not return to those days because people of this country do not desire to back-track.

The clamor is forever for more roads, more schools, more pensions, more protection. These mean more taxes. Honesty and fair play become an imperative need. You own what you have largely through the system which has permitted you or your forebears to accumulate. You have been protected from confiscation and depredation through the same system. Therefore support it in honesty and fair play. I'll admit many weaknesses, but as we do our families, stand by them through thick and thin, so must we do our government.

I do not say blindly endorse every move, but I do say play fair. If you are able to take care of yourself, do not ask your government; if you can borrow at the bank, do not get a government loan; if you are able to earn a large income, do not try to evade the tax. It will mean more money turning the wheels and you will no doubt receive benefit in the end.

We have a very complicated system. I wish it could be simpler, yet I still think it's the best one for America.

On occasion she could write with rapier wit. Consider her account of a local banquet:

When Dr. J. W. Workman turned on the words at the nurses' banquet the avalanche which followed swallowed up the occasion, the doctors, the nurses and everything except W. S. Campbell, secretary of the Chamber of Commerce.

We were breathless before the power of his arguments, descriptions, and conclusions . . . but his is so swift and strong and clever that breathless is the only word which expresses it.

This was generally concluded with self-deprecating humor:

Expecting only humane treatment, being among doctors, nurses and friends, when they called on me my brain took flight. If it had been removed from my skull and detached from my spinal cord for the assembly to inspect it, it would have functioned fully as well. (That's my alibi.)

The chuckles she provided were often at her own expense. When writing about being introduced to musician Nino Martini at a reception following his Fayetteville concert, she wrote: "I asked the usual questions: 'How do you like this crowd?' He replies 'All right.' I said 'Can't you beat that' to which he replied 'Wonderful. Perfectly gorgeous,' and I was content."

Gardening was a frequent topic for her columns. "Gardening ranks almost on a par with religion, if I may say." She once devoted several successive columns to gardens she saw while visiting daughter Anna Teasdale and family in St. Louis. Even such occasions did not escape her sword-like pen:

I recall once at Hampton's Court, in London, built by Cardinal Woolsey, a gardener asked me "Do you have any flowers in America?" I was duly incensed then but after visiting the St. Louis gardens I feel I should return and have him brained.

Softening her tone a bit she said:

. . . if I owned any one of these gardens I'd hate to take a chance on Heaven.

Above all, her columns reflected her deep immersion in the life of her community. Throughout her tenure, the newspaper clearly, and sometimes obstreperously, voiced opinions on political and civic affairs. Its slogan was, "The public welfare is this newspaper's first concern."

"She used her newspaper to wield influence," recalled Fayetteville resident Betty Lighton. As the years progressed that influence grew. This was not without hazards. "Everytime I blow off I also blow up some smothered issue, prejudice or feud, or else," Roberta said. While she was the columnist, it was left to the editors to write the editorials. "It is a fallacious notion," she said, "that a newspaper should or could be an isolated affair. Its life-blood should flow in the veins of the community in which it lives."

Whereas some local newspapers tended to see their role only as promoters of their communities—excluding the bad news—the *Northwest Arkansas Times* under Roberta's leadership saw itself as the community's watchdog, the prick of its conscience. While Roberta was ever the promoter of her area, she was never without suggestions for things to be done, and she never hesitated to complain when they weren't done.

Events would soon put this belief to the test; any political naiveté was about to be put to rest. "Some of her most devastating columns," as Walt Lemke later described them, would be written in the 1930s about "politicians who forgot their duty to the people."

The battle was set to begin that would test the publisher's mettle.

CHAPTER VI

The Publisher and Politics

In our political system, where the majority rules at the ballot box, the minority rules in much of the political process. This was never more true than in the early years of the twentieth century in Arkansas when the Fulbright family moved to the state from Missouri.

They came from a border state that had not seceded from the Union in the Civil War, and where there was a two-party system, to a state that had seceded. Arkansas had known a decade of turmoil during the Reconstruction period. The Radical Republicans controlled state government until the 1870s, the decade of Roberta Waugh's birth. In fact, the year she was born, 1874, was the year that the so-called "carpetbag" constitution of 1868 was replaced by a new Arkansas constitution written by a Democratic majority. While Roberta was growing up in Missouri, a political tradition of Democratic Party control in Arkansas developed. One byproduct of such a tradition was the opportunity for control of election machinery by entrenched local politicians. This type of political dominance was very much in evidence in rural Arkansas for the rest of the nineteenth century and into the twentieth century.

Harry Lee Williams, an east Arkansas editor and publisher in the 1920s and 1930s, wrote at length about this in his book *Behind the Scenes in Arkansas Politics*. He noted: ". . . This control or machine rule as we have come to call it . . . passed down to succeeding generations and is still in vogue . . . in at least a dozen counties I could name . . . there are several delta counties and at least two hill counties in central and northern Arkansas, where the 'machine' has controlled with force."

In the single-party dominance of the period, it was not difficult for the diligent political practitioner to build such a machine through control of the Democratic county central committee. Its power to name election officials and certify elections was virtually absolute. Two levers that helped in machine operation in that period were prohibition and the poll tax. Bootleggers seeking protection for their stills and other operations could produce coveted pints or five-dollar bills for voters or influence. Political machine patrons paid poll taxes for the willing and frequently for the unwilling or unwary. The poll-tax book, listing all qualified voters in a county, was available to election officials who might find it necessary to add a few extra voters to their precinct voting register to "legitimize" a ballot count.

Washington County, in the prohibition decade of the 1920s, easily could have been one of the machine counties mentioned in *Behind the Scenes*. It had a well-organized group of Democratic central committee members and officeholders that could control most elections at the county and city levels. With that control came the power to offer jobs, build roads and bridges, adjust tax assessments, influence the judicial system, and protect law breakers.

Maude Hawn, a reporter for the *Daily Democrat* in those years, recalled a "very corrupt county government with a sheriff about as bad as anyone could have. During prohibition there were lots of bootleggers, and federal agents would come in and raid them, shoot holes in the stills, but that didn't stop them." Former circuit judge and state legislator Maupin Cummings remembered one of the operators. "Dee McConnell had a still. The feds would raid him, but before long it would show up again in operation." According to another Washington countian, Chancery Judge Thomas Butt, there was a county machine in that era known as the Gover machine. The man behind it was Jeff Gover, a farmer who built his political power from his role as county committeeman. His son, Harley Gover, was the sheriff referred to by Maude Hawn.

In the 1920s when the Gover machine was building its political power base, Roberta Fulbright was busy building her economic power base without too much thought of acquiring political power. However, one linchpin in her business holdings was her newspaper. It offered her a voice and influence on the Fayetteville, Washington County, and Arkansas political scene when she was ready to use it for that purpose. She found her political voice in 1932–33 for several reasons: the resurgence of the Democratic Party on the national level; the election of an Arkansas woman to the U.S. Senate in 1932; the beginning of a citizen revolt against the blatant political corruption in Washington County; and her decision to write a column of comment in the paper on a fairly regular basis.

A staunch Democrat, she and editor Lessie Read were invigorated by Franklin Roosevelt's 1932 race for the presidency. The newspaper ran pictures of him and his family almost daily during the 1932 campaign, and Lessie frequently praised him editorially. Their conversations about the candidate and the campaign reflected Roberta's strong opinions about public trust and responsibility. Lessie thought her publisher's ideas and beliefs should be shared with the public. When, finally in March 1933, the month of Roosevelt's inauguration, Roberta accepted her editor's challenge and began to write "As I See It," one of her first columns was an affirmation of both the new president and his wife.

> We believe in Roosevelt because he has suffered and because he has thought much for those who do suffer. We believe in him because he has overcome much. We believe in him because he is willing to negotiate, to confer and to reason and we know no better qualities. So we are today pledging our allegiance to Franklin D. Roosevelt, thirty second president of these United States.
>
> It heartens our drooping spirits that there is a woman in the White House so well qualified to preside that she may forget all the stupid rules and greet her guests and kiss her kin. Hail to the Roosevelts! A new day has dawned and the New Deal is on.

On inauguration day three days later, she welcomed the new administration metaphorically.

> Today we will mark a milestone in history. Today the Democratic mule will be fitted under the collar, the tugs will be fashioned, the bit in his mouth, the lines in the hands of President Roosevelt and the creaking wheels of the

Democratic machine of state will roll into being. I doubt not that this mule will do a heap of braying and kicking but we do expect him to pull and to stay hitched. We hope he is tough mouthed so that he won't be easily turned aside. Mules always come into their own when there are tough hard jobs to do. That's their nature. Digging ditches and removing obstacles are natural to mules. The GOP elephant is munching discontentedly "around the corner" consuming quantities of peanuts still, while flapping his sail-like ears and twisting his trunk in a bit of a peeve. I'm always in cahoots with the mule.

Roberta would continue unwavering support of Roosevelt throughout his lifetime. She identified with the belief he expressed in his first campaign that private economic power is a public trust, and she often wrote columns echoing this philosophy.

I'm getting a bit uneasy about "What I See" when I discover what other people see in what I say but I still believe in seeing.

I don't quite know what I do see when it comes to government and I'm afraid I see through a glass darkly. I don't know if I am a capitalist, socialist, communist or what. I think I am a mixture . . . I think many things should come out of surplus wealth and not out of the mouths of the hungry. There are human rights, social rights and political rights. In a test, human rights should take precedence, I think. The hungry should have food before the rich have luxuries. I cannot believe the doctrine that human beings are born free and equal. No, I can't make myself believe that. Some are born with such fine capabilities and such wonderful opportunities, others with unutterly meager chances both from within and without.

I do not believe that even governments can make things equal but somehow, somewhere in my moral being, I think the strong should bear many of the infirmities of the weak. Yet for the weak to adopt the idea of being carried on the backs of the strong makes them even weaker and to deaden their best abilities so the problem becomes a bit more complex. While I do not believe governments can equalize life, I think the function of government should always strive to that end. I think the natural resources of a country should be vouchsafed for all not given to the few.

Now if only governments themselves were wiser and stronger. But while they represent great strength because they are the combined strength of the nation, they are also weak because they are composed of individuals who have human weakness.

Having fought a lonely battle to win a place in the male-dominated Fayetteville business community, Roberta was delighted when another woman, Hattie Caraway of Jonesboro, surprised the state political establishment with not one but two election victories in 1932.

Roberta had known Hattie's husband, Thaddeus Caraway, who served two terms in the U.S. Senate beginning in the 1920s. He was planning to seek another term when he died November 6, 1931, of complications following surgery.

Seven days later, Gov. Harvey Parnell appointed Caraway's widow to fill the seat until a special election could be held January 12, 1932. Party leaders with an interest in becoming candidates in the regular primary struggled briefly as to whom to support in the special election. Deciding the widow Caraway posed the least threat to their future potential candidacies, they made her the Democratic Party nominee in the January election, and she won. It was widely assumed she would hold the seat for her husband's unexpired term and then step aside. Roberta, a strong supporter of the new Senator Caraway, was elated with the victory and visited her in her Washington office a few months after the special election.

Hattie Caraway had little time to enjoy her victory, because the Democratic primary election in which her seat was up for a six-year term came in August 1932. Six male opponents expected to fight it out for the seat and were shocked and surprised when Caraway entered the race. Given very little chance, she won the election with the rhetorical help of Sen. Huey Long of Louisiana, who made a whirlwind speaking campaign in her behalf immediately before the primary.

In the heavily one-party state this primary victory was tanta-mount to election, so she had time in the fall to campaign for the Roosevelt-Garner ticket. She came to Fayetteville during her campaign tour. Roberta was her hostess for the visit and enter-tained her with a small dinner party at the family-owned Washington Hotel. The next day Lessie Read wrote this editorial:

> Hattie Caraway, the mild mannered woman senator, who won out in popular vote over her six men opponents is paying her first visit to Fayetteville.
>
> She was elected on her own after a complimentary appointment. One of the things upon which she insisted when Senator Long offered to aid her . . . was that he not plead for votes on the grounds of chivalry or sympathy but merely on how she voted.
>
> . . . Mrs. Caraway resents the attitude of people who seem to think that Senator Long can control her vote. "I cannot help it if he votes as I do!", she smiled last night while talking to a few friends . . . "but he understands perfectly that I am under no obligation to vote as he does or do as he says." Mrs. Caraway has a keen wit, a personal charm, a captivating smile and mind of her own. No picture does her justice.

It was one thing for Roberta to write as an observer of the national political scene and quite another to become involved in politics at the local level as a commentator and participant. In 1932, events began to set the stage for the publisher to be so involved.

In the August 1932 Democratic primary, the political pot that usually simmered on a well-controlled back burner of the county machine began to boil over as losing candidates started to chal-lenge the election practices of the county Democratic central committee. Before the mess was cleaned up four years later, Roberta and her editor would become deeply embroiled in local political battles.

The first challenge to the machine came after the August primary when veteran legislator R. J. Wilson asked for a canvas of the vote in which he was defeated. He claimed 1,500 to 2,000 illegal votes were cast. The central committee denied the canvas, so Wilson filed suit in circuit court contesting the election. Within a week, defeated candidates for sheriff and assessor also filed contest suits. Their petitions to the court were signed by twenty-five well-known citizens and detailed a series of voting irregularities such as "the vote in Vineyard Township, where there are no more than 65 qualified voters and 132 votes were cast, 116 for the defendant (Harley Gover sheriff-nominee) and 12 for the plaintiff (J. K. Phillips)."

The real problem for the plaintiffs was the machine's man on the circuit court bench, Judge John S. Combs. When lawyers for the defendants filed demurrers to the charges, Combs ruled for them, agreeing there was insufficient evidence to sustain the claims. The plaintiffs appealed to the Arkansas Supreme Court and got a ruling in their favor, and the suit came to Combs's court where continuances and other legal obstacles kept it off the docket.

In December, after the general election, Republican candidates tried the same sort of contest and went through similar frustrating experiences in Judge Combs's court. Unable to have their day in court, the rejected candidates and their supporters began to hold public meetings and formed a group called the Voters Protective League in December 1932.

That same month, state comptroller Griffin Smith sent auditors to Fayetteville to examine the records in the office of retiring county judge T. L. Slaughter. This caused quite a stir and gave rise to daily rumors. The *Daily Democrat* had no editorial comment but did state in a news story about the audit its desire to be fair.

> The "Democrat" desires to give both sides in the present county inquiry and its columns are open to anyone appearing at the hearing who feels the testimony developed by the questions asked does not give complete opportunity to be heard by the one being questioned.

Roberta had not begun to write "As I See It" when the election contest developed or the audit began, but she was increasingly drawn into it. She would pick up information on the developing upheaval from Lessie on her visits to the newspaper office or by phone; from chats with her Washington Hotel manager Sam Peck and from business associates who stopped at her table during her frequent lunches at the hotel; from University of Arkansas president John C. Futrall and other faculty friends at social affairs; and from conversations with members of the various women's clubs to which she belonged. When she began to write "As I See It" in 1933, however, she had nothing to say about the rumblings against the machine.

She did impress local leaders with her written and conversational comments on governmental affairs in 1933—to the point that many encouraged her to run for Congress in 1934 against Rep. Claude Fuller, who had the support of the machine. She considered it seriously to the point that the *Daily Democrat* ran a story in early May with the headline "Mrs. Fulbright Considers Race. Is urged to run for Congress but has not yet decided." The story noted, "Mrs. Fulbright has been solicited by quite a number of people both men and women and some groups." A week later a news story announced she would not be a candidate, and three days later in "As I See It" she gave the reasons:

> My name became almost inadvertently attached to the idea of a candidate for Congress. I'll admit it had its lure for me as it does for most folks. I have entertained the idea for some days but I realize that I do not know the intricacies of good politics not even bad politics.
>
> I am lame in the knee, so cannot "stand" for election as they do in England and by the same reason cannot RUN as they do here. I could sit in Congress and I believe I could represent this district comfortably but I believe I must leave politics to the politicians.
>
> I truly appreciate those who so generously came to my support. It warmed the cockles of my heart no little but I fear the strain of the campaign would shorten my tenure on this sphere.
>
> So rendering unto Caesar the things that are Caesar's, I resign my desires and ambitions to those who know the game and like to play it.

It was not that simple for Roberta Fulbright, businesswoman and newspaper publisher, to remove herself from the political game. Having been identified as a leader with candidate potential, she became a player who did not run but who guarded the goal of good government with her newspaper.

She did not rush to judgment. Her business involvement tended to make her a political pragmatist, but only to a point. That point was when pragmatism collided with her sense of civic responsibility and duty and her moral commitment to honesty, decency, and fair play. The heavy-handed practices of the Washington County political machine gradually pushed her to that point.

There was a lot of sound and fury in 1933 on the part of the aroused citizens, but no real progress. In June, the Voters Protective League drew five hundred people to a meeting where a resolution was passed seeking the resignation of Judge Combs and three county officials, including Sheriff Harley Gover. It scored Combs for "aiding and advising" in election irregularities. It served only to rile Combs who characterized the resolution as "dirty, filthy, slimy, scurrilous, libelous and scandalous."

Reformers were encouraged in October 1933, when a grand jury, acting on the audit of the county judge's office, returned indictments against Sheriff Harley Gover's father, Jeff Gover, for perjury. The basis for the indictments was fraud. One charge claimed "$45,366 paid for a bridge that could have cost $14,780." But the indictments were in Judge Combs's court and defense motions to deny charges and delay action received favorable rulings from the court.

Finally in April 1934, Pros. Atty. J. W. (Jim) Trimble gave up and asked for dismissal of all indictments, putting the fat in the fire again. Comptroller Smith scored the action in an angry blast that got statewide newspaper coverage, saying: "The Fayetteville fiasco is a disgrace to civil government . . . until public sentiment becomes more militant, public plunder will continue." The *Arkansas Gazette* had a highly critical editorial, which Lessie Read reprinted, in addition to expressing the *Democrat*'s dismay that "adverse publicity is all that Washington County seems able to achieve by its various election contests, court charges that never come to trial and public protests of one kind or another filed by the politically organized . . . What can the people of Washington County do?"

Ever sensitive to unfavorable publicity that might fuel new efforts to move the University of Arkansas from Fayetteville to Little Rock, county residents moved to organize the Good Citizenship League of Northwest Arkansas. Several organizations, including the Voters Protective League, folded membership into the new group which was broken into smaller units in various county communities. This all occurred while Roberta was pondering the race for Congress.

Once her decision on that was made, she and her editor turned their attention to the new crisis. They decided women might be the answer. The Washington County Democratic Women's Club, which Lessie chaired, decided to try and find "county commit-teemen acceptable to women Democrats in each precinct." The idea, which sounded fine in discussion and meetings, was to have women identify potential committee nominees and circulate peti-tions to place their names on the ballot. In practice it didn't succeed. Even though one of their neighbors, Ella B. Hurst, was a candidate for the state House of Representatives, women of that day found it hard to trade their aprons for petition and pencil and their gardens and clubs for door-to-door canvassing. The timing wasn't good, either. The idea was proposed only a few weeks before the filing deadline. The failure of the effort brought the first "As I See It" on the machine problem.

> I looked over the political fence not long ago and I saw
> several things I'd never seen before. For one thing, I found
> out beyond a shadow of a doubt, that the most coveted thing
> in a candidate's mind is ELECTION MACHINERY. Far more
> than press, school or pulpit it is favored.
>
> By election machinery, I mean judges and clerks in every
> precinct in every election. Those judges and clerks for the
> primary come by way of the county committee who
> appoint these officials . . . I have heard (sub rosa and I am not
> vouching for this) that there is in this county an association
> of election returns officials, who pay dues and do all things
> needful to insure the election of their favorite candidate. By

these means and those of a similar nature, one's permanence in office, once secured may be made almost permanent. From this office a strong effort was made to interest women in the selection of desirable committeemen but they, like those of old, were tilling a field, attending a tea, playing bridge or some other excuse, even as those bidden to the feast while those who are IN and who really mean business go out in the highways and byways and gather their own crowd in and compel them to judges and clerks desks to get their men elected. The fate of Democracy hinges on the ability to get honest votes and an honest count. Be not deceived, we must bear our own responsibility for these things.

In reality, about the only positive effect that public outcry had in the summer of 1934 was the big drop in poll-tax receipts, down to six thousand from eleven thousand in 1932. The Good Citizenship League didn't get a full slate of candidates for the Democratic primary. But the machine took no chances with those who did file. It allowed no minority election officials to the challengers at the election. This led to a protest by Roberta in her column. "I can't perceive why it would not have been just plain fair for the minority in the Central Committee to have had representation at the polls in the form of a judge. I just can't figure it. I may be wrong. I'd like it explained. FAIR is right to both."

She did have some cause to celebrate when the votes were counted. Ella Hurst led the ticket in her race for state representative. The attempt to involve the women in the election process had some effect. Roberta called Ella's feat a "feather in her cap and the cap of the county."

The following day she wrote about the primary in a conciliatory way but still clucked her tongue in oblique criticism of the machine.

> The Democratic Primary has "came and went,"* and we
> bow in congratulations to those who are "staying in." We like

---

*The colloquial expression "came and went" was a favorite of Roberta's throughout her career; although it is most closely identified with her when she later applied it to Homer Adkins following his gubernatorial campaign visit to Fayetteville.

them all, always have. They have been good to us many times.

The machine age is upon us, "machine displaces man" is the comment heard and read over again in regard to our woes.

Men, in any machine, become instead of men only cogs and bolts, screws and nuts. Surely poor roles for the lords of creation. I believe they were intended for high domain, for individual action and thought. . . . Our times have become so mechanized that individual rights have suffered almost to extinction. The masculine qualities of leadership, independence and self support are having a combat with combined forces of machines of every type, metal, mental and political.

The Washington County machine chose to ignore the publisher's lament and acted like a true machine, tightening the nuts and bolts of its control in the 1934 general election. Because it had fewer poll-tax receipts to manipulate, the machine was forced to look for a new method to control the general election when the Good Citizenship League candidates announced as independents. The new tool was the corrupt practice pledge. This pledge was required by law to be filed before primary elections. It had not been required in general elections. The election commission was not announced until October. When the commission received the petitions of the independent candidates, it ruled them ineligible because they had not met its requirement of filing the pledges thirty days before the election.

But the spark that ignited the flame under the *Democrat* editor and publisher was the omission from the ballot of twenty-seven candidates for justice of the peace, nominated in the Democratic primary, an omission revealed on the eve of the November 6 election. The nominees came from eleven townships. Here again a perversion of the corrupt practice pledge was used. These candidates had filed such pledges in July and had never before been required to file again before the November election. They were of the opinion they were being punished for circulating petitions to put a county salary act on the ballot. That act would have allowed the quorum court to lower county salaries. The machine had fought the proposal in court, but Chancery Judge Lee

Seamster put it on the ballot. To compound the indignity of the omitted candidates, in some instances on election day, the machine handed out typed lists of candidates to be written in for the positions left vacant by the removals from the ballot.

Two days after the election, Lessie wrote a call-to-arms editorial titled "University City," a subtle reminder of the need to protect the pride of Fayetteville. She called for all to rally around the cause of good government. The next day she reported:

> The telephone rang late, long and loudly last night. Some calls came from the city, some from the county, some from Fort Smith and some from Little Rock. It was from black and white, rich and poor, Democrat and Republican and mugwump. Little Rock people were emphatic that nothing could restore the state's faith in this county except a public declaration of both people and politicians on behalf of clean politics and good government . . . one man said "when our ballots fail we can always use bullets." We are hoping to avoid that but we're not saying there is no danger.

Lessie continued to fan the flame of public indignation for several days, obviously with her publisher's backing, and the battle was joined; the crafty pols and their protective circuit court judge were now arrayed against two determined newspaper women. Lessie, the tall, angular editor, was the fiery crusader. Roberta was the stocky, solid wall of moral indignation. It wasn't possible in the 1930s for women to be privy to the usual forums of community and policy machination. That took place in the offices or stag gatherings of male business owners and politicians. Denied that access, Roberta, in concert with her editor, allied herself with those she considered defenders of the public trust, convinced herself of their moral uprightness, and used the power of her paper to support what and who she thought was best for the political well-being of Fayetteville and Washington County. She wasn't timid in her approach, even in the face of personal and legal attacks.

It would take almost two years to break the hold the machine had on the city and county. Neither of the other two leading papers in the county, the *Progressive Star* of Fayetteville or the neighboring *Springdale News* joined the fray. In fact, the *Star* tended to support the machine and to attack the *Democrat*. As luck would have it, development of several federal indictments of local and county officials and their trials in 1935 provided the ammunition for the steady editorial salvos of the *Democrat* editor and publisher, two of which landed them in court before the battle was won.

Roberta's intense involvement in the political battles led the staff at the newspaper to set up an office for her on the second floor—she had not maintained one before—and she announced it in her column.

> Do you know I am ensconced in a new office over the *Democrat*—Room 200? My door says Roberta Fulbright, President. So Franklin and I are trying out our schemes. I never really wanted to be an honest to goodness business woman and I am in mortal fear of becoming one. Some of my helpers have decided that's my only role and while any other field would thrill me more, here I am.

In December, word came that Fayetteville police chief Neal Cruse and city attorney Rex Perkins were subjects of a federal grand jury investigation in the federal district court in Fort Smith. The charges were conspiracy in connection with an auto theft ring in Washington County. The Fayetteville Civil Service Commission attempted to suspend Cruse several times only to have Judge Combs reinstate him.

The indictments returned by the grand jury against the auto theft ring, that implicated Cruse and Perkins, enabled the *Democrat* to keep public interest aroused. The paper made frequent editorial reference to "the good government group" or "honest elections committee" activities. The first test of the crusade came in the March 1935 city election for mayor and one contested alderman position. The Good Citizenship League supported the winning candidates and rated a banner *Democrat* headline, "Clean Sweep for Good Government." Roberta was happy to see that "people will respond to the proper stimulus and honest publicity is that stimulus."

The theft ring trials came in June in Fort Smith. Perkins was freed on a directed verdict from Judge Heartsill Ragon. The trial for Cruse and a plumber, Homer Christman, who made dyes for the stolen vehicles, ended in a mistrial. But new ammunition was delivered in October when federal indictments charging violation of internal revenue law on the importing and manufacturing of whiskey were returned against Sheriff Harley Gover; his brother, Deputy Sheriff Ellis Gover; and three conspirators, including the farmer-bootlegger Dee McConnell. The charges alleged that a still owned by McConnell had been confiscated by federal officers and stored in the Washington County jail with Sheriff Gover and that Gover had helped McConnell put the still back in operation. Gover made bond, and heading the group going in on his bond was Vol Pullen, chairman of the county Democratic Central Committee.

Public indignation was high but not effective enough to get local circuit court action on the charged officials. Judge Combs claimed the court had no money for a local grand jury. Roberta fumed:

> We are almost accustomed to being ruled by the "indicted." First one then another holding offices are indicted in the federal courts . . . and then state and county courts refuse to investigate or pursue those charges, those in high places of power and preferment go on the bonds of those indicted and the good old American game of passing the buck is in full swing.
>
> . . . All of this proves to my mind that there is a ring so closely woven that fear of a break brings all forces into play . . . It is not lack of funds, my friends, it is lack of courage and honesty and integrity and even imagination. The funds come when those who desire them say come!

A couple of days later she called for a mass meeting to pump for the removal of the indicted officials. The public did not respond to the call, but the prosecuting attorney, Jim Trimble, was persuaded to ask Judge Combs in open court to empanel a grand jury to consider the Gover indictment. He appeared in court and drew a banner headline—"Gover Removal Asked by Trimble"—when he filed a request. A month later, in response to the petition for removal, Combs said he would not act until after the federal trial. A big crowd gathered for that hearing and when Trimble presented his petition, crowd members cheered. Combs threatened contempt citations for any further outbursts and directed the indicted sheriff to make arrests if necessary. Sheriff Gover made a show of going to the back of the courtroom and handing guns to two deputies. An incensed Roberta wrote of that scene and concluded:

> So there is power. There are rights but they do not belong to the citizens. They are in the hands of those with the guns in office.

The gun of office was taken out of Sheriff Gover's hand in early 1936. The series of cases in Judge Ragon's court kept Fayetteville on a yo-yo string. In January, Gover was found guilty on a felony charge of conspiring to violate liquor laws. That same month, in a retrial of Chief of Police Cruse and Homer Christman, the jury found Cruse not guilty and Christman guilty in connection with the auto theft ring. Another jury had found five other men guilty on these charges.

The guilty verdict for Gover led to new calls for local court action after he appealed the verdict. Roberta finally challenged Combs by name in a column for the first time.

> The middle syllable of the word politics is "pass the buck," the next syllable is "take no responsibility." Now as I see it, the case of our sheriff is plainly up to Judge John Combs and if I completely recall, he said if the sheriff were convicted he would then remove him from office. This presents this case to the circuit court convening next week.

As might have been predicted, Judge Combs declined to act. But a defense witness for Gover in his first trial took the matter out of Judge Combs's hands as Gover's second trial with Dee McConnell came to federal court. Earl C. Edgar said he had lied in the first trial when he testified that Gover had destroyed the McConnell still and sold it for junk. He fingered Ellis Gover as the one who had persuaded him to perjure himself. McConnell threw in the towel and pleaded guilty February 6, and later in the day Gover also entered a guilty plea.

Judge Ragon at first delayed the Gover sentencing. He later gave him thirty months in a federal reformatory. Ragon ended his court's year-long involvement with Fayetteville and Washington County with a blistering rebuke to the town when he sentenced Homer Christman, the illiterate plumber, to sixty days in jail. He said at one point:

> I am afraid the people of Fayetteville are a little too complacent about what is going on up there. This poor ignorant man saw a chief of police riding around in that car until it got too hot. Christman saw a deputy trading in stolen cars. The city attorney was mixed up in it. Here were three officers of the law charged with enforcing the law and he saw them mixed up in plain, downright stealing.

Judge Ragon also said that his federal district court had looked like a Washington County court for the past year. All major daily papers in the state, led by the two Little Rock papers—the *Arkansas Democrat* and the *Arkansas Gazette*—picked up the story. To be made front-page news of this nature was galling to Roberta and her Fayetteville compatriots. She wrote of "the shame of the blame of it." Her paper issued a call-to-arms in a front-page editorial. It also reprinted an editorial from the *Arkansas Gazette* under the heading "As Others See Us." The *Gazette's* editorial appeared in the space usually reserved for "As I See It." That editorial lectured Fayetteville on its responsibility to the state because the university was located there.

In his public scolding, Judge Ragon also expressed dismay at what had happened to Harley Gover:

> Here is the tragedy of a young man, sheriff of that county, coming in to receive a sentence, a fine looking young fellow with every opportunity in the world.
>
> It's tragic. I don't believe he would have ever been in this position today if he had not seen elder men and more substantial men doing the same thing.

Gover resigned a week after his guilty plea. At the urging of Roberta and others, Gov. J. M. Futrell appointed Herbert (Buck) Lewis, member of a respected Fayetteville family, to fill the vacancy. The newspaper and the town turned back to a public rally to whip up sentiment against the remaining county officials and Judge Combs. Two thousand people heard a fiery oration from Comptroller Griffin Smith and shouted approval to a resolution calling on Judge Combs to resign. As usual the judge ignored the request.

The first test of leadership for the *Democrat* and the good government group came in a city Democratic primary in February. Rex Perkins, undaunted by his alleged link with a car theft ring, sought reelection as city attorney. He was opposed by Price Dickson, who had the support of the Good Citizenship League. The *Democrat* printed a front-page "contributed" editorial that alluded to Perkins circulars that attacked the Fulbright family and called Dickson a "tool" of the Fulbrights. Lessie also ran an editorial with an excerpt from Judge Ragon's castigation of Fayetteville officials and its statement that "the city attorney is mixed up in it." Dickson won decisively, and Roberta was gracious in victory, writing ". . . of the recent city elections I will make no comment. The people have spoken so much louder than I that I add nothing but my approval."

Perkins didn't let her enjoy her victory long. Within two weeks he had filed a forty-thousand-dollar libel suit against the *Democrat*. The suit was filed late Saturday afternoon after the *Democrat* had gone to press. The editor and publisher learned of it from friends and a story in the Sunday edition of a Fort Smith paper. The front-page "contributed" editorial and the repeat of Judge Ragon's remarks in Lessie's editorial were cited as the libelous articles and twenty thousand dollars was sought on each of the two counts. Compounding the problem for Roberta was the fact that Judge Combs would be hearing the case.

The lawsuit bothered Roberta but did not deter her, and she shared her thoughts in "As I See It" several times and subsequently to a second suit filed in late March against Phipps Lumber Company. This suit sought fifty-five thousand dollars in damages for two children burned when a gas tank exploded and burned one seriously. (The suit acknowledged the explosion occurred when "through childish curiosity, a boy had lifted the lid off a gas can and lighted a match to see what was in it.") Roberta responded:

> The lawsuit against the paper filed by City Attorney Rex Perkins is the price we pay for raising our voices in behalf of decency and honesty in government.
>
> Lawsuits would hold very little terror for me if I were assured of honest proceeding in court. Respect for the courts and law is the foundation of good citizenship and cannot be maintained without honest courts . . . So I'm still game for a lawsuit if only I can have an honest able judge, an unbiased jury and honest lawyer.

Five days later the Phipps suit was filed, and she would write again:

> As you may have observed, law suits are showering about our heads like shells from a machine gun . . . It has been grapevined to me from one lily white soul, that they would sue me "until hell froze over," whether they won anything or not. So there's their notice friends, and as you can easily see, it is trouble, money and worry for me.

Her friends rallied to her support, quite literally. The Perkins suit was on the docket for the court session opening April 27. On April 25, more than one thousand persons attended a Good Citizenship League rally. Speakers included Sam Yancey, director of the Western Methodist Assembly of Fayetteville, and Rev. John Asbell, Roberta's minister. Representatives from the Women's Civic Club, Business and Professional Women's Club (B&PW), American Association of University Women (AAUW), and the Legion Auxiliary were on the platform. Once again all present approved a resolution to ask Judge Combs to resign.

On the first day of court, the *Democrat* had a report on the presentation of the resolution under a headline "Dramatic Scene Opens Circuit Court" and had this report of the happenings:

> In a dramatic scene witnessed by several hundred people, Judge John S. Combs refused to disqualify himself as judge

of the Washington County Circuit Court, declaring "there is no real reason for the request."

Rev. Sam Yancey, leader of the movement to oust Judge Combs, engaged the Judge in a few moments of sharp repartee before he retired from the courtroom.

In the exchange, Yancey said, "I have lost faith in you and your court."

Combs replied, "The people of the county have not."

Predictably, Judge Combs, who so often granted defense demurrers for "machine" defendants, denied those filed by the *Democrat* lawyers on the grounds that the editorials only repeated what a federal judge had said. He also would not grant a continuance until June so that Bill Fulbright could join the defense team.

However, that was when the suit was tried. Combs would allow no significance or referral to the good government campaign, saying he knew of no such campaign. The defense case depended not only on that, but also on testimony from trials in Judge Ragon's court. Combs ruled all this inadmissible and gave a directed verdict against the *Democrat*. He instructed the jury to consider nothing but the amount of damages. Jurors could not agree on any sum and were finally dismissed. Though Combs promised it, there was no retrial. The Phipps lawsuit did not come up in 1936, but it did play a key role in the 1936 Democratic primary that saw Roberta abandon support of Ella B. Hurst, who was running for a state senate seat.

Roberta found it hard to believe the judge had not heard of her good government campaign.

> Of course there is no known way for a layman to prove that a Judge knows anything but we had supposed that knowledge of the *Democrat*'s campaign for good government was fairly widespread. We will endeavor in the future to make this county campaign more definite and more widely diffused . . . so that a wayfaring Judge may become more aware that there is a campaign in progress to rid the county of exploiters, gangsters, self perpetuating officers, ringsters and so on. In short, war against corruption in high places.

Then it was time to turn all the editorial artillery on the August Democratic primary. It was also during this time, according to Allan Gilbert in *A Fulbright Chronicle,* that "anonymous phone calls, obscene letters, threats and innuendo became almost daily occurrences for the Fulbright family." Fulbright employee John Clark, who regularly accompanied Roberta on her rounds, began carrying a handgun. Still, said Gilbert, Roberta persevered:

> In keeping with her promise to make her reform campaign more definite, Roberta launched a three-part strategy in early summer of 1936 aimed at the August party primary: (1) to publicize the misdeeds of public officials; (2) systematically counter charges mounted by the opposition; and (3) encourage voters to study the issues and more importantly, to vote.

Sensing the turning tide, the machine needed to control the sheriff and the Democratic county committee, for Sheriff Buck Lewis was proving to be a strong candidate for reelection. It turned to a former sheriff, Henry Walker, who almost didn't make it on the ticket. County committee chairman Vol Pullen said Walker did not pay his filing fee by the deadline. Walker said he thought his check had been mislaid by Pullen and appealed to the committee, which overruled Pullen, and the battle line was drawn.

Roberta took the attack to Walker. She reminded her readers:

> During the tenure of a former sheriff, Mr. Walker, it cost this county in round numbers $20,000 per year or approximately $1,500 per month . . . we are now getting our sheriffing done for $900.

Later, when Walker was campaigning on a poor-man image, she reported on a little research:

> Henry says he is poor. We find in the records, forty-eight (48) pieces of property since he got on the county payroll. This does not include his sawmill.

She went on to list the legal description of each piece of property.

In advertisements in other papers and in circulars, known in those days as "broadsides," Walker slammed Roberta with an accusation of jury fixing in an old suit against the Phipps Lumber Company and Jack Fulbright by a Florida development company. While Jack was at Phipps he had bought some lots near Coral Gables in the era of the infamous Florida land boom, and after the original developer went out of business and the lots turned out not to be valuable ocean-front property as claimed, no further payments were made. A successor development company brought suit for those payments. Walker claimed a "fixed" jury rendered a favorable verdict for Phipps. It had happened, apparently, but without Roberta's knowledge. She decided to stand and fight. In probably the longest column she ever wrote, she answered the allegation. She titled it "No Lies Thank You" and included a subtitle, "The Coral Gables Affair." She began by declaring:

> There is one thing I can't resort to, even to elect officers whom I think would be the salvation of Washington county. I cannot resort to lies.

She then recounted the story of the failed investment and subsequent suit. She said that "every man in my employ knows I not only always disapprove of bribery but absolutely forbid it when from time to time the hopelessness of justice has been borne in on us and it has been suggested." She said she had been sick in bed when "a former sheriff and a Walker deputy and jury members had solicited the bribe" of her employees, and she did not learn of the incident until much later. Then she put her own spin on the allegations:

> I felt in my heart, it was a body blow to me designed by them to gag me and stifle the paper. For a moment I was staggered, then I said to myself, "I have not done one thing. I am innocent." I see more clearly than ever the cause of decency, law and order must be served . . . I will continue and increase my fight for honesty.
>
> . . . Now readers, more than once escape through bribery has been proffered to my representatives and other business firms here and always has been pictured as very easy and very cheap. I have always said no. I think it has been so much the custom that those who engage in it have ceased to consider

the right or wrong. Their whole concern is how much can be extracted.

These are some of the fruits of the tree of corruption which seems to have spread itself over our fair county . . . the buying of this particular jury by those near to me is a by-product of the great fundamental rottenness of this county. A jury for sale, a judge who sits as a trial lawyer always in cahoots with one side against the other and whose mind is so prejudiced as to shut out all semblance of justice; the illegal purchases of poll taxes; the stealing of elections; the protection of crime by those sworn to prosecute it; the growing powerful and rich from the returns of that protection; the attempted extortion in trumped up damage suits. These are some of the phases of rottenness in this county, on account of which I have risked my peace of mind and the very existence of my interests in an attempt to help clean up.

This column was pure Roberta Waugh, smart, proud, combative, canny, and determined to carry the day. Here she turned to face squarely two demons: the resentment she knew many felt because of her business success and her discomfort with the compromises it had taken to attain that success. She wrote that she always said "no" to bribery. She did not say what her representatives might have said in other instances when bribery was offered "more than once." If she had looked the other way, it was to be no longer. She was tired of the duplicity the corruption spawned and vowed to root it out.

She was as good as her word. The *Democrat* attacked poll-tax fraud by printing the entire Washington County poll-tax list several weeks before the election, so errors could be seen and reported, and by seeking the opinion of a respected former supreme court justice, J. M. Hill, on illegal poll-tax assessments and the penalties for violating the law. The paper gave much of its front and editorial pages to a facsimile of his opinion and a fraudulent poll-tax assessment example.

With their candidates in such hot contests, the machine-controlled Democratic central committee used its last weapon, the primary ballot. It was printed without the names of good government candidates for committeemen. The omission was revealed the day before the election. The *Democrat* in a front-page editorial and in Roberta's column blasted the chicanery and urged write-in votes for the omitted candidates. The paper expressed the opinion that the "crooks are trying to steal today's election. Especially are they trying to perpetuate the Central Committee so that two years from now it may 'do its duty' for John Combs."

The good government campaign didn't do well with the write-in votes but it scored a stunning victory otherwise. Buck Lewis beat Walker by a five-hundred-vote margin. I. R. Rothrock, whom Roberta had endorsed, won a close race for county judge over a Cruse family member.

The wheels had finally come off the machine. Writing of the successful effort of his grandmother, Allan Gilbert said:

> In the beginning of her reform campaign, it is probably fair to say that Roberta and her editor, Mrs. Read, were rank novices in the art of media warfare. They learned as they went, by trial and error, digging information out of public records and organizing both attack and response in a manner calculated to keep leverage on the issues, even through the doldrums of the torpid summer. They got better as they went along, and it is equally fair to say they ended up as experts.

And Roberta told her readers:

> Friends, before this election there was a concerted deep-seated and far-reaching effort to overpower the press, gag the paper and shut my mouth (not altogether successful).

Of her editor, she said:

> Lessie Read may have faults, but they are not lack of honesty, courage or energy.
>
> I wonder where this country would be without its women.
>
> I just can't help wondering.

It might also be said Roberta learned to play hardball politics. The lawyer for the plaintiffs in the Phipps lawsuit over the injury to the two boys angered her, particularly since one of the children was so clearly at fault. George (Ab) Hurst, husband of Ella Hurst, filed the suit. It was not long before Maupin Cummings filed against Mrs. Hurst in the state senate race. Cummings recalled that Roberta called him to affirm her support for his candidacy. The reason given for opposing Mrs. Hurst was that she would only be a mouthpiece for her husband, and Roberta used that suggestion in one of her columns. A day later in the *Springdale News,* Ella Hurst lashed out against the *Democrat* and the good government group, saying she had lost their endorsement when the lawsuit was filed and claiming, "those people immediately threatened me with opposition and with loss of their support if Mr. Hurst did not withdraw the damage suit. Up until that time they were strong for me." Cummings won the race.

Roberta was grateful for the election victories and proud of her paper's role.

> We are proud of the *Democrat's* part in this campaign for honesty. We risked our money, our time, our business prestige on this. We did not get everything but we are pleased.
>
> We had help, good help and we appreciate every bit of it. We had the organized women of the town who did yeoman service . . . there are many others who lifted a load and to my mind this sort of stand is what a paper should do and mean in a community. May it always stand for the people against the few, "unawed by influence; unbribed by gain."

The battle was won, but the war was not quite over. Judge Combs was still on the circuit court bench, and Claude Fuller was still in Congress.

Roberta took off on a trip east after the primary, but her troops moved quickly to solidify their position. Two highly respected county residents, Steve Ratliff and Bill Yates—though not committeemen—stood for election as chairman and secretary of the central committee. The *Democrat* noted that the rules allowed non-members to seek those offices and in an editorial reported that Ratliff had said, "So long as I am chairman, I promise not one legally-nominated candidate for office will have his name left off the Democratic ticket."

In 1937, Pros. Atty. Jim Trimble of Berryville kept his name before the public with a series of cases filed in chancery court against former county officials, including Henry Walker and Harley Gover and their bonding companies for unaccounted-for funds. In 1938, he filed for circuit judge against Judge Combs and in the primary carried every county in the judicial district in a resounding repudiation of the man who did not know there was a good government campaign.

Roberta obviously thought the election victories indicated that the clean-up had removed all danger of poll-tax fraud in spite of widespread evidence across the South that this was not the case. The year of those triumphs that warmed her editorial and political heart, she took exception to the campaign to repeal the poll tax. When President Roosevelt wrote to Brooks Hays, the state Democratic national committeeman, supporting the repeal effort, the publisher, who seldom disagreed with her president, took strong exception to his position.

> I can't believe even our President realizes how difficult it is
> to have an election in Arkansas. It is my belief that registra-
> tion alone will make it easier to manipulate elections . . . the
> privilege of voting is not a natural inherent right but a state
> given one and the state has a right to impose a minimum tax
> for that privilege.

This position was a departure from her libertarian views about free will and the liberty of thought and action. She obviously felt she had won the recent political battle against corruption in part through the tangibility of a poll-tax receipt and the listing of the purchaser's name on a public list that she could publish. She wasn't willing to risk having her foes learn how to subvert to their purposes a new system of certifying voters.

She did not speak out on local races in 1938, though she did endorse Jim Trimble for circuit judge and her friend Clyde Ellis in his race against Rep. Claude Fuller. Both won, Trimble handily, and Ellis by 109 votes.

She explained her restraint in a pre-primary column.

In the absence of the bitter fight of two years ago and the fact there are several good men in county races and they are our neighbors; we feel a hesitance at naming any one.

She also continued her active support of her friend, Sen. Hattie Caraway, who was opposed by Rep. John McClellan in the 1938 Democratic primary. In one column she said, "I prophesy that she will be Senator when 1944 comes around. She's a person to be proud of, one to support, one of the famous women of the world."

In a later column, she had a bit of fun with McClellan's choice of an out-of-state bride.

It sort of seems to me that Congressman McClellan forfeited his right to the women's vote of Arkansas when he deserted our boundaries for a bride. There was not a woman in Arkansas on whom he could cast his approving smile. I'm all for him going to Carolina to get his votes. Why should Arkansas women cast their votes for a man who couldn't cast them a smile? Women all know what I mean. This is women's stuff.

Having made her appeal to women, a month later she turned her attention to the men:

The best efforts of both sexes are needed in order to steer this planet off the rocks. So Sons of Women Be Men, and give honor where honor is due. That is the test of sportsmanship at all times in all places. Be Sports.

Whether or not the men voters were "sports," Senator Caraway did defeat McClellan. Roberta could prophesy, but she could not foresee that in 1944, she would not be supporting her friend, the woman senator, and she would not mind that the winning senatorial candidate had married an out-of-state bride.

She mused about her strong interest in politics in the summer when Senator Caraway was running.

I fancy many of my readers wonder why I take an interest in politics to really espouse or oppose different candidates.

Perhaps I don't know myself. It is one of those urges from within that must find expression without but I am not running for office, none of my family is running. Public money has always had me on the wrong side of the ledger, paying rather than receiving.

It was true at that point no one in her family was even considering running for office. Four years later one of her sons would run, and the courage and commitment of Roberta Fulbright, the political savvy her fight had given her, and the groundwork she laid for more honest elections in Washington County would be key in that son's victory. It was an election that led ultimately to the name Fulbright being known and respected internationally—a fitting tribute to this stalwart woman's abiding interest and involvement in politics.

CHAPTER VII

Of Other Things

The highly charged political battles were not the only crises facing Roberta and the citizens of Washington County in the 1930s. The crippling effects of the nation's Great Depression —the collapse of the stock market; the succession of bank failures; the closing of businesses and industries; and mounting nationwide unemployment, hunger, and homelessness—hit hard locally.

As the depression deepened, jobs and money became scarce. Housing was a luxury that many could not afford, although carpenters worked for $3.50 a day, and a house could be plumbed for $40. Retailers around the Fayetteville square began to feel the pinch. A man's dress shirt sold for 69 cents; a woman's cotton dress for a dollar. A loaf of bread was a nickel, and coffee was 32 cents a pound. In a county heavily dependent upon its fruit crops, a bushel of apples brought 50 cents, the same price as in the 1860s. At the Red Cross Drugstore, Morris Collier was selling a chicken salad sandwich, sundae, or soda for 15 cents.

In only a few months' time in 1930, more than one hundred Arkansas banks failed. None of these was in Fayetteville, but the First National Bank took over the assets of Jay Fulbright's former bank, Arkansas National Bank. Roberta's earlier disposal of stock in Arkansas National was both fortuitous and fortunate. Along with other banks across the country, the Fayetteville banks were closed from March 4–16, 1933, or in the vernacular of the day, they were placed on holiday.

As President Franklin Roosevelt took office and began his New Deal programs, a nation held its collective breath. Roberta assumed an optimistic posture:

> We are turning a corner today. We can't quite see around
> it. But water still flows down hill and through our mains.
> Cows are still giving milk; gas is in the mains; chickens are
> laying eggs. Fruit is growing, better than usual, I'm told, and

the trees are budding. There is a big market for smiles and the supply does not nearly equal the demand, so let's begin to manufacture a few. As a community we are still sound. Sound men are at the helm; sound citizens in the home. Faith, hope and charity still may abide.

Still, she did not agree with all recovery policy:

A moratorium on debts seems a bit superfluous, to my mind. Several persons who happen to owe me have been participating in a holiday of that type for some two or three years, and it appears to me that natural and economic laws see to it that those who cannot pay do not pay.

Citizens Bank, where Roberta became the president following the death of Frank Gray, survived the depression, and on January 1, 1934, its deposits were insured by the Federal Deposit Insurance Corporation. The Bank of Elkins, also a part of the Fulbright interests, was one of the first banks to reopen after the nationwide "holiday." Roberta—who succeeded John Clark as president of the bank—along with cashier J. E. Bunch and his assistant Clyde West guided the bank through the depression by keeping its best customers in the fold. Years later Bunch would say: "That Roberta, what a charmer she was. She could wrap the entire board around her finger and make every member think what she wanted done was his idea. But above all we respected her because she was a darned good business woman."

Despite the tough times of the 1930s, Fayetteville's population grew to more than seven thousand. This growth came while many other areas of the state were losing population and industries in the throes of the depression. Gradually, the city began to show benefits from the myriad of New Deal programs and from its status as the home of the University of Arkansas.

Not only was Fayetteville the county seat of Washington County, it was also the area's trade center. It survived as a railroad shipping point and as a marketing center for the diversified agricultural economy which still included reliance on orchards, truck farms, and the canning and lumber industries. The depression did bring a decline in the once-thriving apple industry. Plagued by collapsing prices, pests, and disease, it never fully recovered.

Yet it was the agricultural economy which helped the area survive the depression. By growing their own gardens and raising their own cattle and poultry, the area residents were able, in large measure, to provide for themselves. Many worked at two jobs—if they could find them—to make ends meet.

The largest payroll in the city was that of the university. The depression brought about a paradox in the life of the school. While state appropriations dropped and enrollment increased by only three hundred students from 1925 to 1935, the physical plant grew. Thanks to President Roosevelt's public works program, new agriculture, engineering, and chemistry buildings became a part of the campus. A new library opened, and a new men's gymnasium replaced the structure Jay Fulbright had donated.

The university gained a 22,500-seat football stadium under the supervision of the Works Progress Administration. It was the football team which brought some cheer to the depression years, particularly a first-ever 1933 victory over arch-rival Texas, 20-6, at Austin.

While a strong supporter of the president's recovery efforts, Roberta showed some minor irritation with the administration's Henry Wallace when he came to town in 1934.

> Secretary of Agriculture Wallace drew a large and enthu-
> siastic audience. The cotton situation is beyond my ken.—I
> was a bit irked at his patronizing postscript: "The ladies must
> take a hand and the preachers . . ." Women play major roles
> in time of depression and my estimate of a man's judgment
> suffers when he does not realize this.

The Fulbright enterprises weathered the depression—although Bill Fulbright again feared they might go broke—and benefited from the gradually improving economy, providing Roberta with a sense of satisfaction. A phenomenon of the depression, recalled Allan Gilbert, was the demand for soft drinks, a plus for the Fulbright bottling works which added other brands to its original Coca-Cola offering. The Washington Hotel added a new roof garden with flower boxes, colorful outdoor furniture, and grass rugs. The new facility provided views of Fayetteville from three directions. Several parties followed the opening, but at the first, the landlords—the Fulbright family—were guests of hotel manager Sam Peck and his wife, Henryetta.

Roberta was a strong booster for her hometown and never missed an opportunity to sing its praises.

> A university city draws to itself more of culture and fine atmosphere than other places of equal size to begin with. Then, those who come to study are in their pristine freshness and impressions are very lasting and fond. Added to this are our lovely hills, the purest water in the country, the lay of the land, the set of the trees and above all those rare persons whom we love and cherish.

At the same time, she always had suggestions for improvement: to build a library and a park and to clean up piles of junk along the city's approaches.

Her desire for a new library and her service on the library site committee in 1935 led her to offer the donation of a lot facing on Lafayette Avenue opposite Mont Nord as a site for the proposed library. While the city planning board and a group of allied civic clubs rallied behind the offer, the Fayetteville City Council voted 6-2 against a resolution to request Public Works Administration funds for the building project, expressing fears that millage money for the hospital and fire fund would be lost if the library millage were tied together with the fund. The proposal died.

While public excitement over the proposal was at its peak, Roberta went to Santa Fe, New Mexico, to attend the annual fiesta. Upon her return she commented on the events.

> I never considered that my proposed lot was a particularly good one for the purpose, but a committee from the executive board came to me and suggested I offer it.
>
> My contention has always been that it's risky to give anything to anybody, individually or collectively. It takes grace to give and grace to accept, one of which is generally lacking . . . it would be nice to have a library.

In addition to the Great Depression, the 1930s brought another momentous event: the end of prohibition and the return of legal liquor sales. In 1915, Arkansas had become the sixteenth state to pass a state prohibition bill which went into effect January 1, 1916. Following the 1932 election, Congress passed the Twenty-first Amendment repealing prohibition. Arkansas voters joined the national majority favoring repeal. Jumping on the national bandwagon and responding to a call for new tax revenues, the Arkansas legislature passed the Thorn Liquor Act in 1935 legalizing liquor and 6 percent beer.

Long a proponent of outlawing liquor sales, Roberta would say later: "I was brought up a rank and belligerent prohibitionist, the only way really to be brought up. My husband and I were teetotalers and fought for temperance in our little town in Missouri."

Among readers of the *Daily Democrat,* opinion was more closely divided. In the newspaper's poll, they voted 392-389 in favor of dry. More than once in "As I See It," Roberta editorialized on the dangers of alcohol.

> I was brought up on prohibition. I believed it, sponsored it, and practiced it until we had it on our statutes about 15 years and I had a certain swerve of reason. I decided the forbidden fruit had become the most coveted in the garden. The nation finally repealed that amendment designed to prohibit (which did not do it.) Now after a year of repeal, I feel like crying "Give prohibition back to us."
>
> Human nature seems to have gone on a debauch. I am aghast at the lengths to which they go for oblivion, escape, hilarity or whatever it is. I know not what, but I cannot yet see why "folks put stuff into their mouths to steal their brains"—that is still beyond me.
>
> Forbidden or not forbidden, drink seems to lure and is a demon to be wrestled with.

On another occasion, after a visit to Missouri, she remarked:

> The absence of any enthusiasm over the advent of beer in Missouri seemed very noticeable. At one of the large hotels in Kansas City recently, only one table in a whole room was seen to be partaking of beer.
>
> Maybe we have learned something after all through the

efforts at prohibition. No honest effort is ever lost—that's my belief.

Hers was an interesting position, to say the least, considering the fact that following the repeal of prohibition the *Daily Democrat* began to carry advertisements for the sale of liquor, and the Fulbright-owned Fayetteville Ice Company obtained a local beer distributorship. It was a dichotomy which she sought to explain.

Some "are distressed to find liquor ads in the paper," she admitted. But Americans had repealed prohibition, she explained, and legal sale of liquor was now the law of the land. She added that while she, personally, could see no good in the consumption thereof, she likewise was well aware that prohibition had not worked, and that "control" and abiding by the rule of the law was surely the wisest course to follow. "I rather resent the attitude," she went on, "of those who say, 'A good paper, but . . .'" She asserted that she always intended to do her level best for the community, but that she didn't intend to do it at someone else's direction.

"I have no apologies," she wrote, because she and her paper were pulling "for the best interests of this community" as hard as anyone. Clearly, she regarded personal belief and business opportunity as two separate matters. She saw nothing amiss in such an attitude.

She also felt compelled to point out that, "It is pretty well attested that the beer of today is non-intoxicating and the light wines seem innocuous enough."

With each business and political battle joined and won, Roberta became a more influential figure in Fayetteville. The broad base of Fulbright business interests, her public voice expressing itself through her newspaper columns, and her own affinity for a wide circle of family, friends, and business associates made her a power in business, government, and University of Arkansas affairs. As with any powerful figure, public opinion was both pro and con. Fayetteville's citizens either responded positively to her strength or resented her power. There was little middle ground. Many were admiring of her business acumen; others were opposed to her strongly expressed editorial opinions. But all agreed that she lifted the sights of what was good for the town.

She paused to reflect on it all in her column.

> A few things I've learned—that business has an element
> of selfish brutality in it. It's difficult to do business with your
> friends and also difficult to be too friendly in your business.
> All of this of course with qualifications. I've lost a friend or
> two by loaning them money, or rather by trying to collect a
> loan, which seems to be a big pity. I've learned that a woman
> has to prove herself over and over again, while men take
> each other without question. I've learned that everyone is
> jealous of his or her position, whatever it may be; in fact, I've
> found the common weed of jealousy growing in all sorts of
> soil, even on rocks and in streams. It must be reckoned with
> in dealing with the human species. There are none above it,
> none below it, in some form.

Despite her intense involvement in cleaning up alleged corruption in Fayetteville and Washington County, there were other matters demanding her attention.

Jack Fulbright's wife, Madeline, died in 1930 in New Mexico where she and Jack had moved to undertake their ranching venture. Her body was brought to Fayetteville to lay in state at Mont Nord; her death another grievous blow to the family. Jack returned home and went to work again for Phipps Lumber, this time as a buyer. He did not remain long. Still not content, he traded his share of family holdings for the Boniwell-Calvin Steel Company of Kansas City in which Phipps Lumber had acquired an interest because of debt owed.

After settling in Kansas City, he married again—to Jean Sweeney—and began the process of reestablishing the profitability of Boniwell-Calvin. Jean handled the books and the billings for the company. Their visits to Fayetteville to see Roberta and to participate in family gatherings were duly reported in the *Daily Democrat*.

Bill Fulbright had remained in Europe for several months following his graduation from Oxford, continuing his tour of the continent. "My mother gave me about 200 dollars a month while I was in Europe," he said. "It was quite a lot of money at that time." When he returned from Europe, he worked in the family businesses and traveled frequently to Washington, D.C., to manage an estate for a friend.

It was during one of these trips that Bill Fulbright met Elizabeth (Betty) Williams, daughter of a cotton broker and member of a Main Line Philadelphia family. Soon Bill decided to move to Washington and enroll in the George Washington University (GWU) Law School. Upon completion of his studies, he went to work in the antitrust division of the Justice Department, later joining the GWU faculty as an instructor.

Bill Fulbright and Betty Williams were married June 15, 1932, in Bala, Pennsylvania, a Philadelphia suburb. Roberta went to Bala for the wedding, stopping in Washington, D.C., on the way to spend two weeks with Bill.

Bill and Betty made their home in Washington. Roberta hosted a reception for them in Fayetteville so Betty could meet all the friends and family in Fayetteville. "My mother," said Bill, "was very happy. She saw Betty as the best of women."

Roberta, bothered for a long time by rheumatism, went to the resort town of Hot Springs in June 1933 to "take a course of baths," according to the *Daily Democrat*. A few days later she wrote that Bath House Row was "the finest one in the world, I'm told." Hot Springs, she proclaimed, made Austria's Baden-by-Wien—where she had also taken the baths—seem like an "old swimming hole."

Several days after Roberta went to Hot Springs, her father, James Waugh, died, June 22, 1933, at age eighty-two, at the home of his son Charles in Rothville. He had suffered a paralytic stroke.

James Waugh was a member of the Rothville Baptist Church where he served for many years as a deacon. Always a taciturn man, he could be persuaded to share stories of life on the farm. Surely he recounted, too, the hair-raising experiences he and his family endured in Missouri during the Civil War. It was his creative bent that led Roberta to think of the Waughs as artistic and creative.

Roberta's father was a master builder—an expert with a framing square recalled his grandson Dick Waugh—and often in demand for his construction talents. Dick remembered a family trip made in the early 1930s from Eureka Springs to Missouri when six family members crowded into a Model-A Ford. The younger Waugh was seated in the back directly behind his grandfather, who was vigorously chewing and spitting tobacco. By the end of the trip, Dick Waugh's reflexes were "acute."

There would be two other weddings to occupy Roberta's time in the 1930s. The twins Helen and Bo, now college age, attended the University of Arkansas. Active, vibrant young women, they pledged Pi Beta Phi sorority, and Helen served as the sorority president.

Roberta was fond of one of their friends, John Wallace, and allowed the twins to go places if John went along. One of their favorite pastimes was riding around town in their large four-door tan LaSalle. John sometimes arranged dates for them at fraternity dances. They were popular with suitors and frequented the dances in the women's gymnasium at the university where the chaperones would not allow the lights to be turned down. Their solution to this dilemma was to bring their dates home to the front porch at Mont Nord.

Helen married first, June 2, 1934, to Hal Cooper Douglas of nearby Bentonville, in an outdoor wedding at twilight at the foot of the stone steps leading to Roberta's rock garden at Mont Nord. Bo was maid of honor. Older brother Jack came from Kansas City to give the bride away. A reception was held in the garden, with music provided by a string orchestra.

Hal Douglas, who received his law degree from the University of Arkansas, had practiced law in Fayetteville for two years with G. Clifton Wade before joining the Federal Bureau of Investigation. The young couple began married life in Atlanta, Georgia.

Bo served for a time as manager of the Fulbright-owned radio station KUOA. On March 16, 1936, she married Gilbert Carl Swanson of Omaha, Nebraska, who had been sent to Fayetteville to manage his family's Jerpe Dairy Products Corporation plant. Jerpe was a forerunner of Swanson Foods, one of the country's leading food-processing companies.

Bo and Gilbert had a small wedding ceremony at Mont Nord. Her only attendant was Helen, who served as matron of honor. The ceremony was conducted at an improvised altar, built by local florist Ray Adams at the foot of the double colonial stairway. Following the ceremony, the family had an informal party at home before going to the Washington Hotel for a larger reception and wedding supper. An eight-piece orchestra played for dancing.

The newlyweds moved into their newly furnished home in Fayetteville's Oak Park addition. The same year that Bo and Gilbert were married—1936—Betty and Bill Fulbright moved back to Arkansas. They purchased a one-hundred-and-fifty-acre farm at nearby Springdale and moved into the farm residence known as Rabbit's Foot Lodge. Rabbit's Foot was a unique structure, built of chinked logs and clay caulking. It had wide porches and a Japanese-style roof. Soon the new farmers were raising cattle, chickens, hogs, and vegetables.

The following year, Helen and Hal Douglas returned to Fayetteville from Washington, D.C. Because Roberta was showing early signs of heart problems, Helen and Hal moved in with her at 5 Mont Nord. Bill and Hal assumed responsibility for overseeing the Fulbright business interests, and Bill joined the University of Arkansas Law School faculty as a part-time lecturer in constitutional law and equity. Helen took on the responsibility for management of the household at Mont Nord, no small task because of the size of the house and the continual "open house."

The 1930s saw the births of seven more grandchildren for Roberta: a son Kenneth Fulbright Teasdale, to Anna and Kenneth Teasdale; a son Jay Fulbright II and daughter Pattie (Patty) Fulbright to Jean and Jack Fulbright; daughters Elizabeth (Betsey) Williams Fulbright and Roberta (Bosey) Waugh Fulbright to Betty and Bill Fulbright; a son Gilbert Carl Swanson to Bo and Gilbert Swanson; and son Douglas Fulbright Douglas to Helen and Hal Douglas.

Roberta was delighted with the growing brood. "They are truly worth all the cost," she said, "which, counting the care, pains and agony of bringing their fathers and mothers through, is considerable."

She was pleased, too, with the purchase of a farm. She bought a piece of land across the road from Rabbit's Foot and set about making a cabin into a weekend retreat. It was a one-room cabin, with an L-shaped living area and kitchen, a screened-in porch, and an outhouse.

Roberta moved a pump organ to the cabin in order to continue her practice of exuberant hymn playing. She also had a wind-up Victrola so she could play her favorite records on the old phonograph machine. Despite her stocky frame, she even managed to entertain her grandchildren by dancing to "Over the Waves." The kitchen had a wood-burning iron stove in which she built a fire each morning to cook breakfast much as her mother, Pattie, had done. Initially, she obtained water from a nearby cold, clear spring; later she had a hand pump. Eventually, water was piped to the cabin, but the outdoor toilet remained a fixture.

"This is how we did it," she told her grandchildren as she performed the routine chores and recalled for them her own early childhood in Missouri. To the readers of her column she said, "the essentials of living are simple and few and I often think we tend to complicate."

She and Betty set about churning butter, rendering lard, making preserves, and "generally enjoyed countryfying each other," recalled grandson Allan Gilbert. But Betty's idea of country included such amenities as finger bowls and bright chintz curtains.

If Roberta ever had any misgivings about her Philadelphia-bred daughter-in-law adjusting to small-town life, they were soon dispelled. Betty, who possessed the poise and sophistication of her Main Line upbringing, could be, in the words of one observer, "just as plain as pig tracks with anybody she happened to meet." For her part, Betty always felt her mother-in-law was on her side, and they enjoyed their time together.

Betty's mother was another matter. From Mrs. Williams's viewpoint in Philadelphia, the state of Arkansas was an outpost, located somewhere "way out there." On one occasion when she opened her Philadelphia newspaper and saw pictures of cotton bales afloat in a 1930s Arkansas flood, she telegraphed Betty that she must "come north immediately and bring the two children." Betty responded that the floods were still seventeen hundred feet below them and three hundred miles away. Later, when a hurricane struck New England, Bill and Betty wired her mother that she had better come to Arkansas to avoid being hit by a falling tree.

When Betty's mother arrived by train for a visit, she disembarked wearing papers covering her shoes for protection against the snow. It didn't help that once when Mrs. Williams arrived at the railway station in Fayetteville, Betty went to the station in Springdale. There Betty fell heir to a load of baby chickens, refused by a local farmer. She took them home and ensconced them in the basement by the furnace where their noisy cheeps were carried through the heating system to the bedroom where her mother was sleeping, or at least attempting to sleep. Given this situation, one can only guess how Betty's mother regarded Roberta's primitive cabin nearby.

Granddaughter Betsey Fulbright Winnacker spent her early years at Rabbit's Foot, and it was her childhood treat to spend the night on an army cot on the screened-in porch at Grandmother Roberta's cabin. Patty Fulbright Smith also loved to spend summertime there, despite the presence of a "huge snake."

Roberta's time at the cabin was generally limited to summer weekends and special occasions, but it provided a relaxing retreat from her intense involvement in the local political battles. The Fourth of July was a special time for the Fulbright family, with everyone gathering at Rabbit's Foot for an old-fashioned picnic. Suzanne Teasdale Zorn would always remember these gatherings as "fried chicken parties" when chicken and watermelon were plentiful. A nearby stream was dammed up, providing a swimming area. It was cooler at the farm than it was in town, and the setting provided a festive atmosphere for the always lively Fulbright get-togethers, where there was no shortage of food and conversation.

Although managers had been installed at all of the Fulbright businesses to supervise daily operations in the years following Jay's death, Roberta was still very much involved not only in the newspaper, but in the other businesses as well. She carefully followed the entrepreneurial style which had served her husband so well, yet with a somewhat conservative bent. She served as president of the Fayetteville Mercantile Company; Fayetteville Ice Company; KUOA, Inc., radio station; Citizens Bank; and Phipps Lumber Company. She felt a sense of pleasure and relief when both Bill and Hal returned to Fayetteville to assume the reins of management. Lessie Read, her good friend and staunch ally in the political wars, retired from the editorship of the newspaper in 1939. James E. Anthony served a brief stint as editor in 1939, followed by James Bohart, who had served on the newspaper staff since 1929 and had begun the paper's first sports section.

Despite Roberta's involvement in business and politics, she did not neglect her other activities, participating in the Christian Church (Disciples of Christ), the Chamber of Commerce, the Ozark Playground Association, the Altrusa Club, the Twentieth Century Club, Pen Women, the Wednesday Club, the Friday Club, the Perennial Garden Club, the Women's Civic Club, and the Idle Hour Club, though she surely had few idle hours. She also gave her support to the League of Women Voters, the Women's Democratic Club, the Symphony Society, and the University Press Club.

Betty Lighton, whose mother, Laura Lighton, was a member of the Friday Club—a women's social club—along with Roberta, remembered the club meetings vividly. As the Friday luncheon meeting time rolled around, the women would suddenly materialize, as if out of thin air, precisely at noon. Together, they made their way up the walk of the home of their hostess who, regardless of meeting place, had laid out the best linen, silver, and china for the event. In Roberta's case, this duty most often fell to daughter Helen, now the homemaker at Mont Nord.

Because of her role at the newspaper, Roberta frequently received invitations to attend other local club and civic functions, and she always tried to be there, believing that such activities were the lifeblood of the community. Besides, such events appealed to her ever-social nature. Without fail, she would write in glowing terms of each function attended. As a result, the invitations multiplied as one organization after another sought to be included in the favorable mention.

It is no wonder, then, with these myriad activities and an insatiable desire for long hours of philosophical discussions with family, friends, politicians, and university professors, that she showed the first signs of a developing heart condition. She called this period in her life, "The thrills of P. M.," with P. M. standing for "Post-Meridian" or "Past the Middle" of life. If this were cause for her to slow down, there were few signs of it. Some of her most turbulent, yet ultimately rewarding times were yet to come.

On the eve of these events she told of an endearing letter Kenneth Teasdale's great-great-grandmother had written to her son many years before: "A hundred years," Roberta observed, "has made fewer changes in the sentiments of mothers than anything else . . . But the heart of the letter holds the same great yearning for the welfare of the son."

This observation would prove prophetic.

CHAPTER VIII

On Campus

The first time Willie Oates met Roberta Fulbright, "she scared me to death and I'm not easily scared." Willie had come to Fayetteville from Arkansas City, Kansas, to enroll as a freshman at the University of Arkansas in 1937. En route to Fayetteville, the train she rode first backed into Fort Smith, Arkansas, before embarking on its forward journey through the mountains to Fayetteville. Perhaps this gave the train's engine a head start on its upward climb to the university community. In any case, Willie's train ride and her introduction to Roberta Fulbright, both, made an impression on the young woman.

Born Will Etta Long, but known to all simply as Willie, she met her future husband, Dr. Gordon Oates, at the university. She also pledged Kappa Kappa Gamma sorority, which is where she met Roberta Fulbright.

The formation of a Kappa Kappa Gamma chapter at the university gave Roberta a great deal of pleasure, for it was an association which had always been dear to her. Only one of her daughters, Anna, pledged Kappa Kappa Gamma and that had been at Roberta's alma mater, the University of Missouri. The other three daughters, all of whom attended the University of Arkansas, pledged other sororities.

Because Roberta's daughter, Lucile, died the day before Kappa Kappa Gamma was installed on the Arkansas campus, April 9, 1925, Roberta was not actively involved in its beginning. Still, Willie Oates found that Roberta's presence was a very strong force in the sorority house.

"The sorority members respected her," recalled Willie. "She had a lot of dignity." She was also an imposing presence to the young women, especially the sorority's new pledges. Her strong voice, sturdy physique, dark hair just beginning to turn gray, and, as Willie Oates described it, her determined jaw gave her an aura of authority.

On her first guest night at the sorority house, Willie and her roommate, Nancy Newland, were sitting on the floor awaiting dinner.

"We were laughing," said Willie. "I have a very loud laugh."

"Who is that black-headed girl in the red?" inquired Roberta, who was sitting nearby, a formidable figure, in an overstuffed chair. "I want to meet her."

Fearing the worst, Willie was relieved when Roberta, upon proper introduction, told her, "You're loud, but I like you."

From that time, throughout Willie's collegiate years, Roberta served as her mentor. She encouraged the young pledge to take public speaking and to participate in all campus organizations and activities. Willie accepted her advice eagerly and joined everything she could, a practice followed ever since, bringing her notice as Arkansas's most recognizable and indefatigable volunteer and fundraiser for charitable organizations.

"I remember her telling me when I failed at something: 'Willie, it's not a failure, it's a challenge,' and she encouraged me to go on to something else."

Roberta had some additional advice: "There's something more to college than looking for a husband." She advised Willie to be sure she received her degree. And she added, "Don't ever let a man buffalo you," no doubt recalling her own early experiences with the businessmen of Fayetteville.

When Willie was not selected for drum major by the band director, Roberta harrumped, "He's military. I could have told you, you wouldn't get anywhere with him. I hope you stomped out." Telling Willie she had the voice for it, Roberta encouraged her to try out for cheerleader, and this time Willie was successful.

"If she were alive today," said Willie Oates, "she would be all for the power of women."

That belief is reinforced by a column Roberta wrote not long before Willie arrived on campus.

> Men always boast a man-made world. Women really made it and let the men play the big parts, for they can't function without applause, although I contend women have the leading parts after all, minus the glamour. If you can find

a bigger part than bringing the race into the world and sustaining it! We are glad that some men are willing to let women figure in their books, in their lives, and in their world. My idea is that it takes two to make the life cycle complete and no apologies are due either side.

Roberta's friendship with Willie was typical of the joy she found in her association with the university students, and occasionally she shared her experiences with her readers.

> Sometimes we of the older generation salve our vanity by observing that those who are coming on are not quite our equal in many things. This, I'm convinced, is giving ourselves too much credit.
>
> I've been associated with functions of many sorts for a long while, but I was introduced to a new efficiency in management when the other night, I tendered my house for some rush parties. Secretly I was thinking I would have a lot to do and would be bothered no end, when, lo, they breezed in late in the afternoon in fresh smocks, and ordered the whole thing in toto, not overlooking a detail and not asking a thing.
>
> It just came off and it came off as planned. Later, everything fell back into its accustomed place and you could not have told there had been a crowd around. They know how to take advantage of the times; they can bring into play all the new devices and gadgets with ease; they are really ahead of the older generation in efficiency.
>
> So let's not fool ourselves or worry ourselves overmuch, but just have great faith in them and give everything that our years and experience will yield and that they will take.

The young sorority women were not Roberta's only interest on campus. All of the students intrigued her. "If I am thankful for one thing more than others it is that I have been privileged to live where choice groups of young people are coming and going. I'd love to know them all by name and by homes and by their ambitions."

The presence of the University of Arkansas dominated life in Fayetteville, and Roberta took a keen interest in all of its activities. She lent support to the journalism department, and undertook an annual practice of having journalism majors—members of the University Press Club—publish an annual issue of the *Northwest Arkansas Times*. She attended Press Club meetings and other departmental functions. For many years, she was a regular at lectures, musical programs, theatrical productions, and other cultural events hosted on the campus. At the President's Ball in 1934, she and Dean W. N. Gladden led the grand march.

Roberta Fulbright relished the conviviality of university events. She related one such occasion to which her son-in-law Hal Douglas agreed to drive her:

> . . . I said, "Just wait here while I go down the [receiving line] and I'll be right out." He said, "Oh, no you won't. You'll get in there and get to loving it." He knows me better than I know myself.

One of the things that always drew her to the university, she admitted, was that "I am attached . . . of all things [to] the old-timers on the faculty."

"She was a very intelligent person," said Dr. Robert Leflar, author of a history of the university. "She understood them [the university officials], sometimes knew them better than they knew themselves." Also, stressed Leflar, through her newspaper Roberta often controlled the appearance in the community of the university's success or failure.

"It is our crowning possession," she once wrote of the university, and she maintained a proprietary attitude toward it. She even came home early from a trip to St. Louis in 1938 in order, she said, to enjoy "the baccalaureate sermon, the commencement address and the processional which each and every year makes goose bumps rise up all over me as I view the majesty and beauty of that academic pageant. This scene in our matchless amphitheater, I do not believe is surpassed in these United States."

Over the years she wrote often on the value of education and the opportunities the university afforded its students. "She [the university] probably shares the romantic love and memory of more of our outstanding citizens than any other institution in the state," Roberta contended.

She once related to her newspaper readers the occasion, at a Farm Bureau banquet, when she discussed education with one of her tablemates.

> I sat by a man from Eastern Arkansas . . . and says he, "I believe I'm agin all this universal education. Education is dangerous as hell, do you know it?"
>
> I replied that ignorance was the dangerous condition as I had always understood it. "Well," says he, "there's something to that also," and at that we were both stymied, smiled and resumed the eating of our banquet.

Over the years, the state's legislative body came in for its share of Roberta's attention, particularly its actions toward the university.

> The 1933 legislature has come and gone. When I was a young housekeeper I used to forever be complaining of my help. My mother once said to me: "My child decide whether they do you more harm than good and act accordingly." As a rule I was forced to the conclusion that they did more good. Thus it is with the legislature. After all our complainings, I believe they did us more good than harm. . . . The University, which is our ewe lamb, was attacked with hammers but is still standing and functioning right over the hill. So we repeat, they did us good.

She kept a watchful eye on periodic attempts in the legislature to move the campus from Fayetteville. She always feared that any negative publicity about Fayetteville or Washington County would prompt another round of efforts to move the university to Little Rock. This was especially true during the political battles of the 1930s when Fayetteville was criticized for not having its house in order.

This concern prompted an editorial:

> Little Rock never fails to point to our university. She may herself not be above reproach in the matter of morals. . . . Her young people may be such that they are a menace to those of smaller towns. But that does not mean University City dare offer an environment not suited to the youth of the state. Our county and our city ever must use great care

to avoid saying anything that can give any other section, especially Little Rock, a club with which to chastise.

When the threat of moving the university gradually receded, she wrote, "In my recent visit downstate, a very prominent financier and citizen said so feelingly that he was glad the recurring efforts of some years back to move the University are over. He said: 'To me it was ridiculous.'"

At the same time, she expressed appreciation to the legislature for the "wise and expedient manner the University budget bill was put through" both houses. She was taking no chances.

In fact, she made it a practice to say thanks to the legislature. As financial aid grew, she said this about the university:

> It is our heart, we—Fayetteville—the arteries and veins. We are delighted at the treatment it received at the hands of the legislature. In the old days we had to struggle for appropriations in a way this generation knows not of. Money, as a matter of fact, flows in rivulets these days, while we used to catch it in a cup.

As the effort to move the entire university faded, it was followed by suggestions to move the Law School to the capital city. Roberta responded:

> We see Little Rock has not entirely changed her spots or system and is already beginning to yearn for our University. The first blast of propaganda to remove the Law School to the already crowded city of Little Rock came Sunday. This is not what we want. This solution does not clock in any way.

Although sometimes lavish in her praise, she was not hesitant in offering criticism if she felt criticism was warranted.

When a provincial professor took exception to northerners on the faculty, she opined: "A university is no field for such tripe. This is concentrated prejudice and the essence of sectionalism. The Mason and Dixon line should be as dead as last year's calendar."

On one hand she could support unequivocally her young sports editor Bob Wimberly in a sports story critical of university athletic policy. On the other, she reserved the right for some pithy comments herself: "The Arkansas-SMU game at Fort Smith was notable for the large number of politicians and Methodists in attendance. Sort them out if you can." Then she added: "The crowd was large, the day perfect, the uniforms colorful, the band— well, the band was there."

Homecoming was a special event for Roberta each year, in large part because so many of her family members returned home for the occasion. Three of Roberta's children lived away from Fayetteville: Jack in Kansas City; Anna in St. Louis; and Bo in Omaha, where she and Gilbert moved in 1939 when he returned home to work in the family's business headquarters. "Lively, vibrant, volatile Bo," as Allan Gilbert described her, found separation from her close-knit family painful, and she always looked forward to any trips home. Thus, homecoming always brought forth some of Roberta's most rhapsodic prose:

> We who are blest by having the University in our midst are
> the center of more folks' fond memories of School home
> than any other place in the state I feel sure.

When homecoming came in mid-November, Roberta felt compelled to give university officials some advice: "I do wish (and I drop the hint) that Home Coming could be when the maple trees are in full flower, not quite as bare as now."

Though she usually had a ready supply of words for any occasion, she was not able to couch her mention of football in the usual sports vernacular; it must have made her sports staff cringe. She could, on occasion, be positively lyrical.

> The Homecoming game was full of color, the day was
> perfect, the trees and buildings in the fading sunlight made
> a picture long to be remembered. The row of gray poplars
> around the Greek Theater lent a beautiful and classic touch
> to the scene.
> The band boys in blue from Rice added tone and color.
> The band boys in red from Arkansas, with "Hail, Hail,
> the Gang's All Here," was another brilliant touch of tone
> and color. The Rootin' Rubes were lovely in white and

silhouetted against the crowd were constant entertainment. The crowd was a mosaic, in reds, blues, blacks, whites and browns: was a picture of rare design. Even a majestic airplane circled the field and scattered red and white confetti over the players.

And the game was good. As a former football star remarked, "The men who really do the work down the middle of the field get no applause, only the ones who carry the ball over the line get the hand." I replied: "So it is with life. Only once in a while someone makes a touchdown. Most of us labor down the middle of the field without notice or applause, with only the inner satisfaction that maybe we have 'played well our part.'"

Some years later, when the university was undertaking a well-publicized search for a big-name football coach, Roberta wrote:

Football, basketball, tennis, track should be adjuncts to a University structure, not absolutely the structure.

. . . Now I enjoy a good football game, have had two sons to play but I am not ready to see it substituted for a University course.

The search was concluded with the hiring of John Barnhill of the University of Tennessee to a ten-thousand-dollar-a-year, five-year contract. As Barnhill led the football team to a winning season in his first year, Roberta was quick to say that the coach and his players deserved support and praise.

But before Barnhill's arrival, Roberta was about to become a player, herself, in one of the university's most lasting dramas.

CHAPTER IX

The University Presidency

On September 12, 1939, University of Arkansas president John C. Futrall was returning to Fayetteville from a trip downstate to Little Rock where he conferred with officials of the university medical school. Around 6:30 P.M., near the small town of West Fork, less than ten miles south of Fayetteville on treacherous U.S. Highway 71, his automobile, reportedly traveling at high speed as he rounded a curve, suddenly veered into the path of an oncoming truck. Futrall was killed in the accident. Only one of five occupants of the truck was injured seriously.

While the cause of the accident was never determined, newspaper accounts reported that Futrall, accustomed to driving a heavy car, was in a lighter vehicle and possibly failed to keep to the right when rounding the curve. Some people theorized that Futrall was blinded by late afternoon sunlight; others surmised that he suffered a heart attack. Whatever the cause, the sudden loss of its longtime president came as a severe shock to the university community.

The day following his death, Roberta paid tribute in the *Northwest Arkansas Times*: "During his tenure the University has emerged from a rather inconsiderable school to an institute of tremendous proportion . . . His place will be difficult to fill. We may not see his like again."

Futrall came to the university as a Latin professor in 1894 and became head of the department of ancient languages the following year. With him came the advent of competitive football at the university, and he served for a time as the coach. He was selected for the presidency in 1914. An austere, aloof man, his long tenure—while marked by significant progress—was not without the usual controversies which inevitably crop up in an academic setting. In 1933, the state legislature passed a resolution charging that Futrall was "domineering" and demanding that the board of trustees fire him. Faculty members unanimously approved a resolution expressing confidence in their president. The matter died.

Another time of tension occurred after Carl Bailey assumed the governorship in 1937. As reported by Dr. Robert Leflar in his history of the university:

> Giles E. Ripley, Dean of Men, presided over a difficult disciplinary case in which several students, including some in which Governor Bailey was personally interested, were expelled. Ripley would not back down from the expulsions and Futrall supported him. Ripley resigned as Dean of Men but continued as a full time physics teacher. Dr. David Y. Thomas wrote some "Letters to the Editor" asserting that certain official actions of the governor violated the Arkansas Constitution. Bailey was irked. There were rumors that the governor was trying to figure out a way to get rid of his "enemies" on the faculty.

In the spring of 1939, Governor Bailey, who served as ex-officio chairman of the university board, had convinced the state legislature to increase the number of board members from seven to ten. At the same time, on the contention that the original seven board members had been improperly appointed, he chose to appoint a totally new board. Among the appointees was Hal Douglas, Roberta Fulbright's son-in-law.

"Governor Bailey," Robert Leflar said, "was bright. He had an appreciation of academic matters beyond that of most politicians." As governor, Bailey was regarded as a visionary, pushing for improved education and expanded industry. While he was responsible for raising the state appropriation to the university by 35 percent during his tenure, his action reconstituting the board was viewed by many as an intrusion in academic affairs. Now, with Futrall's death, he and his appointed board would select the new president.

Because it was the beginning of the fall term, Governor Bailey and the trustees wanted to select Futrall's successor quickly. Canceling all engagements for the next ten days, the governor went to Fayetteville to remain there until after the funeral, September 14.

The governor would give no public indication of his choice for the position. Some of his friends said he favored elevating someone from the staff, but had expressed no preference among staff members. Numerous professors and department heads were rumored for the post, including Dr. Arthur M. Harding, director of general extension, and Dr. Julian Waterman, Law School dean and university vice president. Privately, Bailey offered the job to Waterman, who declined, reportedly saying, "I'm in favor of Bill Fulbright and I think you are too."

Robert Leflar and his wife learned of Futrall's death upon their return from an automobile trip to California. "Whereupon," said Leflar, "I drove to Julian Waterman's home at once. We talked about the university, the presidency and Bill Fulbright. We thought he should become president."

As Dr. Leflar wrote, "A quick campaign on the campus produced substantial support for Fulbright's selection."

At the same time, forces favoring Fulbright were at work in Little Rock. Allan Gilbert, in *A Fulbright Chronicle*, recounted it this way:

> Bailey's friendship with the Fulbrights was intimate to the extent, Hal Douglas recalls, that he was included on several parties at Roberta's "Cabin," across from Rabbit's Foot. Bailey was acquainted with Bill Fulbright, too, therefore, and undoubtedly impressed with young Bill's credentials.
>
> Although legend has it that Roberta interceded with Bailey for Bill's appointment, that move originated somewhere in Little Rock. Hal, who was on the Board of Trustees, recalls that his first inkling that Bill was being considered came via a phone call from Raymond Rebsamen, Little Rock businessman and fellow trustee, a day or so after Futrall's death. Rebsamen wanted to know what Bill's reaction to such a proposal would be.
>
> Bill's response was that as far as he was concerned Dean Julian Waterman, the acting U.A. president (and Bill's mentor) had to be first choice. Little Rock advised Hal that would be acceptable, and Hal was asked to broach the subject with the dean. Hal talked to Waterman over coffee at

the Mountain Inn and Dean Waterman, while flattered, turned down the offer.

He explained to Hal that he had grave doubts that Arkansas was ready for a Jewish University chief executive. Instead, he added his unqualified endorsement of Bill for the presidency. With that, the die was cast.

Reportedly, the university news bureau had readied vitae of eleven candidates for release to the press. Bill Fulbright's vita was not among them. However, both the *Arkansas Democrat* and *Arkansas Gazette* reported that Fulbright was being mentioned as Futrall's probable successor. His election, the newspapers noted, might depend upon whether or not Waterman would accept the job.

The board of trustees met at 4 P.M., September 18, first adopting a resolution expressing respect to the memory of Dr. Futrall and naming the student union in his honor. Then, Governor Bailey recommended thirty-four-year-old Bill Fulbright for the presidency. The nomination was approved without formal dissent. Next, Governor Bailey appointed Futrall's widow, Annie, to the board to succeed Fulbright's brother-in-law Hal Douglas, who, because of the family relationship, had submitted his resignation and withdrawn from the meeting before the Fulbright nomination.

The conclusion among some university officials was that Roberta Fulbright had arranged Bill's selection. Allan Gilbert reported the reaction on campus:

> Bailey's plucking of Bill, somewhat like a rabbit out of a hat, came as a surprise and shock to the Fayetteville campus, largely because no one else seems to have thought of him as a candidate for the job. Bailey, though, was not only a friend of the Fulbrights, but a zealous Razorback fan. . . . Bailey clearly felt that a former U.A. student and football hero with Bill's academic credentials was first cabin material for the job. Artistically and educationally, as well as politically, the appointment made sense to Bailey.

Bill Penix, who arrived in Fayetteville from Jonesboro to enroll as a student at the university that fall, remembered years later that

Roberta was "the dominant force in that community." Still, Penix—who was the university correspondent for the *Arkansas Gazette* and several other news organizations—said, "I do not think in 1939 that Carl Bailey would have made an appointment because Roberta Fulbright said so. Bill Fulbright was a good student and athlete, the kind of person who would appeal to Bailey."

At the September 18 meeting, the board—in addition to selecting Fulbright for the presidency—adopted a rule requiring that all faculty members over sixty-five years of age must retire, an action seen as a move by Bailey to rid himself of some of his opponents on the faculty. While Fulbright succeeded in postponing this rule, he was in the view of some on campus "tarred with Bailey's black brush."

When asked for her reaction to her son's appointment, Roberta said, "It seems like a dream. To me, he's still just a little boy." She did not, however, comment on the selection in "As I See It," choosing instead to devote several successive columns to news of the growing war in Europe.

Contrary to the popular belief that Roberta had a long-standing record of support for Bailey, she did not support him when he ran for the governorship for the first time in 1936. He was one of nine Democratic candidates seeking the post. The Democratic Party regulars couldn't decide which candidate to back.

Initially, Roberta supported Pulaski County judge R. A. "Bob" Cook, urging her readers to "join a landslide" for Cook. "Life is a big adventure," she said, "and nothing I can think of would do Arkansas more good than to have at her helm a man of Judge Cook's caliber and ability."

Gov. J. M. Futrell, in the meantime, first endorsed state senator John C. Ashley, but this endorsement lasted only a few days, and as the election neared he endorsed secretary of state Ed McDonald.

If the governor could switch, so could Roberta, but not without some dismay. In what she titled a political diary, which she published in her column, she revealed her ambivalence.

August 5—I think I am in the same boat with 90% of the muddled population on state politics. In this section we are always particularly concerned for the fate of our University, politically speaking. That question always wields a big stick with us in the Governor's race.

August 6—It looks like the landslide I thought would pile up for Judge Cook is now piling up for Attorney General Carl Bailey.

August 7—The landslide I thought was for Bailey now looms for Ed McDonald, Secretary of State.

August 10—The state machine is greased, oiled and has got to rolling . . . I hesitate to predict, prophesy or even wish. Heaven only knows which one would be best for our state. I give up.

I've always had faith in our present Governor Futrell and I'm holding on to it.

Roberta's faith in Governor Futrell is interesting in light of funding cutbacks to the university during his tenure. But he had supported Roberta and the Good Citizenship League by appointing Herbert Lewis as county sheriff in 1936.* Despite Futrell's last-minute endorsement of McDonald, Attorney General Bailey emerged the victor. The indecisiveness of the party regulars and the lack of a runoff contributed to his win.

Roberta greeted the turn of events this way:

> Our Governor-elect Carl E. Bailey is to be a guest in our fair city today. I hope he likes us as well as we expect to like him. He is young. We like that. He is courageous. Courage is the tops for a governor, or governor-elect or any office. . . . If courage and honesty are combined in one person, that will produce faith and we may then expect mountains to be removed and rolled into the sea. We give him our hand.

---

*Prior to that, in 1933, Governor Futrell had named Roberta Fulbright to a twenty-nine-member commission to finance and maintain an Arkansas exhibit at the Century of Progress International Exposition in Chicago.

Roberta was away on a Caribbean cruise during most of a 1937 campaign when newly elected Governor Bailey ran against U.S. representative John E. Miller in a special election for the U.S. Senate seat vacated by the death of Sen. Joseph T. Robinson. Robinson, the Senate majority leader, died in mid-July of a heart attack.

The special election in itself was controversial since Bailey assured himself the Democratic nomination through his supporters in a committee nomination process. Bailey had been an earlier critic of the state Democratic central committee's policy of nominating candidates for special elections rather than holding a primary election. Now, when he assured himself the nomination through the process which he had criticized, his opponents charged it was illegal. Miller, also a Democrat, resigned from the House of Representatives to run as an independent.

Roberta implied obliquely that she would vote for the governor.

> The Bailey-Miller contest also gained much momentum while I was out. I wish I had an x-ray which would reveal the hands underneath both which are holding them up. Then I'd know more about which would best represent us in the United States Senate. As for me, I'm a poor switcher.

When Miller won the race, it was regarded as a reflection of public opposition to committee nominations and a severe blow to Bailey. Roberta wrote:

> We concur with the majority and believe the best man won, but we will look with confidence to our Governor to show himself the statesman and high executive.

One important standard by which Roberta (and, in fact, all of Fayetteville) judged any governor was the level of his support for the University of Arkansas. She recognized the university's value not only as an educational institution but also as a vital economic contributor to the northwest Arkansas area. As governor, Bailey quickly demonstrated that he would take an active role as president of the university board of trustees.

Bailey's interest in the university stood him in good stead with

Roberta. Through this mutual interest, they became political allies, and she finally gave her full endorsement to him when he ran for a second term in 1938. Ironically, Judge R. A. Cook, whom Roberta had first endorsed in the 1936 election, was running again for the governorship. No longer interested at all in a landslide for Cook, she explained her change in allegiance this way:

> Some say "I thought you were for Judge Cook and Senator Levine." I thought they were a good pair. I still think so, but much water has flowed over the dam and today is today.

A few days later, she added:

> These last two years the Governor has fostered and brought to pass much legislation favorable to this locality and this whole section of the state.

As the election drew near, she intensified her rhetoric against Judge Cook:

> In the "Cook Book" of 1938 we read where the veteran politician Judge Cook founded a fund for orphan girls to be educated in Conway. This fund was in the form of a Life Insurance policy which he allowed to lapse after one year. (Some orphans, some education.)
> It reminds me of the big hearted Scotchman who in his will left one thousand dollars to the wife of the Unknown Soldier. Some philanthropist[s] are these.

Following Bailey's victory in the election, she continued to voice his praise. When Bailey visited Fayetteville, he made sure that Roberta was one of the community leaders he called on. In the fall of 1938, she was selected as a member of the governor's goodwill tour to Mexico. On the tour, she said, Governor Bailey "was in his element and in the finest of moods."

So, by the time the vacancy arose in the university presidency in 1939, Bailey now knew her and her son well. Also, his executive secretary, John Wells, had been a university classmate of Bill Fulbright's and could very well have been one of those in Little Rock who recommended him.

Reflecting later on Bailey's selection of him for the presidency, Bill Fulbright said: "He recommended me, maybe to bring some fresh air to the university." Still, he said, "This move surprised me. I myself would have liked to refuse. I was getting $2,700 a year teaching only three times a week; the presidency of the University was a full-time job and it paid $6,000 a year. It wasn't a great job, and I didn't think I was up to it."

Whether or not Roberta suggested her son for the university presidency—an action which she later denied—she did advise him to accept it, as did his wife, Betty. He decided to "give it a try." At age thirty-four, he was the youngest public university president in the country.

"The old guard [on the faculty] resented someone not rising from the ranks; they were hostile," recalled Bill Penix.

Bill Fulbright was aware of the political overtones of his selection as well as the concerns about his youthfulness. "Arthur Harding and others thought I was too young," he recalled. In typical tongue-in-cheek fashion (sounding very much like his mother), he addressed the issue: "Many remarks have been made about my youth. I really mean no offense by it and I am confident that progress is being made every day to correct it."

The university, which had only about fifteen hundred students, was dependent upon appropriations from the state legislature for its financing. As Bill Fulbright saw it, "The president's principal job was to represent the university, to lobby the state administration and the legislature to finance the university." He became a frequent visitor to the state capital in Little Rock, and he traveled the state, making appearances on behalf of the university, emphasizing that education was the key to eliminating the poverty so prevalent in the state. He was regarded as a good administrator, moving deliberately, and willing to listen to the advice and counsel of senior staff. Any lingering resentment gradually dissipated.

Roberta's pride in her son's appointment was reflected in her column:

> You can't impress a Texan, so don't try. I tried my stuff
> down in Marlin, Texas, last week. I told a Texan that I had a

son who is President of the University of Arkansas; never a gleam. I told him I had twin daughters and they were married and each had a boy, and that I had nine grandchildren, and so on; never a glimmer. So I gave up.

In those days university commencement ceremonies were held at twilight in the Chi Omega Greek Theatre. The graduation processional formed at the landmark Old Main and proceeded in stately fashion to the amphitheater. At his first commencement ceremony, when Bill Fulbright passed by Roberta in the academic processional, she was heard to remark, "There went my own little boy." His ascendancy to the university presidency at an early age combined for his mother her pride in her son and her proprietary interest in the university.

In 1941, when young Bill Penix became editor of the student newspaper, the *Arkansas Traveler,* a local preacher was vocal in his condemnation of university students, saying they were bound for hell because of their drinking. Penix couldn't resist the temptation to print stories about these charges in the *Traveler,* at the same time poking fun at the preacher. President Fulbright was not amused and wanted to censor the stories, but the faculty senate refused. Still chuckling about the incident many years later, Penix wryly said, "I probably should not have written as bluntly as I did." This small matter in no way interfered with a lifelong friendship which Fulbright and Penix forged. Penix later served as campaign manager for one of Fulbright's senatorial reelection campaigns.

There were, however, more serious matters at hand. On the campus, both the young president and his students were becoming increasingly aware of the storm clouds forming for America's involvement in World War II. In his speeches around the state, Fulbright urged that the United States give immediate help to Great Britain to fight the German threat. Despite the strong support for isolationism in the country, he advocated U.S. entry into the war. "I was seen as a radical extremist. There was even a time when a neighboring university invited me to speak but quickly canceled the engagement after looking at my advance text," Bill recalled.

Roberta, meanwhile, was making a similar call in her column:

> America, it seems to me, is summoned by all the voices of civilization, past, present and future; by all the cries of humanity and all the forces of right, to throw her weight into the balance for the rescue and salvation of humanity.

She also offered this warning:

> Here's a little inside tip to the next generation: when you emerge from your chrysalis don't be either a woman or a Jew. While they are two of the best specimens of the human race, they can each one stir up more prejudice per square inch, per square person, than any other of the species. It's the unpardonable sin to be either one, unless you are willing to hide your light under the ashcan and let it remain there.
>
> Prejudice completely shorn of reason fires my inflammable nature until a conflagration is all that can appease it. To my mind, this unreasoning prejudice which kindles at the advent of either a smart Jew or a smart woman almost always spells the superiority of both. For the human race "en masse" only gets "het up" over those who beat them, not the inferior ones round about. We never hear anyone holding forth over the subjugated races.
>
> The rule of reason is a good one. Have a reason for your conclusions. Do not let blind prejudices lead you on. Human beings thrust into this world through no act of their own should not be pre-judged. They should individually have a chance. The individual is the thing. The world needs all of the fit ones; so do not judge folks en masse either religiously, sectionally, racially, or politically.
>
> As I see it, the question today is: Shall the individual be considered or the structure built by the individuals—the State. Fascism, Naziism, Sovietism, all say the State. Democracy says the Individual. What say you?

As the storm clouds of World War II darkened across Europe, Roberta's concern grew. Two months before Adolph Hitler's army invaded Poland, and Britain and France declared war on Germany, she wrote:

What worries me is that words, those magic conveyors of ideas, are losing their meaning. The word "Peace" from the lips of Hitler denotes war and aggression. The word "Freedom" among the totalitarian means control of the individual by the super-state—the total absence of freedom as we believe in it. Integrity is at zero hour among the peoples of the world.

Throughout the summer of 1940, Roberta Fulbright wrote much more about Hitler and the European war. But the thunderclouds of war were not the only concern occupying the Fulbrights, mother and son. Another battle was looming closer to home.

CHAPTER X

The Last Word

When Gov. Carl Bailey decided to seek a third term in 1940, defying a two-term Arkansas tradition, he was opposed by a longtime political opponent, Homer Adkins, Internal Revenue Service collector for Arkansas.

Bailey, in some ways an introvert, was, nevertheless, a good campaigner, adept at meeting and greeting his constituents in a favorable manner. Still, he had his work cut out for him in a race against the affable, folksy Adkins, a former sheriff of Pulaski County (the state's most populous county) and Ku Klux Klan official in his earlier days.

Although they had not faced each other directly, the clash between Bailey and Adkins would not be their first. In 1933, Bailey supported Brooks Hays in a losing race against David D. Terry for the Fifth Congressional District seat. Adkins supported Terry. The bitterness of that political fight spawned a rivalry for political leadership between Adkins and Bailey that continued for more than ten years. The alliances formed in support of these two politicians created some of the most persistent factional divisions in Arkansas political history.

Boyce Drummond, in his thesis, "Arkansas Politics," quoted John Wells, a longtime associate of Bailey's, as saying that Bailey and Adkins represented "'anti-theses of political ideas and objectives.'" Added Drummond:

> Adkins has always been the politician; Bailey often rose to the challenge of government. Adkins was a shrewd businessman; Bailey was a lawyer with a deep respect for the legal profession and the law. Given their temperaments, clashes between the two men were inevitable when they both turned to politics.

They clashed again when Bailey was chosen by the state Democratic committee as the party nominee in his losing race for the U.S. Senate in the 1937 special election. Adkins led those opposed to Bailey. When Bailey defeated Judge R. A. "Bob" Cook for the governorship in 1938, Adkins later lamented that Cook had a chance to win, but "he stumped [*sic*] his toe."

Thus the stage was set for a full-scale battle in the 1940 governor's race. Onto this political stage: enter Roberta Fulbright.

As she had been in 1938, Roberta was a vocal supporter of the governor. Because Bailey had involved himself in academic matters, it wasn't long before the University of Arkansas became an issue in the campaign. In fact, in his opening campaign speech at Russellville, Adkins criticized political involvement in education, declaring that "interference with or intimidation of any qualified person working in any phase of the state's educational system cannot be too strongly condemned."

When Adkins came to Fayetteville for an August campaign appearance, the *Northwest Arkansas Times* headlined the report of his speech: "Adkins Talks to Saturday Crowd. Declares Governor Should Not Be on UA Board."

Reported the *Times*:

> Declaring that the University of Arkansas must be taken out of politics, Homer Adkins, candidate for governor, in an address here Saturday night declared if he is elected he will remove himself as ex-officio chairman of the board.
>
> "As governor I will give what assistance I can but I want the faculty to feel free to vote and say what they please. Intimidation of people in educational circles must stop," he declared. In introducing Adkins, local attorney Karl Greenhaw said, "the governor attempted to get the University into politics by increasing the membership on the board three men."

Now Homer Adkins had Roberta's attention. Proving that she read the news reports in her own paper, Roberta's response was immediate. She wrote:

> Well, Mr. Homer Adkins, candidate for governor "has came" and we will also say he "has went."
>
> . . . [Adkins] says he will take the University out of politics. An institution which was conceived in politics, born in

politics, nurtured by the same process throughout almost a century of its history, will not be easily extricated from that same influence.

Let's examine his method; if elected by political vote he will be a political governor, but he says he will appoint a non-political board. "There just ain't no such animal," and we of Arkansas and Washington County know it.

So when anyone tells you any state institution is going to be out of politics, just don't believe it, for it is not true and never will be true. Our concern as voters or politicians, if you will, is to choose good legislators and a good governor and that will mean good state institutions. Our University is of course a prize of high order, but friends, it[s] needs must be sustained by political methods and I make bold to say in the main good politics has been its portion. We hope this continues.

The next day she wrote again:

I can hear someone say, "We knew you would be for Governor Bailey. He appointed your son to the Presidency of the University." Well, granted. Of course we were for him before he did that, we never asked him to do it, never mentioned it to him, nor had anyone else mentioned it. It was the governor's own idea. We are appreciative of the honor, truly, but it has in no way changed our belief in what we said in the last campaign.

We believe the governor has the makings, the potentialities, if you will, of a statesman to a greater degree than any man in Arkansas.

Mr. Adkins I do not know, have never met.

That same day Governor Bailey was in town as the speaker for a celebration honoring former governor Archibald Yell. Bill Fulbright represented the university on the speaker's platform.

A few days later Roberta brought up the governor's race again:

So the old adage: "Do not change horses in the middle of the stream" seems to apply. At any rate do not swap a wheel-horse for a pony nor a tried executive for one whose most impressive promise [is] to welcome every man, woman and child to his office at all times.

The next day the *Northwest Arkansas Times* reported in a front-page story that Arkansas senator Hattie Caraway had announced at a statewide rally in Little Rock that she would vote for Homer Adkins. Long a supporter of Senator Caraway, Roberta made only one public comment on the endorsement. Referring to the support for Adkins by officials at the federal level, she said: "We still believe in the sovereignty of states and resent super-control. I like our United States Senators but I can't say we need them to direct our voting."

She went on to add:

> Governor Bailey's record of things done, as opposed to Mr. Homer Adkins' promises of doing nothing but saying "Howdy" should put all debate out of the question.
>
> Arkansas will not fail to return Governor Bailey to the office he has so ably filled.

Governor Bailey's reelection was not to be. Buoyed by support from the Arkansas Farm Bureau and an anti-third-term sentiment, Adkins won the primary. The *Northwest Arkansas Times* reported on the day following the election that Adkins was in the lead by thirty thousand votes over Governor Bailey and two other candidates with some precincts still to report.

Adkins carried Fayetteville and Washington County by more than 60 percent. His final statewide margin was about 31,500 votes. In the heavily Democratic state this meant Homer Adkins would be the new governor.

There are those who, in hindsight, expressed surprise that Roberta would come out so forcefully and bluntly against Homer Adkins. Surely, they reasoned, she must have realized how she was jeopardizing her son's position as university president, and surely, too, she must have realized that it was unlikely that Bailey could overcome heavy anti-third-term sentiment. Those theorists did not know Roberta Fulbright. She had proved to those in Fayetteville, at least, that she didn't back off from a fight and she didn't hesitate to speak her mind. If anyone expected her to back off now that Adkins had been elected, they, too, would be mistaken. Roberta conceded Adkins's victory, but in her own fashion.

Arkansas voters evidently love to have their hands shaken and promises of a welcome for themselves and families at the capitol above any refunding of their debts, building of their highways or lowering of their freight rates.

We are all terribly personal. It belongs to us as humans and we react to small flatteries. Voters remind me of children, to be personal again. I've tried like sin to keep business going for my children, money in the bank, and food on the table, and sometimes all they can think of is that the food was passed on the wrong side or the spoons were not in line with the knives. The big things are forgot.

Now we at the paper are amenable to the will of the people at all times, we hope with grace and gumption.

Governor Bailey's services to the state still seem big and important and the vote against him seems very surprising. No doubt the idea of a third term made its appeal against him. Too often in Democracies those who do exceedingly well go unrewarded. This is deplorable, but our congratulations to Mr. Adkins.

Although I have not met the Governor-elect, Mr. Adkins, he is pictured as a genial, fine man and I am looking forward to making his acquaintance. Our fellow townsman, Mr. Karl Greenhaw, we consider a friend.

We wish for and predict a splendid administration for Mr. Adkins.

Despite her concession to Adkins's election, it was clear she would never be an admirer of Homer Adkins, nor he of her. The new governor did have something he wanted to accomplish in his administration, and in no way would Roberta consider it splendid. Surely aware of Roberta's acerbic comments, he soon turned his attention to the university.

"One of Adkins' main objectives was to rid the university of some of Bailey's political friends, including Fulbright," wrote university historian Dr. Robert Leflar. "It is possible," added Leflar, "that Adkins had already made up his mind to get rid of Fulbright, but this comment (that Adkins would be only a hand-shaking governor) was widely attributed to fixing his determination." Immediately following the election the only question that remained, according to Bill Penix, who observed the campaign firsthand as a journalist, was "How soon was Adkins going to get Bill Fulbright fired?"

If Governor Adkins still felt, as he had in his opening campaign speech, that interference with qualified educators was to be abhorred, there was now no indication of it. Concerned about the developing situation, the university alumni association, meeting in Little Rock, October 19, 1940, issued a statement praising Bill Fulbright's "efficient and successful management." Charles D. Frierson, a state senator from Jonesboro and alumni president, presided at the meeting.

Just as Bailey had done, when Adkins assumed the governorship, he sponsored legislation to reorganize the board. While he did agree to remove the position of governor from the ex-officio chairmanship of the university board of trustees, as promised in his campaign, he pushed the legislature to reconstitute the board so that he could appoint all of its ten members.

Rather than call for a vote in the senate where Governor Adkins had an anticipated majority, state senator Maupin Cummings of Prairie Grove, whom Roberta had supported in Good Citizenship League days, and Charles Frierson of Jonesboro, who had presided at the alumni meeting supporting Bill Fulbright, attempted to forge a compromise. Saying they had an understanding with the governor that, in return for legislative cooperation, Fulbright would not be removed for at least a year, Cummings and Frierson convinced three board members to resign, permitting Governor Adkins to make three appointments.

Governor Adkins, denying later that he had made such a promise, said he agreed there would be no changes during the 1941 spring term. Since the terms of three members expired that spring, he was able to appoint a total of six new members of the board. The new members were polled in advance as to their position on the university presidency. It was, in effect, a litmus test. For the first time in the university's history, there were no board members from Fayetteville.

The *Northwest Arkansas Times* reported that the board would probably remove Bill Fulbright and perhaps two other administrative officials of the university. On May 16, 1941, on the eve of the new board's first meeting, university students held a rally protesting the impending upheaval. During the furor both those supporting Governor Adkins and those backing Fulbright adopted the battle cry, "Keep politics out of the university." An editorial in the *Arkansas Traveler,* the student newspaper, supported Fulbright, as did a number of the state's newspapers. Meanwhile, there was uncharacteristic silence from Roberta's corner.

The first meeting of the new board was scheduled for May 17 in Little Rock. Pres. Bill Fulbright was not invited to attend. Rumors continued to spread that there would be administrative changes at the university. Governor Adkins, reiterating that politics had no place in education, and declaring that he had no knowledge of any personnel changes, said any decisions would be the board's own. The new chairman of the board was John G. Ragsdale of El Dorado, an Adkins appointee.

At this initial session the board changed the name of the football stadium from Carl Bailey Stadium to Razorback Stadium. No action was taken on Fulbright. Still, rumors of his removal persisted, although all board members said they received no suggestions on personnel from Governor Adkins. However, Sen. Maupin Cummings believed that Dr. Arthur M. Harding, whose name had been mentioned earlier as a Futrall successor, and others were lobbying for the job. Chairman Ragsdale was openly campaigning for Harding. The next board meeting was scheduled for June 9 in Fayetteville, commencement day.

The *Northwest Arkansas Times* carried no further news articles about the potential firing, reporting only that the board meeting would be held at 9 A.M., June 9, on campus. In the days leading up to the meeting, Roberta made no direct mention in her column of the anticipated removal. Instead, she referred to it obliquely. In expressing her hope that a young man of her acquaintance would attend the university, she added parenthetically, "no matter who's president."

Betty Fulbright planned the usual social gathering hosted by the president on the evening before commencement. Wives of five of the six Adkins appointees declined the invitation, a clear signal of things to come.

On the morning of June 9, Roberta returned from Michigan where she had gone for the graduation of grandson Allan Gilbert from the Cranbrook School.

The board of trustees meeting was called to order almost an hour late by chairman Ragsdale. President Fulbright, present for a discussion of routine matters, was then asked to leave. During the ensuing discussion about the presidency, board member Jay Dickey of Pine Bluff argued on Bill Fulbright's behalf and called him back into the meeting, but he stayed only briefly. While Fulbright waited in his office in another part of the building where the board met, the trustees voted 6-4 to seek his resignation. Two emissaries from the board informed the young president that he would be given the opportunity to resign.

Recalled Fulbright: "But I didn't like at all the idea of resigning myself. I thought it irresponsible to just leave behind all the work I had been doing as president. I had nothing personal against the new governor, but I thought we should make clear the fact that he wanted to fire me."

He told the board: "In order that there be no misunderstanding about the situation, you fire me."

Again, the board voted 6-4 for removal. Bill Fulbright's services would be terminated June 30; two other officials on the Fayetteville campus were also dismissed.

The motion to remove Fulbright was made by Marvin Hathcoat, an attorney from Harrison, appointed to the board by Governor Adkins. The motion was seconded by Hugh Park, a Van Buren newspaper publisher and also an Adkins appointee.

Park's action came as no surprise. On two occasions in the summer of 1940, he had editorialized against Governor Bailey. On the second occasion he printed his opinions in a full front-page editorial accusing Governor Bailey of plunging the University of Arkansas into politics by adding three new members to the board. According to Park's accusations, Governor Bailey claimed the new members were needed because alumni wanted to be represented on the board. "Soon," accused Park, "he [Bailey] and 'the alumni' had selected them a new president [Fulbright] and the governor had absolute dictatorship control over every professor and every student in the state's pride and joy—its university." Ironically, Park's own appointment by Governor Adkins to a revamped board came as the result of the new governor's maneuvering to form a board of his own choosing. After Fulbright's ouster and the resulting storm it stirred, Park defended his actions, saying in the six-week period between his appointment to the board and his vote for the president's removal, "there has been ample time for organization of a citizens or a 'political' bloc to prevent an ouster of their president and others. No such protests have been received by the board. . . ."

Voting to dismiss Fulbright were board chairman Ragsdale, Hathcoat, Park, Dr. Euclid Smith of Hot Springs, John Snapp of Fitzhugh, and Fred I. Brown of Little Rock, all appointees of Governor Adkins. Voting against dismissal were Jay Dickey of Pine Bluff, Harry L. Ponder of Walnut Ridge, Henry Yocum of El Dorado, and Louis McDaniel of Forrest City. All were appointed by former governor Bailey except Ponder, who had been a board member for about twenty years and was reappointed by Adkins.

Following Fulbright's removal, Dr. Arthur M. Harding was nominated for the presidency and elected unanimously. His salary was set at seventy-five hundred dollars annually; Fulbright had been paid six thousand dollars yearly. Fulbright had no comment following the meeting; nor did Dr. Harding, who was called into the meeting thirty minutes before it adjourned. Board members refused to comment after the meeting, referring reporters to Secretary T. C. Carlson.

The board instructed Carlson to withhold any announcement until after the early evening commencement ceremonies. However, word spread quickly on the campus where there was anger at what was viewed as new intervention in university affairs. At 6:45 P.M., when Fulbright arrived for the ceremonies to introduce commencement speaker Dr. E. C. Elliott of Purdue University, he received a standing ovation. In reviewing Dr. Elliott's long tenure at Purdue, Fulbright said, "A tree cannot prosper when its roots are tampered with." This prompted a second standing ovation.

Although Fulbright made no public comment on his removal, he greeted Dr. Harding at a campus reception, congratulating him on his appointment.

The board, meanwhile, still had not provided an explanation for its actions. While the main players in the drama remained silent, Roberta's *Northwest Arkansas Times* reported under a banner headline that evening:

> Several changes in University of Arkansas faculty personnel were made today but official announcement will be withheld until tonight.
>
> Dismissals of President J. W. Fulbright, Horace E. Thompson, assistant director in charge of agriculture extension service, and Boyd Cypert, business manger of athletics, were voted by the expected 6-4 count, it was authoritatively learned by the *Times* this afternoon. As was preconceived, Mr. Fulbright will be succeeded by Dr. A. M. Harding, director of general extension.
>
> No official announcement was made by the board of trustees at the conclusion of the morning session, which held up a scheduled noon alumni luncheon until 12:30. The group authorized T. C. Carlson, board secretary, to make an official announcement after tonight's commencement exercises. It is assumed that "reasons" for the dismissals will be disclosed at that time.

The following day the newspaper, in an editorial entitled "Our Fuehrer," said:

> It is high time for all citizens of Arkansas, and especially those of Washington County, to ponder deeply the significance of the most dramatic shake-up in the history of the University. Not even governors take such unprecedented action without there being important and deep seated issues involved. It is incredible that a great institution which spends over 2 million dollars of the taxpayer dollars annually should be disrupted merely to satisfy a personal friendship.
>
> To go back to the beginning Homer Adkins made a special point of promising to take the University out of politics. Since his election he has proceeded to "take over"

Henderson State Teachers College, Arkansas State Teachers College, and now the University of Arkansas, the three largest and most important educational institutions in the state. We may well ask, "Why should he desire the complete domination of these institutions?" The answers must be found in the desires and aspirations of Governor Adkins.

Governor Adkins is, according to his own oft repeated statements, an uneducated man with no knowledge of the magnitude, the complexity, or the significance of a University, yet he proceeded to place it in the hands of his political allies.

It is noteworthy that Governor Adkins carefully avoided appointing a single Trustee from Fayetteville, the first time that has happened in the history of the institution. This would not be accidental.

If we recall the recent experiences in Mississippi, Louisiana and in Germany, we find that politicians seeking to create all powerful machines invariably subject the educational institutions to their complete control or destroy them. Universities are breeding places of truth, liberalism and intellectual independence. Unless they are controlled and the young people indoctrinated with proper political attitudes, they raise embarrassing questions to those seeking irresponsible power. It is therefore quite logical that an ambitious Governor holding an important office for the first time should desire control of the important educational institutions. If he can discredit and destroy the prestige of the university he thereby eliminates his greatest potential critic in the state.

Religion and education are the bulwarks of democracy. Invariably the kingfishers and fuehrers protest mightily their allegiance to both while laying plans for their annihilation.

When Hitler protested and promised that he sought only peace and goodwill the world believed him. Do you believe him now?

It was a blistering editorial. While Roberta bore no ill-will toward Dr. Harding, who was appointed her son's successor, her feelings about Governor Adkins were bluntly expressed through her newspaper's editorial. It is not known whether the unsigned editorial was written by Roberta or by her editor Jim Bohart. Clearly, though, it expressed her views. These views were even more plainly stated in "As I See It" in a short and none-too-sweet column:

> I would like to make an addition to the statement which seems to have rankled the heart of the present governor.
>
> I repeat. Arkansas prefers a hand-shaker to one who does constructive things.
>
> There is a vast and tremendous difference between building and wrecking. Some Arkansans cannot discriminate. All over the state institutions are feeling the axe of the wrecker.

In his centennial history of the university, Dr. Robert Leflar had this to say about Roberta's forthright comments:

> Needless to say, this language was not calculated to heal any breaches, nor did Roberta Fulbright have any intention of trying to heal breaches. She was not mad at the newly named President Harding, who she thought had merely taken advantage of a bad situation which he did not create, but she was after Adkins' scalp.

On June 11, the *Times* also editorialized against the board's postponement of the announcement of Fulbright's firing. At the same time, it complimented its own reporter Jerry Neil, who, the editorial said, "got his story—of a University of Arkansas Board of Trustees meeting in a men's restroom."

The next day the *Times* bemoaned the loss of a new women's dormitory, the plans for which were voted down by the board of trustees.

Roberta's ire over her son's firing was shared locally where most citizens thought Fulbright to be a good president. It was all politics, they believed.

While popular opinion long held that Adkins's desire to fire Bill Fulbright was based on Roberta's earlier outspokenness, others believed Adkins simply wanted to rid the university of some of Bailey's political friends, following the timeworn political philosophy, to the victor belongs the spoils. Dr. Robert Leflar later wrote that "one of Adkins' main objectives was to rid the University of some of Bailey's political friends, including Fulbright." Allan Gilbert concurred:

> Hers weren't comments to enflame a passion for revenge. But Adkins undoubtedly had a bigger reason for disliking the Fulbrights than Roberta's As I See It column, though that stands as a useful symbol. The historical concensus [sic] on the firing is that Gov. Adkins, irritated by Roberta's newspaper comments against him, had Fulbright ousted as an act of retaliation. That's legend. It had an added nuance. A Southern political fundamentalist, Adkins believed in rewarding one's supporters—at the expense of the opposition, where possible. He believed in using politics for power and favor, and he had a fervor opposed to those with advantages of wealth and education handed to them. He didn't think much of higher education and he didn't like what Roberta and her son Bill seemed to stand for. It is significant that Adkins not only stacked the board at the U.A. in Fayetteville, he meddled in affairs of higher education across the state. The Fulbrights proved too handy a target to overlook, and part of that "package" unnoticed by most historians, Mrs. Fulbright's son-in-law, Dr. Gilbert, University physician since the early Twenties, was summarily relieved of his duties, too.

In any event, "The firing," Bill Fulbright remembered, "wasn't pleasant to the ego. I would have stayed there." He had served as president of the university for slightly less than two years. Now, many thought, because of his mother's strident voice against Governor Adkins, he was without a job.

Once again he returned to the Fulbright family business enterprises as president of the Fulbright Investment Company and Phipps Lumber Company. After his return to Phipps, he added to the family's holdings with the purchase of the wagon department of the Springfield Wagon and Trailer Company. He was fully prepared to settle into his role as Bill Fulbright, businessman.

He said nothing publicly at the time about his mother's supposed role in his firing. An undated handwritten statement in the Fulbright papers in the Special Collections Division of the University of Arkansas Libraries yields these thoughts:

> In so far as my mother has been concerned I had no apologies to offer. She has had six children of her own and now has ten grandchildren and at the age of 67 can scarcely be said to be the dangerous political ogre sugested [*sic*] by rumors, emanating I presume from the governor or his friends.★

A half-century later Bill would look back on his firing and sum it up this way: "Bailey was my mother's friend. My mother supported Bailey. Adkins didn't like it. He couldn't do anything to my mother. He could only do something to me."

In all probability, as Allan Gilbert indicated, Adkins's desire to put his own man in the university presidency entered into it. "Gov. Adkins wanted A. M. Harding," said Bill Fulbright.

The events in this turbulent two-year period contributed much to the passage in the 1942 general election of the Thirty-third Amendment to the Arkansas Constitution which limited a governor's influence on the board of trustees. The amendment set appointment limits, staggered terms of appointment so that the governor could make only one appointment to the board each year, and considerably restricted the governor's power to remove board members.

While this might have been the end of the episode, it was not.

Toward the end of Governor Adkins's first term, a group of Carl Bailey allies met in Little Rock at the home of prominent businessman Raymond Rebsamen. Among those present were Bailey, Roberta and Bill Fulbright, and Donald Murray, an Arkansas newspaperman who, as editor of the *Jonesboro Daily Tribune,* had supported Bailey editorially during his gubernatorial campaigns. The topic of the meeting, according to Murray, was how to defeat Adkins in his quest for a second term.

★Roberta had ten grandchildren by 1941 and reached age sixty-seven in that year, so it is possible the note was penned at that time.

"The consensus of that group," recalled Murray, "was that Bill Fulbright was the logical candidate and everyone agreed that he should run. He was dubious about the idea at best."

Years later, Murray could still picture Fulbright leaning on the fireplace mantel, a drink in his hand, obviously weighing the decision.

Murray remembered that Roberta approached her son and said, "Well, Billy, what do you think?"

With an emphatic gesture, Bill replied, "Goddammit, Mama, I don't know."

Bill Fulbright did not run for the governorship. If he did not know whether or not a political race was for him, he was soon confronted with a decision again.

In the spring of 1942, Third District congressman Clyde Ellis, a former student of Bill Fulbright's at the university and whose election to Congress Roberta had publicly supported, decided to seek election to the U.S. Senate. Congressman Ellis, whose ten-county district covered the northwest area of the state, including Fayetteville, went to see Bill to encourage him to run in the Democratic primary for the vacated congressional seat.

"I had never thought about a career in politics," mused Fulbright, "but it was true that, as a professor, I used to pontificate on how an educated leadership was indispensable to the political health of the nation."

This time Bill gave the suggestion serious consideration. As he had done before accepting the university presidency, he talked the decision over with Betty and Roberta. Betty favored the race and, "My mother was all for it," he remembered, ". . . and she told me that if I didn't run she would. 'Now is your chance to give back what you got from the Rhodes scholarship,' she said."

"If she hadn't been a woman, she would have run," Bill said of his mother. But she knew the odds against the success of a female candidacy. As she had done in 1934, she demurred, this time in favor of her son.

Bill Fulbright, who had only been in three of the counties covered by the congressional district, set out with Betty to tour the district. He was encouraged by the offers of support he received.

He made the decision to run. His principal opponent, Karl Greenhaw, was Washington County campaign chairman for Homer Adkins in his 1940 race against Carl Bailey. As governor, Adkins appointed Greenhaw to the Arkansas Supreme Court to fill the unexpired term of a deceased justice. Greenhaw's political indebtedness to Governor Adkins became a liability in the race with Bill Fulbright, whose firing at the hands of Adkins generated sympathy and support.

It wasn't long until Greenhaw tried to make some of Roberta's earlier words an issue in the race. In a political advertisement in Roberta's own *Northwest Arkansas Times,* Greenhaw trumpeted: "The Candidate's Mother Speaks! Mrs. Roberta Fulbright, Columnist and Publisher, Says, In 'As I See It':

> We of Northwest Arkansas feel that he [Greenhaw] would fill the Senator's office, when that time comes, with dignity and grace.
>
> The Senatorial toga would fit his broad shoulders well. I think I voice the entire sentiment of this section.

The column quoted by Greenhaw was written January 14, 1941, and referred to a possible appointment for Greenhaw to the Senate that year to succeed John E. Miller, an appointment that didn't take place. It also appeared before Bill Fulbright's public ouster by the university trustees appointed by Governor Adkins, Greenhaw's ally.

The temptation for Roberta to respond must have been great. Yet she remained silent as she did throughout the race. Although the power of the press was readily available to her, and while she generally took a position in political races, she did not use her column as a partisan podium, realizing that to do so would be counterproductive.

The power of the *Northwest Arkansas Times* printing plant was put to use, however, producing throughout the campaign a small tabloid newspaper called the *Victory News.*

A recurrence of her heart problems also served to keep Roberta in the background, although this did not keep her from sharing, in private, with her son her opinions on the conduct of the campaign. As she began to recover from her bout with illness, she told her readers:

> Even being compelled to lie and contemplate the ceiling for
> a season, wondering when my pump will click, brings some
> compensation unknown to active days . . . July wasn't bad
> in bed. I may take August and come out in the fall.

Bill and Betty toured the district in a Model-A Ford coupe with a loudspeaker on top. They visited personally with voters; Bill kept speaking engagements. As the campaign progressed, his crowds grew. "It was well-known that I was removed as president of the university, and I think I got some sympathy votes," he said. In the primary, the *Northwest Arkansas Times* reported, "Fulbright polled 7,539 votes in 246 of 285 precincts; Greenhaw, 6,090, and Virgil Willis, Harrison, 4,115. Governor Homer M. Adkins, who made no formal campaign, scored an almost three-to-one victory over three opponents for renomination." In the runoff, Fulbright won his election by nearly four thousand votes, a large margin in the district, and without Republican opposition, assumed his seat in the U.S. House of Representatives in January 1943.

For Roberta, this victory was a satisfying moment, her only regret being that Bill and Betty sold Rabbit's Foot in preparation for their move to Washington, D.C. The days of mother, son, and daughter-in-law being "countryfied" were over.

John Erickson, a former University of Arkansas student who had gone to Washington, D.C., with Congressman Clyde Ellis, remained in the office, as Fulbright's aide. The new congressman's mother, he remembered, came to his swearing-in. From the beginning Erickson found her to be a "very interesting person— bright, forceful in her opinions," and very devoted to her son.

She quickly adopted the habit of writing Erickson with information she thought her son or his staff should be aware of— whether it be news of local or state events, or even a bit of gossip.

Hopeful of getting a seat on the House Agriculture Committee, Bill was instead assigned to the Foreign Affairs Committee. Roberta was not long in writing him about this news. "We were so glad you got on that Foreign Affairs Committee. I just hope it will not curtail your efforts elsewhere, but I'll be content." Adding some comments about her health, she wrote, "I have been in bed all day until tonight. I had one of those beastly dizzy spells which drive me mad. I think I am better."

Two days later, in another letter, she observed: "There is a very great urge on the part of the people for honesty in public office and I'm glad." The word "glad" rated a double underline. A note in the right-hand margin asked, "Have you done any society?"

As a new congressman, Bill Fulbright quickly made a name for himself when he authored the Fulbright Resolution, which laid the groundwork for United States membership in the United Nations.

Still, he kept tabs on things back home. In September 1944, Sam Gearhart, general manager of the *Northwest Arkansas Times,* wrote him: "Your mother and I drove over to Harrison. The day was fine and your mother enjoyed the trip very much." Reportedly, Roberta was interested in purchasing the *Harrison Daily Times* and was promised first opportunity to do so by owner John Newman. No such sale ever took place. Gearhart also reported to the congressman an increase in *Northwest Arkansas Times* advertising rates.

Of the new congressman, local writer Irene Carlisle said, "Men and women of Arkansas 3rd District are close to their Congressman—they have to be. He is their sole contact with national government—They had been hearing about Bill Fulbright off and on for several years. His mother 'owned the town' at Fayetteville and Bill had had a hand managing the family's imposing array of small businesses since he was in his teens." Then she added: "Bill's mother, shrewd, well informed, capable Roberta Waugh Fulbright exercises considerable power in Northwest Arkansas."

Observed Carlisle:

> Few people in Washington County are untouched by one or more of the Fulbright concerns. The *Northwest Arkansas Times* carries in its editorial column the views of its publisher on every subject from the high school play to national politics. Roberta Fulbright's opinions bear a good

deal of weight in her locality and she exercises a sort of benevolent despotism over the community. Mrs. Fulbright's editorials written in longhand and published under her own name under the heading "As I See It" are important shapers of thought in the community.

In 1944, still in his first term, Bill learned of Governor Adkins's intent to run for the U.S. Senate in the upcoming election against incumbent Hattie Caraway, who once again was seeking reelection.

Former governor Bailey had again approached Bill about running for governor, but Bill preferred the Congress. Feeling that his position as a congressman would be untenable if Adkins were elected to the Senate, Bill decided to enter the senatorial race himself. It would be better to make the Senate race and risk the loss than to remain in the Congress and face the possibility of having to work in the same congressional delegation with Adkins. Bailey supported the decision and helped him in the campaign.

"For Bailey and me, this election would be a grudge match," said Bill. It was a race full of ironies. Now Bill Fulbright was pitted directly against his nemesis Homer Adkins in a contest in which, this time, the people would decide the winner. Bill was also running against his mother's friend, Senator Caraway. As for Caraway, she had supported Adkins in his race for the governorship against Bailey, but the political friendship cooled when she issued a statement in January 1942, denying she had previously indicated she would not be a candidate for reelection in 1944. (In another irony, also in 1942, she endorsed John McClellan—her former senatorial opponent—in his winning race for the Senate against Atty. Gen. Jack Holt.)

Three other candidates, "Colonel" T. H. Barton, a wealthy El Dorado oilman; David D. Terry, a former congressman from Little Rock; and J. Rosser Venable of Little Rock, a World War I veteran, entered the 1944 senatorial race. Terry later withdrew. An early poll showed Adkins in first place, followed by the incumbent Caraway; Fulbright was third.

Before the race heated up, Roberta, Lessie Read, and another friend spent a week of relaxation at Petit Jean State Park. Read, who had retired from her editor's post, still wrote an occasional column called "Round About Town." In it, she was not reticent about promoting the candidacy of Bill Fulbright:

> . . . And Fulbright for the Senate.
> So wrote a Little Rock voter to the editor of the *Winslow American* the other day in answering questions concerning "how Little Rock stood" concerning candidates for various offices.

The news columns in the *Times* were filled with reports of Fulbright's campaign activities; editorials supported his candidacy. His opening campaign speech was carried in a full-column, front-page story. A Sunday open house for the candidate at the Washington Hotel was openly promoted. But there was no spillover of editorializing in the news columns, and the other candidates were given coverage, too. As in the earlier congressional race, the *Times* printing plant produced the *Victory News,* a campaign newspaper mailed to voters statewide.

Upon her return from Petit Jean, Roberta had another brief bout with illness. "It is from my bed that I write . . ." she told the readers of "As I See It." She did not attend the summer Arkansas Press Association meeting in Hot Springs. When she reported that *Times* general manager Sam Gearhart and editor Ted Wylie had gone to the meeting, she couldn't help adding: "We entertain the idea that our paper ranks right with the best in the state."

Her columns during the campaign were sporadic; they covered a range of subjects. She continued to promote the purchase of war bonds, and she praised FBI director J. Edgar Hoover, saying, "Thank God for him." She was silent on the Fulbright-Adkins race.

It became, in Bill Fulbright's words, "a mean race." Early in the campaign Fulbright raised a wide range of issues and stressed his support for the state's agricultural economy. Adkins promoted his record as governor, campaigning on a platform of strict economy while supporting the spending actions of the legislature.

The tenor of the race soon changed. Since the election came in the throes of World War II, Adkins, fifty-four, and a World War I veteran, accused Fulbright, thirty-nine, of dodging the draft. Fulbright replied that regulations did not allow the drafting of men who were fathers before the Japanese attack on Pearl Harbor. He also countered by producing letters of support from servicemen overseas.

Unquestionably remembering the effect of her earlier comments in the Adkins-Bailey gubernatorial race, Roberta maintained her silence through most of the campaign. She was also heeding the admonitions of silence by her family. Finally, six days before the primary, she spoke out, but only in general terms.

> A political campaign, so close to one that you can feel it in your face is one of those happenings which try men's souls. It can be productive of some of the most infuriating emotions you can imagine; your temper and patience can be lashed to white heat and your personal demons fairly take over, under the whip of contemptuous lies, rumors, insinuations and unheard of perfidies which seem to be incident to modern campaigns.
>
> On the other hand, some of the most wonderful and exhilarating experiences are encountered in the wake, also.
>
> We are just skipping for the moment, the unpleasant, because our hearts are warmed by the unlooked for, unexpected, but we trust not unmerited, kindnesses, loyalties and services tendered us and our candidate. It humbles me.

As the primary election day approached, members of the far-flung Fulbright family gathered at Mont Nord. The Teasdales came from St. Louis, the Swansons from Omaha, and the Jack Fulbrights from Kansas City. It turned out to be a victory celebration. Bill emerged as the leader, with Adkins, second, and Barton, third. Senator Caraway, who relied largely during the campaign on a letter of friendship from Pres. Franklin D. Roosevelt, and was never a factor in the campaign, was fourth, finishing only ahead of Venable.

There would be a Fulbright-Adkins runoff, and the campaign was not long in gearing up again. Two days after the primary, the Associated Press was quick to point out that the "Paths of Fulbright and Adkins first crossed in 1941 when a Board of Trustees named by Adkins removed Fulbright as university president, charging him with lack of cooperation."

Just as quickly, Adkins denied responsibility for the ouster. His denial did little to alter the commonly held belief, at the time, that he wrongly intervened in university affairs. In almost every community there was someone who had attended the university, and to an alum, they believed that Adkins had trifled with fundamental educational values. Whether these feelings would translate into an election victory for Fulbright remained to be seen.

The candidates jockeyed for support among the state's leading politicians. The *Times* reported that Senator Caraway said from her home in Jonesboro that, "she believed she would make no statement in regard to the runoff." What effect Fulbright's candidacy had on the friendship of Roberta and Hattie Caraway is not known. Caraway remained characteristically silent, and Roberta did not write of it.

Adkins continued to hammer away at the themes of patriotism and Fulbright's draft status. Fulbright again responded with testimonials from servicemen.

Lessie Read pointed out in her column that Fulbright enjoyed support from the Washington, D.C., press, and the *Northwest Arkansas Times* chipped in with its own homegrown editorial support. Roberta finally addressed the campaign a few days before the runoff.

> My children tell this on me: "Mother, you say too much about everything." I replied: "My dears, I do not say *one-half* of what I think . . ." Well, I'm saying a few things about the senatorial campaign and be it said now. I have not said one-half of what I have thought . . . First I want to say I am as proud of Arkansas as I am of Bill. Second, I want to say do not fail to vote on Tuesday. That's our system and we must abide by it.

On election night, she worked off her nervous energy by writing her column.

> My "thank you" list grows ever apace. First: I met a dear soldier home from the Aleutians who lives in Greenland, Ark. He was here on furlough. He tells me this. The soldiers received their absentee ballots up in the Aleutians and he says

they weren't interested in voting but he knew Bill and believed in him so did some missionary work and procured 45 votes for Bill! That touched me to the center of my being. The boys, says he, are interested primarily in getting this fight over and coming home. We must keep faith. I feel grateful.

So many letters come to me to say they are all for Bill, one from a dear lady whom I have not seen in ages saying she recalls when Bill was little and I carried him on my hip.

From Captain Warren Williams who is a prisoner somewhere in Germany through his mother comes this message: "Mother, you can tell your old boy friend Bill that he made print over here and to keep up the good work, we are all behind him."

Ten o'clock election night. The last report was that Fulbright was ahead—so I'm grateful again.

This news was indeed good for the Fulbrights. The *Times* reported the following day that Fulbright was the winner. He carried Washington County 2,799 to 767 and Fayetteville, 1,288 to 260. The next day the statewide tally, with almost all precincts counted, was 110,352 to 79,474. Adkins acknowledged defeat. Although Fulbright would have token Republican opposition in the general election, his victory in the Democratic runoff was tantamount to election. It was an impressive win for the young congressman in his first statewide race.

Said Roberta:

We've had a Senate race in Arkansas. May I say rather fervently, I believe the best man won. Further, I want to say again that profound gratitude seizes me when I consider how many of the fine folks of Arkansas took real interest in this race. This can not be overrated or overstated, and without it the best man would not have won. So, thanks friends.

For Roberta, this was a mild victory statement. It was in stark contrast to her postelection comments in 1940 when Adkins defeated Bailey for the governorship. If she had become embittered by Bill's removal from the university presidency, as some believed, then victory was sweet. She must have been sorely tempted to repeat her earlier barb that Homer Adkins "has came and went." But she did not, although folklore, passed down through the years, asserts that she did.

"There is no doubt in my mind that the critical comments she made about Homer Adkins in the Adkins-Bailey campaign led to his firing," said Bill's aide John Erickson. "I think the University of Arkansas alums were a big reason he beat Adkins in the senate race. They were proud of Bill Fulbright and resented Adkins for what he did."

"The largest single factor in Fulbright's victory," Dr. Robert Leflar would say, "was the manner in which Adkins as governor had stacked the Board of Trustees and ousted Fulbright and his colleagues for political reasons. Mrs. Fulbright's revenge was complete."

"It was in a measure a personal triumph for Mrs. Fulbright," the *Arkansas Gazette* later observed. In any case, she emerged from the experience as a seasoned politician and an astute newspaper-woman. Sam Harris, the AP reporter who became the *Gazette*'s city editor and political columnist, pointed out years later, "In a political way she was aggressive; in a business way she was firm."

Always, she was staunch in support of her newspaper. A few days after the senatorial election, she was back in bombastic form when responding to a perceived criticism by the Farm Bureau:

> It just doesn't matter about me . . . but the TIMES is some-thing very different and I believe in it. It seeks truth and calmly pursues it.

Apparently mollified by a conversation with a Farm Bureau official, she wrote a few days later:

> I suppose I have been writing when I should have been reading and talking when I should have been listening, but reading and listening get dull. Now and then I blow off. As I have said, the *Northwest Arkansas Times* is my seventh child and I fend for it as easily as for any child I have, but I do want right and truth on my side.

Those who knew her personally found her to be down-to-earth, friendly, and outgoing. Those who knew her only from her newspaper column believed her engaging but sometimes sharp-spoken. An individual seen through different eyes at different times in her life, remembered by others in terms of their own personality and life experience, may sometimes seem a contradiction. Particularly a strong-willed, dominant personality like Roberta Fulbright will elicit such observations. Some of her grandchildren, for example, remember her as a warm-hearted, generous grandmother. For others, their overriding memory was not of a nurturing personality, but one who was admirable in strength and perseverance.

In any case, most people found themselves in awe of her personality, influence, and willingness to put herself on the line. Later, biographers of Bill Fulbright would oftentimes picture her as a Ma Fulbright-type character who owned most of Fayetteville and cleaned up its political corruption in the manner of a pistol-packing mama. In doing so, they failed to capture the essence of a personality, born out of early self-confidence, tested in legal, business, and political battles, and confidently secured with her newspaper platform. As is often the case with strong, successful individuals, she was more complex than some writers discerned. She was not brazen or flamboyant as some implied. Rather, she was assertive, self-confident, and ebullient. Beneath her extroverted nature, she was always wary and demanded much, both of herself and others. Raised with few luxuries, she was well endowed with high standards.

Now, at age seventy, her success in business, civic affairs, and politics well secured, she assumed the identifier, "Mother of Senator J. William Fulbright."

Responding to a columnist who wrote that Roberta's chief claim to fame was the fact that she was the senator's mother, her friend Lessie Read came to her strong defense: "But Mrs. Fulbright was distinguished, my dear sir, long before 'Bill' was booted out of a university president's chair into national politics."

Roberta did not try to run Fayetteville, as some accused her, said Lessie. Instead, she proclaimed, "the people have faith in Mrs.

Fulbright's personal integrity and her sense of justice, and in those of her paper. Neither has any axe to grind."

Whether or not she "ran" Fayetteville, her opinions on people, places, and events were closely followed by those who read her column. If any of her readers expected her to modify her outspokenness because of her son's position, her quick response to the perceived slight by the Farm Bureau disabused them of that notion.

CHAPTER XI

The View from Mont Nord

"You could see forever from Mont Nord," proclaimed Roberta's grandson Kenneth Teasdale. At least it seemed that way to the grandchildren who found the Fulbright home high on a hill overlooking Fayetteville to be a center of lively activities.

"Everybody came by that house," remembered Teasdale, who always looked forward to his trips to Fayetteville from St. Louis. "It was not unusual to see eight to ten visitors a day." His sister, Suzanne Teasdale Zorn, savored these visits, too. Her mother, Anna, she said, always referred to them as "going down home."

Granddaughter Patty Fulbright Smith was also an eager summer and Christmas visitor at Mont Nord: "There was lots of activity. I always wanted to go." For Patty, who was prone to carsickness, the trip down to Fayetteville from Kansas City was an agony—particularly since her father, Jack, was not prone to making stops along the way—but always worth the discomfort once she arrived.

As a young man, Kenneth Teasdale was impressed that the house was one in which everybody was equal, even the grandchildren. Grandmother Roberta didn't stand on formality. At mealtimes she didn't sit at the head of the table, choosing instead to sit beside a grandchild.

"If she were sitting next to you and she saw something on your plate she wanted, she took a bite," said Teasdale. Consequently, the grandchildren learned not to dally over dinner. They also learned not to leave anything on their plates. Roberta's memories of early hardships did not permit wastefulness. Patty Smith, who was sometimes dubious when a chicken wing appeared on her plate, was told by her grandmother: "Wings make you pretty; eat them."

The visits of the grandchildren were often marked by their hyperactivity and lack of sleep, not only because of their natural youthful exuberance, but because of their indulgence in the never-ending supply of soft drinks furnished by the family bottling franchise and always available from an ice box at the house.

The grand old house provided plenty of nooks and crannies for mischievous grandchildren to indulge in childhood games. The attic, which always yielded innumerable treasures, was a favorite gathering spot.

Grandson Doug Douglas, who lived with his parents Helen and Hal Douglas at Mont Nord, was sometimes the one who led others to forbidden places, most often the second-floor balcony at the front of the house. Another favorite group sport for the youngsters was to slip upstairs to the sleeping porch and jump from the headboard of the bed to the mattress.

To her nieces and nephews Roberta was affectionately known as Aunt Berta. Even her cousin Martha Stratton Twichell of Rothville —thirty years her junior—called her Aunt Berta. While visiting from Rothville, young Martha treasured a ride on the family pony from Mont Nord to downtown Fayetteville. Such treats always awaited youthful visitors. Nephew Dick Waugh thought Mont Nord was a "wonderful place." As a boy he was impressed by the back hall closet which held a wealth of athletic equipment. Golf clubs, tennis racquets, and even bicycles might be found there.

Once, when another of Roberta's nephews, Earl Waugh, was staying at Mont Nord, he became determined to get into some canned apples he discovered on a shelf. He accomplished his goal with hammer and nails. Rather than chastise the youngster, Roberta quipped, "Give me an enterprising young man anytime."

"She was a wonderful person to spend time with—a lovely, indulgent grandmother," reminisced granddaughter Betsey Fulbright Winnacker. "She didn't say, 'be good,' or 'sit up straight.' She had a secret. You always treat children like people. We were always included in discussions."

"There was no sense that she was running things," Teasdale added. "She just set the tone. She was fascinated by people and she wanted others to be the center of attention. She promoted lively intellectual discussions and encouraged the youngsters to participate."

She instilled in her grandchildren a love of reading. One of her favorite teaching tools was to call each grandchild, individually, into the sitting room to read newspaper editorials to her. "You dreaded it," said Patty Smith. "These were not easy to read for a child; we didn't know the vocabulary."

She had a habit of stretching out on the floor to take a nap, often in the company of a grandchild. Suzanne Zorn remembered joining her grandmother for one of these naps on the living room floor, a location Roberta chose in the summertime in order to get a breeze from the open front door. She would doze blissfully as long as conversation in the room continued. "If the discussion stopped, she would rouse," said Betsey Winnacker. It seemed she was conscious of conversation even in her sleep. "Grandmother included us in everything; we never had hesitation in saying anything in front of her," marveled Patty Smith.

Because he lived at Mont Nord, young Doug Douglas saw his grandmother on a daily basis, and as a result, sometimes saw a different side of her. He viewed her as a strict disciplinarian, an authority figure who was clearly the matriarch of the family. The other grandchildren, too, learned that she could be stern. Generally it only took one look from her to put an end to any mischief.

At age eight, Douglas got a new B.B. gun. As his grandmother said, this made her nervous. She recalled the story of the boy who got a gun for Christmas and recorded subsequent events in his diary—"Rained, couldn't get out with my gun." Next day—"Rained—couldn't get out with my gun." Next day—"Rained today. Shot Grandma." Her grandson, she was happy to report, promised his father, Hal, that he wouldn't aim at human beings.

"I respected her quite a bit," Douglas emphasized. Still it did not prevent him and his cousin Gibby Swanson from doing something mischievous and fleeing upstairs where they knew, by this time, she was no longer able to chase them. More than likely their transgression was to sneak into the living room—forbidden territory except for social occasions. As she reported to *Times* readers, she heard one of her grandsons say to a friend, "Grandmother gets cross sometimes, but she generally comes through."

Douglas, too, remembered the large family gatherings, particularly at Christmas, when Roberta would eschew her habit of sitting with the grandchildren and instead take her place as the family leader at the head of the dining table.

"Those were wonderful times with more presents than you can imagine," said Douglas. Patty Smith remembered that a large Christmas tree and a seemingly endless tumble of presents filled the sun porch. Betty Fulbright was the lone family member who, by tradition, opened her presents early—on Christmas Eve. For the grandchildren who had to wait until Christmas morning after Santa Claus came, the wait was almost unbearable. It became an even more intolerable wait because the family gathered in the dining room for a sumptuous breakfast, usually featuring quail. In a family always inclined toward conversation, the gift-opening was further postponed by long discussions at the table. By this time the grandchildren were in torment.

Smith recalled the Christmas when peeking over the banister from the upper floor she spied a bicycle "from Santa Claus" being removed by the grown-ups from the hall closet for placement under the tree.

The stockings, which were hung for the youngsters, were, in actuality, Grandmother Roberta's hose, and there was always competition to see which child could get the longest one.

Roberta once said that during childhood Christmas redeemed the year for her, "and as an old lady it should do more." As one Christmas approached, she openly hinted in "As I See It" for a new console organ, pointing out that she saw one at the Lions Club Christmas party and adding parenthetically, "By the way, I know a fine lady who wants one for Christmas and SHOULD have it. Santa take note she *deserves* it." She failed to report whether or not she received it.

Christmas gatherings were regarded as such special family times that Betsey Winnacker was mortified one year when she became ill. Nothing was allowed to spoil Christmas.

It was not difficult at Christmas time to talk Roberta into playing some hymns on the piano or organ. Sometimes son-in-law Kenneth Teasdale would sing. "O Little Town of Bethlehem" was Roberta's favorite, granddaughter Bosey Fulbright Foote remembered.

"She had a latent religious strain," mused Betsey Winnacker, whose early childhood memories included taking communion in church with her grandmother. This strain became more evident as the years passed, and she wrote more often in her column about religious faith, passing on her own Christian homilies.

She also had a strong moral streak. Author Tristram Coffin recounted a story—whether true or apocryphal—of a time when she heard that the church board intended to remove the minister she admired. In Coffin's words: "She stormed the board meeting and said she believed in justice and the reverend was not receiving it. The board overruled her objections and fired him. She found the pastor another post."

Four more grandchildren were added to the family in the 1940s. Three—Jay, Patsy, and Helen Carla—were born to Bo and Gilbert Swanson, and a daughter, Ann, to Helen and Hal Douglas. "Life never loses its interest while children and grandchildren function," Roberta would fondly say.

She took her grandmother role seriously. "Pride in grandchildren is a malady for which 'no cure' has been discovered." She always enjoyed recounting stories of her grandchildren's bits of wisdom. When her three-year-old granddaughter Ann Douglas came trooping downstairs at Mont Nord to join Roberta in the morning, the proud grandmother related: "I was taking my quota of pills and she says, 'Grandmother, why do you take so many pills? Oh, I know, because you are a grandmother.'"

Although by the 1940s there were thirteen grandchildren, Roberta somehow managed to give each grandchild individual attention. Kenneth Teasdale remembered sitting on a forked tree which had been turned upside down in the backyard and listening to his grandmother talk while she worked in her garden.

The Fulbright family was "a blood relationship of incredible power," said Teasdale, summing it up. He attributed that largely to his grandmother. "She had more life than anyone. I've never met anybody like her, man or woman."

She was fiercely loyal to her family. If she chastised them

in private—and she didn't hesitate to do so—she was always on their side in public. By now completely strong-willed and self-confident, she had no patience with timidity in others. "Go ahead and do it," was the advice she gave her grandchildren. To her first-born granddaughter, Suzanne Zorn, she was an important role model. "I was inspired by her example. I realized what women could accomplish in business and professions."

Her sense of humor with her grandchildren sometimes took a devilish turn. When Zorn was in her teens and visiting Mont Nord, she dressed up for a date. As she and the young man left the house, Roberta—who was watering the garden with a hose—could not resist the urge to flick some water on her grand-daughter, much to the young woman's mortification.

There were times, Roberta once acknowledged in her newspaper column, when continual cheerfulness could be quite wearying.

> Robert Louis Stevenson says that cheerfulness and gentle-ness surpass all other virtues; and Elsie Robinson, the colum-nist, has written a poem, "Cheerfulness is the tops."
>
> I was thus brought to reflect upon it. One of my chil-dren said to me once: "Mother, you are cheerful but you aren't happy," with the implied meaning that I was sort of a hypocrite. Well, what of it? Have I not beaten the game a bit if I'm cheerful even when I'm not happy? My grand-daughter is a particularly critical little girl. I said to her, "Try liking something. Just say 'I like it.'" Quick as a flash she replied, "It might not be the truth, grandmother." Well, I, being brought to a halt thus said, "I believe I'd rather you'd tell a few stories than to never say you like anything."
>
> So I believe I'm sticking to it. Lie a little if absolutely necessary in order to be cheerful and pleasant. There's no place in this world where a grouch can be successfully used.

Sometimes, as she said, when her age began to "grind me a bit," and her health began to decline gradually, she was not cheerful at all. A former editor at the *Arkansas Democrat* and *Arkansas Gazette*, journalist Robert S. McCord remembered the sole occasion on which he met Roberta Fulbright.

When McCord enrolled at the University of Arkansas in 1947, he had already worked for two summers and before and after high school classes as a photographer at the *Arkansas Democrat* in Little Rock, so he had at least a vague knowledge of who she was.

Not long after he arrived in Fayetteville, he landed the job as photographer for the Razorback Beauty pictures in the university yearbook. Roberta loaned the use of Mont Nord for the photo session. Although McCord had not expected to see her, suddenly she appeared. Not at all garrulous on this occasion, she spoke only briefly, and tersely, to McCord and some of the young women being photographed. Still, temptation prevailed. Never one to pass up a conversation, she talked to McCord about her son, Senator Fulbright, "who was then and still is one of my heroes," professed McCord.

While a student, McCord continued his photographic work. His 1949 photo of President Harry Truman marching with his World War I outfit won second place in the Associated Press national contest for news photography, an honor noted on page one of Roberta's newspaper, the *Northwest Arkansas Times*. McCord became the editor of the university student newspaper, the *Arkansas Traveler*, and also became a reader of "As I See It." He thought the column "wise and liberal." Because it was the late 1940s, he also realized it was unusual that a newspaper opinion column was written by a woman, a rarity in those years.

Roberta projected an image of strength and intelligence to both friends and foes alike. While business competitors and political opponents found the force of her personality to be intimidating and dominating, all who knew her agreed that she was one of the most remarkable personalities they had encountered—a creative thinker, whose insight they grudgingly admired, whose newspaper columns they eagerly anticipated, and whose favor they sought to garner. "I have always hoped," she confessed, "that I do not have sense to know who hates me. Nor to discern who sort of mitigates against me; also sense enough to not return any of these ignoble actions." She was slow to anger, but when she became angry, everyone knew it, especially her opponents and the readers of "As I See It." In those instances tact and diplomacy took a backseat to bluntness.

"She was not domineering, but she was dominating," said businessman Morris Collier. She was frequently the recipient of attention at civic functions and when distinguished visitors came to town, she was most often the one who entertained them. "She loaned dignity to any of these occasions," added Collier.

"There was always excitement around her, like sparks," one family friend observed. "I was very much in awe of her as a child," emphasized Betty Lighton whose mother was a longtime friend of Roberta. "Mrs. Fulbright—whatever generation she lived in—would have been a force."

Her nephew Dick Waugh remembered her as a "marvelously warm and friendly person." By all accounts she was a remarkable raconteur who could recount stories with skill and wit. Waugh, too, remembered her as an accomplished storyteller, "a great observer of others' foibles." She was not averse either to pointing out her own, as she often did in her columns.

She could also laugh at her own expense. It was traditional for the university's *Arkansas Traveler* to publish a tongue-in-cheek April Fool's Day edition. Nothing was sacred; no one was spared, not even Roberta Fulbright. In the 1941 edition, editor Bill Penix wrote a column which he titled "As I Saw It," or "Through Rose Colored Glasses" by Aurora Bullfright.

Penix, who demonstrated a gift for parodying Roberta's style, wrote this:

> I went to Hog Eye today.
>
> Hog Eye is a peaceful little town nestled down in the beautiful Ozarks. It is 100 miles east of Cass and some 75 miles west of Chicken Bristle. And I do believe the grass at Hog Eye is fully a shade greener than the grass in our own little city of Fayetteville.
>
> The mission that took me to Hog Eye was not a selfish one, even though I did purchase some land while there. No, my journey thither was to investigate the plausibility of a plan suggested to me recently by a dear friend of mine, Homer Adkins.
>
> This plan, and if I may say so it is a fine one, is to pick the University up, bag and baggage, and move it to Hog Eye.

An abandoned CCC camp there would provide adequate facilities, yes, wonderfully adequate facilities, for our little University. There the students would be free to study in quiet and solitude, and the enterprise, with careful planning, could be carried on communistically. Each student might be given his own 40 acres and a mule.

This would leave the Fayetteville equipment empty so that the Jap aliens from the west coast might be quartered here. Think what lovely gardens we could have!

This I call an ideal set-up and an idea that only our fine governor could conceive.

May he achieve his goal.

Roberta did not take exception to the satire. In fact, said Penix, "she laughed about it."

Another time, however, her sense of humor did not come to the fore. Young Penix, while drinking beer at George's, a favorite student watering-hole, became annoyed by the odor emitted by the nearby Jerpe poultry plant owned by Roberta's son-in-law Gilbert Swanson. Feeling quite expansive at the time, Penix penned a letter to Roberta claiming that he had talked four students out of burning Jerpe's down.

"I think you'd better do something about it," Penix said of the smell.

Whether Roberta took the letter seriously or decided to teach the student editor a lesson, Penix was soon visited by postal inspectors. Roberta had turned the letter over to them. Penix, who admitted his contrived story, was properly sobered by the episode.

"You ticked Mama off," Bill Fulbright told him. When Penix mentioned it to her sometime later, she laughed, remarking coyly, "They didn't carry you off, did they?"

Despite the battle of wits, Penix held Roberta in high regard. He always enjoyed talks with her; he admired the fact that she had enhanced the family business holdings following her husband's death. Men in the community didn't like it "because it was a woman calling the tune," contended Penix, but "she had more to do with her community than any woman in the state."

Lessie Read agreed. Quoting the saying, "You can't be down in the mouth and up on your toes at the same time," Lessie wrote that it could well be Roberta's motto. "She doesn't like 'down in the mouth' people. She believes that those who achieve must be on their toes. Such are the only kind she cared to have around. Maybe that's why," contended Lessie, that the *St. Louis Post Dispatch* wrote that, "'. . . Mrs. Fulbright is a power to be reckoned with in Northwest Arkansas.'"

"There was always someone visiting or about to visit," said grandson Allan Gilbert of Roberta's days at Mont Nord. "They weren't invited. They just dropped by." The state's leading politicians came to pay courtesy calls, as did local leaders in the community. "She didn't seek it," said Gilbert. "It just developed around her. When you went to northwest Arkansas, you went to see Mrs. Fulbright." It became an accepted practice, not only for the politicians, but for everyone who came to Mont Nord, including salespeople and workers performing repairs, to sit down for a visit. Her egalitarian approach made equals of all comers.

Granddaughter Suzanne Zorn remembered when a young man stopped by the house on a survey of church membership, he wound up spending several hours while Roberta recounted the specifics of her own religious background beginning with her Baptist ancestors and ending with her years of teaching Sunday School in the Christian Church. "He was probably sorry he ever set foot there," said Zorn.

An August 22, 1943, entry in the diary of Marion Hays, wife of longtime Arkansas congressman Brooks Hays, reported:

> The Fulbrights gave a dinner for us recently. Eighteen guests. We gathered at Mrs. Jay Fulbright's; then drove to the Washington Hotel where we had a private dining room. Afterwards, sat in the Fulbright yard and talked. It was very pleasant.

As a college student, Marion Hays had visited Mont Nord on other occasions as a friend of Anna Fulbright. Roberta, she recalled, was always "very pleasant to me." Her connections to the family went back to the time when she was doing her practice teaching in Fayetteville and Bill Fulbright was a student in her seventh-grade class.

Another frequent visitor was Dr. W. B. Mahan, head of the University of Arkansas Department of Philosophy and Psychology. He and Mrs. Mahan came to Mont Nord on many Saturday nights when he and Roberta discussed a wide range of issues and ideas, these spirited discussions sometimes lasting until two or three o'clock in the morning. While Mahan enjoyed the challenge of these lively talks, he would not fully acknowledge Roberta as a true intellectual because she lacked the academic background. When she talked of returning to college, he discouraged her.

"She loved to talk, God, she loved to talk! She'd wear us out staying up at night," marveled Bill Fulbright. Her cousin Martha Twichell also remembered her as a "big talker. She loved to argue."

"Every time I come home from a party," Roberta said, "I realize I talked too much." It never kept her from doing it again the next time. "The gift of gab is most important," she informed grand-daughter Suzanne, who saw that her grandmother possessed a great curiosity; she was interested in everything and everybody.

"Mother," daughter Helen said, "could get on the train to go to St. Louis and know everybody on the train by the time she got there." Ironically, it was Helen who inherited her mother's story-telling skills.

Roberta was as comfortable in the conversational company of men as she was with women, perhaps more so. Ruby Thomas remembered a warm friendship which she and her husband, Herbert, enjoyed with Roberta during the fifteen years the Thomases lived in Fayetteville. Herbert Thomas, later the founder of Pyramid Life Insurance Company, liked to exchange ideas with Roberta. Bill Fulbright once mused that, "Mother and Herbert get together and settle the world's problems."

"Her head was no sack," said Ruby Thomas, putting it in the local vernacular. "It's her mental powers that I remember. I looked up to her; she had presence."

Henryetta Peck recalled similar conversational experiences. She and husband, Sam, who later owned and managed the Hotel Sam Peck in Little Rock, went to Fayetteville in 1929 to lease and manage the Fulbright-owned Washington Hotel, located on the southwest corner of the square in downtown Fayetteville. Roberta was a frequent patron of the hotel dining room where she and Sam Peck often had long, lively conversations. "She had a wonderful sense of humor," said Peck.

Her knack for conversation sometimes resulted in some unusual conversational partners. On one such occasion Roberta accompanied the Pecks on a cruise. Never one to meet a stranger, she initiated a discussion with several men from New York's Tammany Hall political machine.

"They were fascinated with her and she with them," Peck said. "They all sat up talking well into the night." The topics of that late night conversation are not known. In a strange twist of fate, Bill Fulbright served on the Foreign Affairs Committee in the House of Representatives under the chairmanship of Tammany Hall-controlled Congressman Sol Bloom, whose own controlling style Bill found objectionable.

If Roberta felt comfortable in any conversation, that same confidence never extended to mastery over the automobile. While Jay Fulbright had been determined to be one of Fayetteville's pioneer automobile owners, Roberta was more skeptical as to the value of driving. At one point she decided she would try to drive the family Maxwell Roadster. Upon completion of this adventure, she failed to set the brake and the car rolled into a tree at Mont Nord. That ended her driving career. "She wasn't in accord with the automobile," is the way son Bill charitably put it. From that time on, she walked where she needed to go or was chauffeured by family, friends, or business associates.

"Grandmother loved to take rides; that's how she learned what was going on in the county," observed Patty Smith. "She sat in the front seat, put one leg underneath her, and turned around to talk to you, teaching you all of the time." Because she didn't drive, she was never aware of any danger. "She was insouciant when she rode," said Suzanne Zorn. "She loved to go anywhere."

In 1947, striking telephone workers put a real crimp in her style when she found herself without telephone service. She grumped to her readers about "the telephone strike when you can't tell anybody they are wrong." To remedy the situation, she caught a ride with friends Ruby and Herbert Thomas to St. Louis to visit Anna and family. There she could talk to her heart's content. It also satisfied her ever-present desire to travel. "You'd go anywhere at the drop of a hat," a family member told her. "Actually," added another, "you don't have to drop a hat." Because of a fondness for antiques, some of her favorite trips were to New Orleans in search of treasures.

Despite her dependence on others for transportation, she was a frequent afternoon visitor in the homes of friends. On these outings she was seldom seen without a hat and was usually dressed in a plain dark dress, the same simple choker at her neck, and sturdy, sensible shoes on her feet, an acquiescence to her short legs and stubby toes. Her short, wispy hair had begun to turn gray and lay close to her head. It became her habit as she grew older and her figure became stockier to rest her arms across her ample bosom.

She and Lessie Read formed a fast friendship during their time at the newspaper which strengthened over the years and prompted frequent visits and outings. Lessie, too, was a large presence and together they made an imposing pair. Yet they were not without their own acknowledged shortcomings as Roberta described them.

"It is always too bad that neither Lessie or myself can drive a car and I am always afraid it makes us look and seem a little old. I really could drive a horse and buggy," Roberta advised. "I'm a terribly out-of-date old woman. I can't use a typewriter—and I'm ashamed of it." With her usual brand of self-deprecating humor, she declared that had it not been for her inability to drive and to type, "I might have been able to accomplish something."

She also acknowledged she had never learned to smoke a cigarette; "did not have time nor money," she said, "and never learned to drink a cocktail. I was taught I wanted to go to heaven and I still do."

Her busy schedule did not prevent her from observing a daily habit of taking afternoon tea, a practice established during her visits to England. "She was won over by the British," said Allan Gilbert. She kept candy and cookies in the closet for these tea sessions and for gifts. Her "saving ways"—which she characterized as "my natural and acquired economy"—were legendary in the family since her closet often yielded gifts which had been given to her, stored away, and later recycled to friends and family members. Once, when one of the Fulbright daughters sent a package of presents for Roberta, she knowingly said, "Mother, I don't care who you give them to."

Her generous spirit, however, would shine through, ranging from small but significant acts of kindness to gifts of considerable value. When the twins, Helen and Bo, were young, they took delight in teasing their niece Suzanne by sharing with her only a quarter of a stick of gum. On seeing this, Roberta promptly over-ruled them with a whole stick, a small act of generosity her grand-daughter never forgot.

She gave her niece Margaret Waugh Crittenden a lovely amethyst ring. When Margaret protested that she could not accept something of such value, Roberta admonished her that "everyone should have something you don't need." In this same spirit she gave each grandchild something she valued highly to remember her by.

Her interest in gardening never waned. Though she was aided by gardener and handyman Tom O'Kelly, she could garden endlessly. The sight of the tall, thin O'Kelly and the short, stocky Roberta, side by side in the garden was amusing to the family. Despite rheumatism in both knees, she would weed the entire garden while bent over from the waist in a standing position. It was a talent in which her grandchildren marveled.

"Friends," she advised her readers, "make a garden! If not for yourself, make it for your grandchildren." She also found it to be therapeutic. "When I become 'fed up' on politics and finance, even friends and family once in a while, I regale myself with a garden spree," she said.

Of the flowers in her garden, she observed: "They do not talk back, they are not jealous, they do not care which one you attend to first, they do demand a little of you, but they repay you for what you bestow almost without fail." Even in January she enjoyed a garden stroll, picturing the prospects for spring.

When weeds threatened to take over in the spring, she pointed out: "If anyone doubts that I am a Democrat, they should see my garden. . . . The common herb have acquired all the best space and attention, the second raters have about run out the 'elite.'"

She also liked nothing better than to sit down and play the piano. "I'll Take You Home Again, Kathleen" and "Beautiful Dreamer" were her favorites. "No one," she complained, "in 30 years had ventured to say a complimentary word." Then one day she happily reported that one of her grandsons told her, "'Grandmother, I just love to hear you play the piano.'"

"Well, I was pepped up no end," she said.

In addition to her passion for playing the piano, she loved to read. She found time to write her son Bill some motherly advice to do the same.

> I am about thro [sic] with Dorothy Thompson's *Listen Haus*. It is a masterpiece. I think you *must* read it—I'll send it to you.

She also passed on other news.

> We're having a cold snap 6 degrees below last night. I have been living in the dining room yesterday and today only I have been in bed all day until tonight. I had one of those dizzy spells which drive me mad. I think I am better.

Still unable to sleep at night, she spent her wakeful hours reading and continued her nocturnal practice of writing "As I See It." On occasion she wrote about her maladies:

> "As I See It" has been having difficulty seeing it. I have been indulging in one of those spells which make and keep the druggist rich. I went in for a fancy case of pink-eye, appendaged with the most devastating cough and sore throat my enemies could even wish on me.
>
> I consumed in those few days a tube of analgesic balm, one of eye salve, bottle of ST37, a large one of cough syrup, Vick's and Mentholatum, plus table salt and baking soda in large quantities, and aspirin, boric acid, iodine and glycerine.
>
> Do not mistake this for an advertisement for those drugs, for none did much good. They did serve to keep me busy,

but not happy. I still see poorly and feel worse, and am now trying a little whiskey and honey. Next time I'm getting turpentine and coal oil to begin with.

Her columns softened somewhat as time moved on and she became more nostalgic. On growing older, she wrote:

One thing about the march of time, as it slips up on us we have the opportunity to view our mistakes. It's an ordeal. Just when you thought you were smart, you find out you've been all sorts of a fool. Just when you thought you'd won, you discover you are a loser. Just when you think it is your time to receive, you find you are expected to give and give; to retire, and all but vanish through the grim experience of growing old.

Yet—I love to live. I don't know why exactly, but I know I do, and I thank God that I am alive. I do wish that wisdom had made its berth with me earlier in the struggle, for the emphases of life would have changed somewhat.

A man's life does not consist of the abundance of the things he possesses, but it consists of—well, it's darned hard to tell just what it does consist of, but a man's life is more than meat and his body more than raiment. There are values which should be clutched and held with untiring tenacity. Had I known, I could have grabbed quickly at the heart and mind of those entrusted to me, held on with more purpose.

Love is the great adventure, and no matter how it ends it is still the great experience. I would have you readers love with more abandon, fewer inhibitions and less caution, but I would have you not forget that love is long-suffering and is kind, is not puffed up. Risk your all. Be willing to give rather than receive, be a vehicle of eternal giving. Strive to love and not to be loved, strive to understand and not be understood, strive to minister and not be ministered to. Tough medicine, yes; but not taking it is tougher.

Her hometown, where she still kept a keen eye on all activities, and commented on them, too, continued its growth, reaching a population of more than eight thousand in the mid-1940s. Agricultural production continued to drive the county's economy. Retail prices which had plummeted during the depression began an upward surge. Dresses at the Boston Store were selling for $6.98 to $8.98. The citizenry kept a daily vigil on World War II, they bought war bonds, and like the depression years, they tended homegrown vegetables, now called victory gardens.

The onset of the war disturbed Roberta greatly, not only for the tremendous loss of life and the threats of Nazism, but for the destruction of the historic landmarks across Europe she had seen and loved.

> It is a gloomy thought to contemplate the devastation of all those lovely sights. As the songster has said, "Memory is the only friend that grief can call her own." My grief over the war is enshrouded in memories of lovely things that were and will never be again.

At Christmas 1941, she devoted a column to the boys in the military, saying she hoped they would be home in 1944. When the war continued into the winter of 1944, she repeated the column again. "There is rank injustice and inequality, we know, in asking you who are young and brave and strong and haven't lived yet to give it all to the god of war . . ." she lamented. "We suffer because we have not known how to save you. Our own helplessness distresses us." To her readers she said, ". . . the boys of the world are paying the absolute penalty for the faults of the world."

As Allied forces battled their way across France some months later, she was reminded of a rhyme she had written about the French city of Strasbourg, located in the Alsace Loraine region, which was intensely contested in World War I. She had written a poem after a 1926 visit and reprinted it as battles once again raged in France.

> Strasbourg is a city
>> That has changed its residence.
> It used to live in Germany
>> But now it lives in France.
> It has a wondrous clock
>> up in a wondrous tower
> That tells you what you want
>> to know,
> The day, the week, the hour.

> The seasons and the stars
>> Are recorded on its Face.
> What a pity it can't tell
>> To whom belongs Alsace.

Over the years her columns increasingly reflected her nostalgia for her childhood days on the farm in Missouri. "She was one of a pioneer strain of women," observed granddaughter Betsey Winnacker. "She showed great strength." Her grandmother believed in hardship, Patty Smith agreed. "She grew up that way."

As Roberta grew older, she thought more and more about the time when she was young. "I was born in one of the smallest and nicest towns in Missouri," she proclaimed. Her son Jack took her on a sentimental journey back to Rothville in 1948 where she "visited, reminisced and recalled all day."

By any standard, life on the Missouri farm was hard, a daily battle for security and survival. Yet she looked back on it with nostalgia, as a time when courage and forbearance were the traits that counted most.

Her travels to England had stirred her pride in her English ancestry. But she was prouder, still, of her grandparents whose pioneering spirit prodded them to leave the fertile farm valleys of Virginia and join the countless others who settled the west, and of her parents who secured that new life in the west.

She was part of that pioneer spirit. "I myself am a Missourian," she once said, "and the feel of the soil, the curl of the smoke, the scent of the grass and the set of the trees make me know I am part of it." The view from the hilltop at Mont Nord, though of Arkansas, would always encompass that Missouri landscape.

CHAPTER XII

The Passing Years

"The height of Chinese philosophy," wrote Roberta Fulbright, "is for the son to create more perfectly than did the father and thus the race progresses and becomes civilized. There seems much in that concept, to me." Although she wrote those words some years before her son's election to the Senate, they must have come to her mind again with his satisfying election victory.

"There is much of his father in the Senator, in his complete lack of hysteria, his deliberate self-control, his willingness to walk alone," writer Tristram Coffin would later observe. Roberta, too, had seen these qualities in her son and reflected on them with pride.

When Bill Fulbright assumed his Senate seat in January 1945, Roberta was a month shy of her seventy-first birthday. She was bothered by heart problems, low blood pressure, and rheumatism in both knees, as well as what grandson Allan Gilbert referred to as the curse of the Fulbrights: gastroenteritis and insomnia. Gilbert remembered that she kept a box of soda handy in at least three places throughout the house as a home remedy for her gastric distress. Granddaughter Bosey Fulbright Foote recalled being instructed to tiptoe past her grandmother's room on occasions when Roberta was not well. "She was the only person I ever knew who drank hot water. I always supposed it was for health reasons."

Still, she made the trip to Washington, D.C., where, attired in a conservative dark dress, fur stole, and sophisticated dark hat with matching bow, she watched as Bill was sworn into the Senate. "Well, here I am in the world-capital of Washington, D.C.," she informed her readers. "Saw Bill seated. Betty, her mother, the two girls, Betsey and Bosie [*sic*] and myself had seats in the gallery." Then she attempted to put it in perspective: "My inability to comprehend the fact of Bill's having become a senator rather alarms me—but as the old fellow said when he saw the House of Lords:'Gad! How much they look like other men.'"

She remained in the capital almost a month and wrote nine columns with a Washington dateline.

Washington, she told folks back in Fayetteville, was laid out in circles. "That seems typical and prophetic," she said. "One is sometimes inclined to think that long residence here renders the minds of Washingtonians rather circuitous—no beginning, no end, just round and round the mulberry bush."

"Washington doesn't need any robot bombs," she said, referring to Hitler's bombardment of London, "politicians keep the populace well on their way to shelter." She also pointed out that Washington was only about eight feet above sea level, leaving her feeling "like a balloon minus its wind."

As she had done many years before in England, she dutifully reported on the parties, luncheons, and dinners she attended—and even those she didn't attend. She was especially pleased to be invited to lunch at the Army and Navy Club as a guest of her cousin, Capt. Dorothy Stratton of the Coast Guard SPARS. Stratton, a former dean of women at Purdue University, was the daughter of Pattie Stratton Waugh's youngest brother.

She also told of attending a party at the Democratic Women's Club when first lady Eleanor Roosevelt was in the receiving line. "You would go far to find a better looking group of women," she bragged, "and my faith in democracy soared anew."

She mentioned early on that she had not yet had a chance to go shopping. "I really should buy a mink coat, but won't 'cause winter is too far gone, also money," she reasoned. "I think, though, I'll replace one of my old hats with a new one."

She soon brought up the subject of a mink coat again, reporting that she ran into Blanche Wingo, daughter of former Arkansas congressman Otis Wingo. She lamented that she did not get Wingo's married name, but she did not fail to notice something else: "She, though, had a lovely mink coat, really a must in Washington, so I gather her husband is quite all right." Apparently Roberta's fur stole was not filling the bill in the capital city.

She did not go shopping for a hat. "Folks, my age and color and previous condition of servitude just are not catered to in the millinery marts of the capital," she reported. "It's the 'petite' blondes and the slim, slick beauties who can buy hats here." She did buy one, but spared her readers a description. Sometime later she said, "Hats seem out—I'm always in on hats 'cause they improve my looks, or at least I'm convinced they do."

She was in the House gallery when her hero Pres. Franklin Roosevelt addressed Congress. "I, with my incorrigible habit of taking a note or two, took out my pencil and pad and began. This seems verboten ('forbidden' in German). This privilege belongs only to the Press Gallery. Fortunately, I escaped the eagle eye of the law and thus a scene was avoided."

"Columnists are thick up here," she advised, "and I am almost constrained to wish I'd moved up in my youth and tried my hand, for there appear to be good, bad and indifferent."

Roberta had remained loyal to President Roosevelt throughout his presidency, and when he ran for a fourth term in 1944, she had capsuled his opponent Thomas E. Dewey of New York with this pithy observation:

> If Mr. Dewey takes nine coaches to properly convey him and his entourage from New York to St. Louis when he is only a nominee, I wonder if the New York Central railroad could transport him if and when he should become president. It looks formidable.

On January 20, 1945, President Roosevelt was inaugurated for the fourth time. Because World War II was still underway, the scaled-down ceremony was held on the portico of the White House. Bill, Betty, and Roberta were among the guests. This was a special thrill for Roberta, long one of the president's most loyal admirers. "The occasion," she said, "is TOO MOMENTOUS, too full of meaning for my comprehension." Still, she managed to provide *Times* readers with a detailed description.

"I will say I believe the president has cause to rather dislike the press," she contended. "If there's a way to put emphasis in the wrong place, they do. (It makes reader interest.)"

On her return to Fayetteville, she datelined her first column "HOME," then added, "But here I am now at a desk piled high with unanswered letters, unpaid Christmas bills and some utility ones and it is now time for me to have the clubs to which I belong and so on."

Her trips to Washington were infrequent; her interest in Bill's senatorial career was maintained largely by letter from Fayetteville. On one trip to the capital she wrote home to her friend Walt Lemke, "I am enjoying the full days up here and the Senator is standing it very well, thank you."

Roberta always enjoyed the beauty of the trees and flowers in Washington, and used them, in her column, for other comparisons: "It's a city of favors, either being granted or sought, and 'saying it with flowers' has been found very effective."

Visits to the Lincoln Memorial, she declared, always made her faith in America mount, ". . . to stand in the presence of the Great Emancipator gives me comfort—real abiding comfort." She also liked to observe sessions of Congress. On one occasion, when visiting the Senate some years before her son took office, she observed a long technical debate on the value of holding companies. Referring to one senator who held forth for quite a long time, she said, ". . . I think he was against holding companies but I would not swear it."

When back at home she usually addressed her letters to Bill with the salutations, "My darling boy," "Bill, precious boy," or "My dear." Her letters took on a decidedly different tone than that of her column. She was solicitous and sympathetic, yet full of motherly advice, urging her son to buy war bonds and encouraging him to take restful breaks away from the stress and strain of the Congress. "It's forever up to me to be telling folks what they should do and they don't like it," she said.

"You are on my mind," she wrote Bill, "and when I consider what a long strain you've been under I am writing to say Stop! Look! Listen: Do not exceed the speed limit. Go away for a few days if you feel too harassed. Go to Virginia."

"I have a dreadful fear of nerves cracking in this country of ours anyway," she wrote him on another occasion. "Now I'm not expecting any such performance, but do take care of yourself and if you are even a little kin to me you will have a tendency to be hard on yourself. Don't do it. You're ahead of the game, honey, way ahead, so give yourself a bit of a break. You've done a wonderful job."

Referring to Roberta's influence on her son, Kurt Karl Tweraser, in his doctoral dissertation at American University, wrote: "His mother especially provided him a model for coping with failure and for doing one's best even when complete success is not possible. She herself had to overcome recurring temptations to withdraw and to contemplate her virtues."

In the view of Karl E. Meyer, an editorial writer for the *Washington Post,* Roberta was "an imposing woman of strong features, strong views and a strong will." In her column, he opined, she "could be tart and heterodox when she was so inclined." Reflecting on her influence on her son, the senator, Meyer said: "His mother's Missouri liberalism left a mark on Fulbright. So did her love of learning."

One journalist was bold enough to ask her if she followed her son's lead in her writing. With wit, she replied, "Of course as a rule I endorse him in full, but seldom ever try to say so."

She told her son, "As we older grow we suffer for love, but it's the law of life I guess and the one thing I do not choose to be is a baby or a fool—I suspect myself of both at times—However, my role has been a bit stiff."

She was deeply saddened by the unexpected death of President Roosevelt, April 12, 1945, in Warm Springs, Georgia. The *Northwest Arkansas Times* ran an oversized banner headline saying simply "Roosevelt Dies." Listing reactions of local leaders, the *Times* quoted Roberta as saying, "Gone is one of, if not the greatest, single personality in this old world." Yet—while she had ever been Roosevelt's staunch defender—she wrote little in her column about his death. With the rest of the country, she was resigned to moving on. Now a fellow Missourian Harry S. Truman would be president, but this evoked little comment on her part.

By now she had shifted major responsibility for operation of the Fulbright enterprises to others, particularly son-in-law Hal Douglas. Douglas had entered the military as a naval intelligence officer during World War II, but resumed his management duties upon his return, including his role as secretary-treasurer of the

Democrat Publishing Company, parent company of the *Northwest Arkansas Times*. It was his habit, when he came home to Mont Nord at the end of the business day, to spend an hour or two with Roberta going over business matters. She expected nothing less. It was left to daughter Helen to manage the Mont Nord household, no small task, but one which she bore with grace. It was wonderful, Roberta declared, seemingly unmindful of the heavy load, "that my baby girl can cook and serve with distinction and ease."

The family-owned Washington Hotel—still managed by Sam Peck who now also had a hotel in Little Rock—underwent a face lift and was heralded in newstories and ads in the *Northwest Arkansas Times*. Roberta was away in Washington when the revitalization was celebrated. (When she was at home, however, she never ceased to enjoy going to dinner at the hotel, generally going once a week on the day fried chicken and mashed potatoes were served.)

Also while she was away, Arkansas attorney general Guy E. Williams ruled that new governor Ben Laney would have five appointments to make to the University of Arkansas Board of Trustees. The ruling held that four of the board members had not been appointed legally by former governor Homer Adkins. The four trustees—whom the ruling stated had not been confirmed by the Senate—were Chairman John G. Ragsdale, Harry L. Ponder, Hugh Park, and J. H. Snapp. The fifth appointment would come from the expiration of the term of another board member. The ruling was requested by Governor Laney.

Three of the four board members—Ragsdale, Park, and Snapp—had voted for Bill Fulbright's ouster from the university presidency in 1941. Proving perhaps that time did indeed heal wounds, Roberta made no response to this turn of events. But with these removals and Bill Fulbright's victory over Governor Adkins in the senate race, the battle over the university presidency had clearly come full circle.

Roberta immersed herself in the activities of her family, friends, and community. When she returned home from her trip to see Bill's entry into the senate, she accepted a number of speaking engagements. As World War II came to a close, she spoke fervently of peace and postwar world planning. She professed, in her usual self-deprecating way, to difficulty in public speaking: "When I get on my feet my brain takes a vacation, but my tongue is doing time and a half. As I know, I'm considered belligerent, but peace is my theme, so friends and neighbors unless you feel peaceful, fight shy of me."

When she spoke to the Business and Professional Women's Club in Springdale, she noted, "Someone said they wanted to 'cover' my speech. Well, all I can say, they needed an army tent, for persons, things, ideas and implements were thrown together in confusion combined with peace proposals." Though she claimed she was ill-prepared, she was not without detailed charts which she displayed to bolster the points she made. Her aw-shucks disclaimer on public speaking was not consistent with her ever-present desire to stand up and speak, even when she went to meetings as an observer and not as a program participant.

It is not surprising that her schedule led to another bout with illness. When she felt better, she went to Omaha in June 1945 to visit Bo and Gilbert Swanson and family. While she was there, Gilbert persuaded her to undergo ten days of clinical testing. As the tests came to a close, she attempted to use her well-known powers of influence.

"Doctor," she said, "you are a good guesser so why not just guess on these few remaining points."

Firmly, he said, "We do not guess."

The doctor prevailed; the tests proceeded, but she did not reveal the results. When she returned home she reported on another embarrassing moment during her trip.

> Recently I was introduced as the mother of Senator Fulbright of Arkansas. At once I detected they had never heard of Senator Fulbright, never heard of Arkansas, and definitely never desired to hear of me. The populace still needs education, I tell you.

For a time in 1945, Roberta's picture appeared with her column. This practice continued only briefly; the picture disappeared without comment. It was the only time during all the years of her column that her picture was used. There is no indication as to whose idea it was to add the picture, nor to withdraw it.

As World War II gradually ground to a halt in the summer of 1945, she continued her campaign for peace in "As I See It," writing about the responsibilities of maintaining peace in a newly ordered world. On the local front, she turned to more mundane matters in the aftermath of the war. Commenting about the urgent need for housing at the university for returning veterans, she claimed, "The University authorities have been very slow and silent until now and the occasion presses." Of the returning servicemen, she asked her readers: "What can we who have stayed at home do, I wonder, to help stabilize them and re-orient themselves?"

In November, the *Times* carried a front-page story announcing that an international military tribunal had opened the Nazi war crimes trials in Nuremberg, Germany. Closure on the horrors and atrocities of the war was underway.

Roberta continued to hammer away about her concern for meeting the requirements of the postwar period.

> Our own self-righteousness as Americans and our sense of having earned the *right* to be rich and well-fed is alarming.
> . . . We are a fine nation of mixed breeds and tendencies all flaunting the name American and loving it, but in this bitterest period of the world's history, the starkest period of European needs, let us show ourselves *worthy* of our heritages.
> . . . I resent the implication that we women rampage for "silk stockings" and fight for extra bacon—.

When some of her editorial campaigns evoked vocal opposition, she lamented, "About the only fun I get these days is turning the other cheek."

In December, when Bill came to Fayetteville for the Christmas holidays, he spoke to a large crowd gathered for a Christmas program at Central Methodist Church. He told his audience they were living in a new era. According to the *Times* report:

He pointed out the assumption many in the United States have adopted, that we are the only good people in the world and that the bomb should be left in trust with us, is very unpopular all over the world.

Roberta was heartened when, in August 1946, President Truman signed into law her son's bill to create a program of exchange of students and academicians with countries throughout the world which became known as the Fulbright Program. It served to reinforce her own belief that America must bring itself closer to the rest of the world if peace and understanding were to be achieved. One neighbor who didn't quite understand what the Fulbright scholarship program was all about said it was all well and good, but she was sure that Mrs. Fulbright paid for it.

In the meantime, she had returned to her own drive for added university housing for veterans. For those who thought she was carrying the topic too far, she said:

We may not be up on the functions of a state university, but we still believe we know something of the functions of a newspaper and a town. We still maintain the University is an asset of the state, the definite responsibility of the town in which it is located.

. . . I have never let my interest (in the university) lag.

Her interest in goings-on in Little Rock was also piqued when she stated her opposition to the construction of a state-financed football stadium in the capital city, expressing instead her support for a governor's mansion.

She was chosen Arkansas Mother of the Year in 1946, an honor which pleased her and her large extended family. She once reflected: "When God gave us children He gave us a job big enough and important enough to stagger the best of us." Then she acknowledged: "The other side of this picture is that it is the dearest task you will ever be called upon to perform."

While she held firmly to a lifelong belief that maintaining a stable home and raising a family were the most important of all endeavors, she could look at her role as family adviser with some bemusement. She relayed to her readers a remark made by

Sir Wilmott Lewis, and reported in the *St. Louis Post Dispatch,*
which she thought fit her own case.

> Man's life is divided into two periods—In the first he sets
> a bad example; in the second, he gives good advice.
> My children with one accord informed me I had reached
> the second period.

She had given birth to six children, "not one born in a hospital,"
she said. She had experienced the peaks and valleys of mothering
six children; had shepherded her diverse brood through the pitfalls
of growing up and establishing their own families; had seen her
oldest daughter die unexpectedly at an early age; had given love
and attention to a large group of grandchildren; and had watched
her younger son rise from political removal as university president
to a position of respect in the U.S. Senate. "I realize endlessly," she
remarked, "that fate has been kind to me. Life has yielded much
of her best to me . . . but waves of discontent and appalling melancholy sweep over me at times. . . ."

No doubt the early death of her husband left a void which
never again was completely filled despite the large family around
her. Advancing age and chronic heart problems contributed to her
melancholy, too. While business responsibilities now fell to Hal
Douglas and homemaking chores to Helen, Roberta could not let
them go. When Hal and Helen considered moving into a home of
their own, Roberta countered by asking them: "What will I do by
myself in that big house?" The Douglases remained.

Although she did not make a habit of writing about her family,
she did, from time to time, bring them up:

> In my column . . . recently I very inadvertently said I did
> not impress my children properly. I guess I storied a bit—
> I just did not make quite the impress [*sic*] I had featured I
> would—a bit of perverted egotism, no doubt.
> . . . There cannot be found a parent who thinks more
> highly of her brood than I.

She was proud that Jack wrote an occasional column for "As I
See It," but couldn't resist saying, in introducing one column: "He
and I can look through the same keyhole and he will see East and

I will see West, but we enjoy the same meal." When some of her readers asked when he was going to write again, she said, "I take it they crave a bit of pepper sauce and are weary of plain vanilla."

She enjoyed visits with Jack and his family both in Kansas City and Fayetteville. "Jack refuses to be molded—he's ground down by sandstone rock," she commented. "When he comes, religion, ethics, politics, business and sports afford conversation." After one University of Arkansas homecoming gathering at Mont Nord, she remarked: "Jack treated the guests to a good brand of capitalism and anti-New Dealism, not always served at our home. It takes me a couple of weeks to recover. We did have a good time, though."

When daughter Anna was defeated in a race for the St. Louis board of education, she lamented, "but that's the way with little towns like St. Louis." As Roberta saw it, Anna had two handicaps: "First, she was a woman. Second, those Missouri Democrats did not perceive a Missouri-born, Missouri-educated (at M.S.U.) Democrat of the first water."

As the 1946 fall term approached at the university, she again took up her campaign for student housing. Although the university had obtained some temporary buildings, the continuing rise in enrollment caused housing shortages. Roberta suggested that Fayetteville residents, who could spare the space, open their homes to students. Some students took her literally. In August 1946, shortly before the opening of the fall term, she was approached by four prospective students on the subject she had raised: "Those who live in big houses should take students."

"I encountered them," she related, "on my front veranda with the *Northwest Arkansas Times* in hand carrying the news of the release of the 1,500 hutments from Camp Robinson which they apparently had not seen."

The visitors wanted to know why she didn't open her home to students. She related the story to her readers.

A bit of criticism—slight challenge had been generated against *poor old* me and my big house and the houses of my neighbors but especially me and mine. I explained we of our house minister to an immediate family of 24 members, with more in the offing—comings and goings are fairly constant. We have no house help. I am old and the house not adapted to outsiders because of entrances and such.

Their approach irked me just a bit. I have made a prolonged, persistent and unrelenting effort to be a good citizen, to endorse and aid every project of community good within my power—with accent on the students and University in general.

... hope I may have dissipated the tone of challenge they had in their hearts and voices.

While this encounter did not deter her from keeping up her pleas for student housing, she also found a new cause—the condition of Fayetteville's sidewalks which she discovered accidentally.

Just for a change I walked to town for the first time in several years today. I had a heart attack some seasons back, and had been warned as to walking, climbing steps and so on.

... I discovered we have more worn out, miserable sidewalks between Mt. Nord and the *Times* office than we have decent.

"The only thing that old folks are really good for is to make comparisons," she added a few days later.

When the 1946 fall term opened at the university, it was a new era in higher education. The returning World War II veterans and their families found housing in Veterans Village. The *Times* highlighted a story of two generations starting to school together—the father headed toward Old Main on the campus, the son to school in Veterans Village. The son, according to the *Times,* had high expectations, but by noon was discouraged, telling his father in disgust, "I didn't even learn to read!"

Roberta had her own back-to-school story to report.

A first grader in school after the first day. Father says, "Henry, what'd you learn?" Henry: "Not much. I'll have to go again tomorrow."

Occasional bouts of illness again began to plague her and she sometimes enlisted guest columnists, including old friends Lessie

Read and Walt Lemke. In March 1947, she told her readers, ". . . my time is occupied by lying in bed with a bad ticker." Daughter Bo came down from Omaha to be with her mother, who, the *Times* reported, was improving. When she was unable to attend a university lecture given by Louis P. Lochner, former Associated Press bureau chief in Berlin, he gave a fifteen-minute address on local radio station KGRH, saying he wanted Roberta to hear something about the conditions in Berlin.

After a month of illness, Roberta wrote, "I just got past pushing a pencil and turning a page, and I was nearly to the end, I'm telling you."

But she hadn't given up. When a 1947–48 concert series was announced for Fayetteville, she pronounced, ". . . we will try to be there in our best bib and tucker."

She also reported a visit from Jack, who came down from Kansas City.

> He was born with an embryonic atom bomb somewhere in his makeup so he fits this age rather well.
>
> . . . At any rate he doesn't seem much older than I am and we can talk endlessly.
>
> . . . Jack puts out the idea that he would enjoy my column much more if I would write more about Virginia.
>
> . . . I have never visited Virginia so I'm not so very competent on the subject. He does not think that should deter me and of course if I were an honest to goodness writer it wouldn't.

(She did visit Williamsburg, Virginia, in 1946 during a trip to Washington, D.C. Apparently she was referring to the fact that she had not visited the area in Virginia from which her forebears departed for Missouri.)

Her spirits were lifted when the University of Arkansas announced that Bill Fulbright would be one of five persons on whom the university would confer honorary degrees at the June 9, 1947, commencement. There was no small irony in the fact that the event would occur six years to the day when Fulbright was fired as the university's president.

The event also coincided with the university's seventy-fifth anniversary year and the investiture of its new president, Dr. Lewis Webster Jones. In reviewing the university years since her arrival in Fayetteville in 1906, Roberta remarked, "Up to now, as I see it, Dr. J. C. Futrall has left his imprint in bolder symbols than anyone else . . . He was an able man."

Bill's selection for an honorary degree gave Roberta no small measure of satisfaction. "Under pressure I think I can approve the U.S. Senator," she said. She was also gratified by the selection of another of the honorees.

> We also desire to say we feel a sense of uplift and eman-
> cipation to know that a woman is to receive an honorary
> degree from the University of Arkansas for the first time. We
> approve of Miss Jobelle Holcombe, and we feel the shackles
> falling from us.

Holcombe, professor emeritus of English, was a university faculty member for more than forty years.

At the same time, Roberta was lukewarm to the idea of women being admitted as full-fledged pastors in the Presbyterian Church. The idea was voted down at the church's general assembly. (The Northwest Arkansas Presbytery voted for it.)

> We accept the verdict of the majority. Knowing the
> women will forever do much that has to be done, I wish
> some times that men did like women better in high places,
> because they do have the ability and willingness but there
> just isn't enough ego to go around and men can not function
> without it.

Despite her love affair with her hometown, she still was not lessening her campaigns for civic improvement. In addition to her pleas for "decent" sidewalks, she argued for improved streets, a better water supply, increased fire protection, new schools, a new Boys Club, and a combined city, county, and university hospital. She even gave her opinion on routing and beautifying the area's highways. The citizens were not taxing themselves sufficiently, she believed.

> I am reminded that we are a bit like the father who told his son when he went to town from the country, "Son, be in favor of everything until it comes to the money, then fight the location."

She recounted how, for many years, she had supported the widening of the city's streets despite the cost.

> I so often recall what my husband said when we were paving our streets. I think you all know I usually put my complete o.k. on anything which my husband ever did or said. But I recall saying, "Jay, you men are making our streets too narrow." He replied, "They are as wide as we can pay for." Well, I let it go at that but I think we probably could have had them paid for had they been wider and we would have been considerably better off.

Although her campaigns for public works remained unchanged, her interest in politics had taken a different turn. Contrary to the 1930s when she took vocal stands on candidates of her choice, in the 1940s she did not always endorse candidates. This undoubtedly had something to do with her son's elected position in the Senate and also to the shifting of her interest to other things. She did, however, comment from time to time, musing: "A Free Press and a democratic government are an original pair, not comparable to the Garden of Eden and original sin, maybe, but just about."

She did not succeed in becoming well acquainted with Gov. Ben Laney, who took office in January 1945 succeeding Homer Adkins. After a Laney visit to Fayetteville, she said, "I am old fashioned and love to get acquainted with governors. Our Governor Laney can slip in and out with less commotion than I am used to." When Laney ran for reelection, she said only, "Governor Laney strikes us as the one to succeed himself. . . ."

Soon after, she went to Little Rock for Washington County Days at the Capitol, reporting, "I missed seeing the governor. I never have any luck seeing him."

After his reelection she gave him some support:

The governor has struck us as being an honest, wise man whom we are very inclined to honor.

We were a bit fearful that our Northwest did not claim his attention and affection enough, but at this stage we desire to congratulate ourselves again on a friend in court in the person of our governor, as well as our representatives.

When she saw him at a university alumni luncheon she reported, "Governor Laney is always a bit difficult to contact, he's evasive, but he wins us when we reach him every time."

The summer months of 1947 brought a rash of "flying saucer" sightings in the Fayetteville area, as throughout the country, and the *Northwest Arkansas Times* dutifully reported the sightings. "There were about eight cars parked on U.S. Highway 71 north of Fayetteville last night with folks leaning out the windows or standing nearby, their necks craned as they watched the heavens for some of the flying saucers," the *Times* reported in a page-one story.

Roberta refrained from commenting on this occurrence, perhaps because she had no interest in such a phenomenon or she didn't want to poke fun at the citizens who believed they saw them. More likely it was because she had again been forced to bed by illness, no doubt made more uncomfortable by summer weather which saw temperatures ranging up to 104 degrees, the second warmest August recorded up to that time in Fayetteville.

To cheer her up, radio station KGRH played one of her favorite songs, "I'll Take You Home Again, Kathleen." She was also cheered by a visit from her brothers Jim and Charles Waugh of Rothville. She was well enough by late September to attend the annual picnic for *Times* employees.

She remained serious about her responsibilities to the press. She was called upon to judge the feature writing contest for the Arkansas League of American Penwomen. She was supportive of young professional women, particularly those entering journalism. In a letter to Walt Lemke she praised the work of Connie Stuck, a University of Arkansas graduate who had served as editor of the *Arkansas Traveler* and after graduation as the editor of the *Marked*

Tree (Arkansas) *Tribune,* calling her "engaging to the limit." Then she added, "Women are here to stay, I am convinced."

She had the shock of her "young life" she said, when she read in the *Readers Digest* that, "American men do not love women. I had suspected it but David Cohen says it's so. Well, so long as that is the case we better try to make ourselves count." Making "ourselves count" included women running for high office. "Senator Byrd of Virginia is credited with saying a woman vice president would be a good idea. I second the motion." But, she complained, "there is no real method to measure or value the talent of the women of this country."

She could be equally frank in her criticism of women, observing that a female university official, dressed quite fancily for a school social occasion, was surely showing off.

She could also express doubts about herself. Reporting on her attendance at a University Press Club banquet, she said:

> For some unknown reason they gave me a seat by the speaker for the occasion, Mr. Hardy (Spider) Roland. He is the coronary thrombosis of the *Arkansas Gazette.*
>
> . . . I asked him home with me for breakfast, and he did not come.
>
> I look at myself and wonder why I ever thought a column could exist under my dominion.
>
> Well, I have loved writing it and it is habit hard to break. If enough of you will write a card and say "quit" it might work.

Perhaps Roland's failure to appear for breakfast was not due to his lack of regard for Roberta as a columnist, but rather his inability to recover in time from the previous night's celebration. At least one—and maybe most—of the journalists attending the event could not fail to notice that as he delivered his speech, Roland would occasionally stop to sip from a tube leading from his coat pocket to shoulder level. When the tube finally failed to yield the necessary intake, Roland pulled an empty liquor bottle from the pocket, tossed it aside, reconnected the tube to a new bottle which he carried in another pocket, and casually resumed his speech. Seated next to him, Roberta, a well-known advocate of abstinence from alcohol, surely could not have failed to observe this phenomenon.

Although she was under orders to "go slow," she was well enough in the spring of 1948 to return to Washington for another visit. Fascinated as always with congressional debate she went to a Senate session.

> Up in the visitor's gallery I at once pushed over and leaned on the railing looking down eagerly into the chamber, trying to find my little boy when a page very promptly says, "Lady, it's against the law to lean on the rail."
>
> I sat all afternoon to hear Bill speak, but at 5 o'clock we came home and then he finally did hold forth.

She was still dispensing her favorite potion—advice. After sitting quietly at the breakfast table for a few days while the senator remained hidden behind the morning newspaper expressing concern over what he read, she could not resist.

> I told Bill at breakfast, though I don't think he ever heard or answered, that I had just read that Oliver Wendell Holmes, the greatest judge of all times, never read a newspaper. Bill may have grunted, I don't think so, but he steams up a bit harder than an old mother craves, but "crises" are a dish at every meal and are always described as "very critical." All I can do is to recall that they are recurrent, not always fatal, though I can't see that helps too much.

Not to be outdone, Bill had a rejoinder a few days later when he told someone, "Ma only knows what she reads—in her own paper, mostly her own column."

"So," she said, "I'm getting a little rusty missing my own column."

She was not the only family member to dispense advice. Anna wrote her during the Washington visit.

"Mother, do not be afraid to miss some things."

"Good advice, I'll admit, but hard to follow," Roberta replied.

She and daughter-in-law Betty were invited to attend a meeting of the Congressional Wives Club where scholarly programs on current issues were generally the topic of the day.

The invitation was extended by Marion Hays, wife of Congressman Brooks Hays, who knew of Roberta's penchant for such discussions. But this day's program turned out to be a demonstration by a local butcher on the different cuts of meat. Despite the fears of their hostess, Roberta and Betty were quite captivated and left after the meeting with their own freshly cut pieces of beef in hand. To her readers back home, Roberta wrote glowingly about the program. Always mindful of the influence of the agricultural economy on her community, she said of the demonstration: "Sounds nearly like a farm course, doesn't it?"

Another event she did not miss was the Gridiron Tea. There, she reported, she saw President and Mrs. Truman. She was also overjoyed by a visit from her old political ally, former governor Carl Bailey and Mrs. Bailey. Five months later, in Little Rock, Bailey died suddenly of a heart attack. Wrote Roberta:

> He was one of the essentially great of Arkansas, if I am a judge. I always felt that great urges surged within him, great ideas pursued him. He was possessed of an unusual courage.

When four men contended for the Democratic gubernatorial nomination in the summer of 1948—Sidney McMath, Jack Holt, Horace Thompson, and James (Uncle Mac) MacKrell—Roberta's only comments were:

> I declare to you. I believe all of the handsome men in Arkansas decided they'd like to be governor. I guess their friends encouraged them. Well, I hope the handsomest man wins.

These light comments were a far cry from her earnest support some years earlier for Carl Bailey.

In November 1948, she accompanied Bill—whom she now referred to as "Senator Bill" in her column—to Little Rock. Her pride was evident. "I am just saying he is one of the most diligent and studious boys in the United States Senate." While they were in central Arkansas, she was amused to report that two young boys asked for Bill's autograph, "because he had played on the Razorback team."

She also reported that she and Bill had dinner with Mr. and Mrs. J. N. Heiskell at their home in Little Rock. Heiskell, the venerable publisher of the *Arkansas Gazette,* was well known as the dean of Arkansas newspaper owners, and dinner with him was "a rare treat to us who are connected with the press," she said. "I make bold to say he knows more about the state than anyone living here."

While in Little Rock, she went to hear Bill's speech at the Rural Electrification Administration (REA) dinner. Since the presidential election pitting Pres. Harry S. Truman against Thomas E. Dewey was just a few days away, the REA dinner reminded her that "Truman says Dewey says, 'TVA is wonderful but we must never let it happen again.'" When President Truman emerged an upset winner, Roberta, mindful of their shared Missouri roots, expressed admiration for his competitive spirit and his unwavering determination when he believed he was right.

Although the Fulbright family was now spread to faraway locales, Roberta remained the strong center of family activities, and every family member who possibly could continued to gather at Mont Nord for the university homecoming and for Christmas. Bill Fulbright's administrative assistant, John Erickson, often accompanied him to Fayetteville for Razorback football games. "She would have a big party at Mont Nord for his friends," said Erickson, who remembered, too, that parking around Mont Nord was always a problem during these large gatherings.

"I just believe we generate atomic energy in modern quantities about as well as any unit one can find," Roberta remarked after twenty-six of the family arrived for Christmas in 1948. She grieved, nevertheless, that her children and grandchildren had been denied the benefit of Jay Fulbright's company and counsel. She never ceased to miss his companionship.

She continued to take an active interest in the operation of the *Northwest Arkansas Times,* where she carried the title of president. In 1940, the paper had moved to new quarters on the corner of North East and Meadow streets in downtown Fayetteville. In 1945, longtime employee Sam Gearhart was made a stockholder in the Democrat Publishing Company and was named vice president in addition to his duties as general manager.

Sam Schwieger had succeeded James Bohart as editor in 1943, but stayed only briefly—moving on to accept a better business opportunity—and was followed by Ted Wylie, who remained at the helm for more than twenty years. Wylie, a graduate of Columbia University's school of journalism, worked on several Arkansas papers before coming to Fayetteville. After watching him play baseball at the annual *Times* picnic, Roberta wryly observed that he "has the talent for being the cleanest man to play ball and run a paper I know and withal we look forward to what he is going to say and believe him." Grandson Allan Gilbert served as sports editor and staff artist. There were thirty-two employees with forty-six others working primarily as carriers and routemen. By 1949, the annual payroll reached one hundred thousand dollars.

In an eleven-year period, the newspaper's circulation doubled. In 1938, forty-four hundred families read the *Times;* in 1949, that number reached nine thousand. The *Times* was going to 98 percent of the homes in Fayetteville and 70 percent of the homes in Washington County.

"Her one big love besides her family," said Bill of his mother, "was that newspaper."

But by 1949 she was considering retirement from writing her column. "I keep saying that I am writing 'Finis' to 'As I See It' but something keeps prodding me." But before she said "Finis" she always had another project she wanted to push. On this occasion she was promoting the idea of the city planting flowering trees and shrubs.

Apparently her threat to quit evoked reader response, for a few days later she wrote:

> "As I See It," I am forever about to quit attempting to take up space, but forever there comes something I am still interested in writing. I desire at this time while it is pressing on my mind to thank you, my friends and readers, for the support you have so generously given me through the years.
>
> The writing of this little column has been a great pleasure and outlet for me and you have made me happy regarding it. It has sustained me in a manner difficult to describe, yet very real to me, and difficult to get on without.

So she continued on, plugging away several days later on some of her favorite civic topics: widening the streets, constructing additional water facilities, adding neighborhood playgrounds, and building a city library at ground-floor level to replace the one housed on an upper floor where she had difficulty climbing the steps. She also wrote of the need for a convention hall. "Why in heaven's name," she asked in exasperation, "do we never have any money or credit?" In the same vein, she said prophetically: "As I see it, the great struggle of the future promises to be for a place to park."

She retained her childhood fascination with weddings, reporting glowingly on the local wedding of Jean Thomas, daughter of Ruby and Herbert Thomas. As Roberta described it, "the wedding party floated down between rows of exquisite bouquets and ribbons with tulle parasols to soften the rays of old Sol." This time, unlike her experience as a child, Roberta got to sample the wedding cake which she described as "perfection."

An outbreak of polio plagued Arkansas in the summer of 1949, as it did the rest of the country. In less than a month, Washington County reported eleven new cases, and the city of Fayetteville, reported the *Times,* was doing its best "to improve sanitation and to prevent a more serious outbreak." By fall, funds for the polio drive were being collected in local area movie theaters.

Also in 1949, Gov. Sidney McMath asked Roberta to serve on the publicity committee of the first Governor's Highway Safety Conference. He also named her to a statewide committee to receive and direct distribution of gifts in the Arkansas unit of the French "Merci Train." The train was a way for the French people to say thank you to America for its help in World War II. Her "duties," according to her column, involved making a trip to Little Rock to greet the train. There were only two committee members from northwest Arkansas, she pointed out, "so I figured they did not anticipate many words or ideas from this section (two meek little women)."

Her frequent calls for world peace and postwar cooperation among nations were rewarded with an appointment to the Atlantic Union Committee of Arkansas. The committee promoted the aims of the Atlantic Union Council, an organization advocating unity among nations bordering the Atlantic Ocean and identified with the Atlantic Pact. "Let's be careful who we denounce and what we do. We can not withdraw from the world, we can not even imprison everyone who does not think as we would advocate," she said.

Later she confessed, "My two occasions of shame for America are when we turned down the League of Nations, then unleashed the atomic bomb . . . both the results of political influence." She repeatedly stated her case for peace as the cold war intensified across the globe. She apologized, however, for not giving the Atlantic Union Committee the attention she felt it deserved. "I plead guilty and am sorry," she admitted.

"One thing I can never subscribe to is that life is dull," she said. Whether attending local civic and women's club functions or school programs in the small communities surrounding Fayetteville, she always expressed her enjoyment of each event. After attending an afternoon concert of the Northwest Arkansas Symphony, she described the concert as "a sort of miracle," and the conductor "a marvel." She wished, however, for music which was "a little more familiar. Folks don't enjoy being reminded a whole afternoon that they don't know a thing."

When she had to miss the dedication of a new printing plant for the university's journalism department because she was visiting Anna and family in St. Louis, she wrote Prof. Walt Lemke: "To tell the truth, I have more faith in the press than I have in arms."

Her interest in her hometown never lessened even when she was away for awhile. A few days after her note to Lemke, Anna wrote him that, "She is so engrossed in Fayetteville these days that no place else offers much interest."

"This little town," Roberta said of Fayetteville, "has run off and left me. I am like our baby who was under the table recently and we kept calling her. She replied, 'I don't know where I'm at.'"

As young journalist Bill Penix had so accurately perceived a few years earlier in his parody of Roberta's columns, she always wrote in superlatives when describing Fayetteville and the northwest Arkansas area. In her eyes, the pastures were always greener, the flowers more prolific, and the foliage more colorful than anywhere else. Descriptions of automobile trips in the countryside took on the air of visiting a fairyland. Everything about the events she attended was described as delicious, delightful, exceptional, or enchanting.

As she became more reflective, religious themes began to appear frequently in her columns. Sometimes these took the form of sermonettes on love, prayer, and appreciation. Roberta, Lessie Read once wrote, ". . . believes strongly in the power of love. She also believes in the power of work." And, indeed, she "sermonized" about it often.

Roberta acknowledged her dependence upon her hometown, saying, ". . . altogether we hate to think of having to leave it one of these days." As her health permitted, she continued to attend all of the school and community functions to which she was invited in the small towns of Washington County. These forays took her back in time to her childhood when such events were the lifeblood of the community.

But when visiting Anna, she was not totally oblivious to what was going on in St. Louis. She reported to the folks back home that she saw "more Southern Baptists downtown than I did dogwood trees in blossom. I used to be one and they look like they used to. You can tell 'em when you see 'em. They're bent on being right."

In 1949, the John Brown University Press in Siloam Springs, Arkansas, published a volume of Roberta's poetry, *Sea (See) Foam and Dashes of Spray,* written from observations during her travels abroad. The poems were not intended originally for publication, but were written as a travel diary to record her impressions during her trips. The idea for publication came from her children who came upon her verse-filled notebook and wanted the poems published in book form as a holiday greeting to friends and family. The book was edited by Lessie Read with cover design by Charles D. Glaze and Allan Gilbert.

Some of the poems were in rhyme; others were not. Most aptly described as a book of verse, the poems had an Ogden Nash-like character about them. "I have a friend," she acknowledged, "who loves to talk about Iambic Pentameter. I have no idea what it is."

On one European trip she wrote "Chocolate and Lace."

The women make lace
    and turn many a trick
But they save their face
    By their chocolate thick.

Perugia chocolate's
    very famous
It's very rich and thick.
    And if you are not careful
It'll make you very sick.

On a trip to the Swiss Alps, she recorded her impressions in a
poem entitled "Real and Ethereal."

The real blends into ethereal
    Where sky and mountains meet
In filmy clouds that float above
    The lake that flows at our feet.

Lake and clouds so far apart
    and yet so much the same,
Sometimes the one, the other is
    By just the other's name.

And the thing we call this solid earth
    Which hovers in between
Is oftimes trees and flowering spray
    With perfume all unseen.

So might not this sodden thing called "me"
    Through the touch of that magic Hand
Be born into boundless beauty
    As the flowers are born, from the land?

The log brought in an hour ago
    Cut from the fallen tree
Is now sailing with the clouds
    Revelling in Infinity.

Some time ago 'twas earth and sky
　　And slumbering very deep
But the touch of that magic Hand
　　Awoke it from its sleep.

Another poem, simply called "Women," was based on her observations in Europe.

Some women wash in the seas,
　　They wash in the city tub.
They wash right down on their knees
　　With a rock on which to rub.

They wash in ditches at their doors
　　With a crying child on the bank.
They live in houses (with no floors)
　　That are dismal, dark and dank.

They are beasts of burden surely
　　Bearing loads and children, too.
Living from the scraps of comfort
　　Left when men and beasts are through.

Their skins are like good leather,
　　Their hands are rough and hard.
They are more inured to weather
　　Than the oxen in the yard.

They are hitched right into the harness;
　　They carry loads on their heads;
They slave for their men and children
　　And let the men sleep in the beds.

But also the strength of a nation
　　Is in these seasoned souls.
When you've borne burdens and children
　　The strength of your soul is untold.

And a nation grows strong thru women
　　Who become inured to toil.

There's strength and fibre developed
   By living close to the soil.

The publication of the book of verse emboldened her to include occasional poems in her column. Reflecting on her own situation, she wrote "Do Not Be Old."

Age is a condition of the mind.
   If you have left your dreams behind.
If hope has fled and your ambition
   fires are dead.
And you no longer look ahead
   and love is cold.
Then you are old.

But if from life you take the best
   And if in life you see the jest,
If love you hold
   No matter how the years go by
No matter how the birthdays fly
   You are not old.

Nevertheless, her activities, she believed, were about to catch up with her. "I have spread myself so thin and far and wide I am hard to find and I can't even locate myself," she said. Still, she had one more major task to accomplish—a legacy she would leave for women in the press.

CHAPTER XIII

The Women Organize

Roberta Fulbright knew how to seize the moment. In 1949, she sensed an opportunity to do just that in the interest of the women working on newspaper staffs across Arkansas. The result was the founding of the Arkansas Newspaper Women, forerunner of today's Arkansas Press Women.

This stocky woman wore a corset with minimum complaint but she chafed under the corset of convention in a male-dominated society that used women's talents and ability but never recognized that service with a share of power. Chafe as she might, it wasn't in her nature to defy that convention militantly, but she was always looking for ways to circumvent it.

She found a way to do that in the spring of 1949. Her friend Prof. Walt Lemke of the University of Arkansas journalism department, working to promote that department, and L. J. (Bill) Miner, innovative manager of the Arkansas Press Association, teamed up to do something different for the association. Instead of meeting in one of the traditional central Arkansas locations (Little Rock or Hot Springs) for the summer press meeting, they would have a seminar on the university campus. Instead of speeches, bull sessions, and business meetings, there would be lectures, tours of the campus, and interaction with the Fayetteville business community.

To make it work, they needed strong local support, and Lemke turned to the local leader he knew best, Roberta Fulbright. Ever the booster of her town and region, she was a pushover for the idea and promised her support. In fact, she looked forward to the prospect of hosting a meeting of her peers. "There is a peculiar charm attached to newspaper people," she said. "I think it may be because they are accustomed to not being too self-important."

She also saw a chance to float an idea, getting women in the newspaper field together to discuss a professional association. She was familiar with Missouri activities and undoubtedly aware that it had such a group. She knew she had a supporter in Lemke. He had developed a healthy respect for women journalism students who had served as editors of the student newspaper, the *Arkansas Traveler,* and who were now making their mark in the newspaper and public relations fields. On occasion he shared with her news of the progress of these young women. The question was, would the Arkansas Press Association support the idea?

The answer was yes, because of the sensitivity of Miner and the interest of his capable assistant, Eloise Castleberry. Miner did much in his tenure to sell the press association members on the idea of selling themselves to the state's business leaders. Women editors and staffers had responded to his ideas, and he had come to value their contributions. Castleberry, long the APA link to women, was delighted to see the possibility of an organization for them. She gathered the names for a mailing list. There were not many. The first list contained fourteen names of women working full time in an editorial or staff capacity. The names of publishers' wives and part-time staffers were added.

A letter of invitation went out from Roberta. She couched the idea in a careful tone. This would not be a separate professional group, but an auxiliary to the APA. She wrote:

> As you know, the Arkansas Press Association and University Department of Journalism are sponsoring a Press Seminar here on campus June 16–17–18.
>
> It occurred to me that working newspaper women should have a place in this Seminar and should have a larger part in the activities of our state press association.
>
> What we ought to have, I think, is an organization called Arkansas Newspaper Women, or something similar to serve as a sort of auxiliary and a part of the Arkansas Press Association.
>
> I have discussed the matter with Mr. W. J. Lemke, who is the University's representative for the Press Seminar. He has discussed it with Mr. L. J. Miner, secretary-manager of the Arkansas Press Association. Both of these gentlemen approve of the idea. Mr. Miner is willing to give the newspaper women a place on the APA convention program. Mr. Lemke

will help us organize and suggests a newsletter to keep us in touch with what other newspaper women are doing.

I am a little hesitant in writing this letter, because my only newspaper activity at present is the column I write for the *Northwest Arkansas Times*, whereas most of you are working full time as reporters, society editors and the like.

If you think the idea of Arkansas Newspaper Women is a good one, won't you please write and tell me that you'll cooperate? If the response is favorable, we'll organize ANW when the Press Seminar is held here . . . I'll be looking forward to meeting you at the opening of the Seminar June 16.

May I hear from you?

Sincerely,
Roberta Fulbright

The letter was late getting drafted and mailed, going out less than three weeks before the seminar. However, Roberta had struck a vein of pent-up desire, and the recipients didn't need more time. Within a week, seventeen had responded. Only one, Aline Murray of Wynne, took exception to the idea of an auxiliary. Aline, who always held her own and shared equal billing with her reporter and editor brothers, wrote:

> I quite agree with your idea that newspaper women should have a larger part in the activities of the press association but I am not enthusiastic about an auxiliary. Why should there be separate organizations for women and men engaged in the same work with like interests and abilities?
>
> I am always opposed to segregating men and women in business and professional organizations because I don't think it benefits the business or profession and works to the disadvantage of women who are trying to advance themselves and gain recognition purely on the basis of ability and qualifications.
>
> All this doesn't mean I won't join the auxiliary if it is organized. . . . You shouldn't have any hesitancy about taking the initiative in any newspaper activity and I am sure anything you do will be appreciated by both men and women in the newspaper field. Your reputation as a competent business and newspaper woman is too firmly established for it to be otherwise.

The other women, conditioned to rowing instead of rocking the boat, expressed appreciation and enthusiasm. Comments from all were similar to those expressed by several who would later serve the organization as president.

Mary Louise Wright of the *DeWitt Era Enterprise*:

> Indeed, I think an Arkansas Newspaper Women's organization would serve a good and useful purpose . . . At a breakfast for women during the 1947 meeting, I made the suggestion but there was not good attendance and the idea didn't get very far.

Esther Bindursky, *Lepanto News Record* editor:

> I'm fully in accord with your idea of organizing the newspaper women of Arkansas. We have been needing such an organization for quite a while . . . thanks for your efforts in trying to get us together. You certainly have my support.

Margaret Woolfolk, *Crittenden County Times* editor:

> Your proposal to organize a women's group to serve as sort of an auxiliary and part of the Arkansas Press Association sounds good to me. With leadership provided by yourself and help from Mr. Lemke and Mr. Miner, I see no reason why such an organization would not be successful and beneficial to all women of the press.

Roberta's neighbor and friend, Maude Duncan of the *Winslow American,* sent a reply that reveals the idea had been brewing for a while: "I am so delighted that you did conclude to take up the matter. It should be done and by whom but you!" Roberta and Maude Duncan shared a mutual admiration society. Roberta once called Duncan, "a tiny piece of inspired humanity who embodies the spirit of the hills, the quality of its rocks."

Roberta and Dr. Lewis Webster Jones, university president, shared the welcoming duties at the seminar's opening dinner. Lemke was the master of ceremonies. He announced that Roberta would sponsor an annual journalism scholarship award of five hundred dollars for an outstanding journalism student. The award was to be known as the Jay Fulbright award. Roberta's leadership role and her spirited remarks thrilled the women present and set the tone for the meeting to discuss and organize the new group.

Twenty-three women attended. Roberta had written of her hesitancy to call the meeting because she did not work full time, and she declined to take an active role in the organizing activity for that reason. She spoke briefly, affirming her feeling of the need for such a group. Lemke made some remarks and promised support and counsel as bylaws and programs were developed.

Alita Tidrow of the *Smackover Journal* chaired the meeting for the election of officers. Jamie Jones, wife of *Searcy Daily Citizen* publisher M. P. Jones, agreed to serve as the first president. A report of the meeting, speaking of Jamie Jones, noted: "Other organizations such as the Arkansas Federation of Women's Clubs, the Phoenix Club, Presbyterian Women's Auxiliary and Parent Teachers Association have all valued her leadership as president." An active club woman herself, Roberta was pleased with the selection.

That same *Arkansas Publisher* report noted, "Under the leadership of Mrs. Fulbright, publisher, *Northwest Arkansas Times* and mother of Arkansas's junior Senator, J. W. Fulbright, the Arkansas Newspaper Women's Association is now an auxiliary of the Arkansas Press Association. Mrs. Fulbright was made honorary president for life."

"I have great faith and respect for the Press and I trust I may be a symbol of some merit to these fine women," Roberta responded. She also used the occasion to express her opinion on women and the press.

> . . . The Arkansas newspaper women organized on their own and I surely desire to express my appreciation of the life membership accorded me and I hope the group may grow in strength and efficiency. I believe as of old, that there is latent power in both women and the Press. The printed and read word is important regardless of radio, television and phone.

She headed the list of charter members. The other charter members—some of whom listed themselves with their given name and others with their married name—were Lessie S. Read,

Maude Duncan, Isabel France, Edith Sweezy, Esther Bindursky, Mrs. John Troutt, Mrs. Howard Stuck, Gladys Edwards, Marian Love, Mrs. W. L. Love, Mrs. C. H. Rice, Mrs. Guy Phillips, Eloise Castleberry, Mrs. M. P. Jones, Mrs. Walter Raney, Mary Louise Wright, Marjorie Crabaugh, Mrs. C. A. Verbeck, Kate Gillespie, Alita Tidrow, Mrs. R. L. Fisher, Mrs. C. C. Elrod, Mrs. Max Hampton, Mrs. Val Zachariah, and Ethel Hale Cox.

When the fledgling group published the first issue of *Arkansas Newspaper Women,* Roberta complimented them, saying, "Women have a certain sense of news (that's fit to print) of people who are worth knowing, of events which are crucial or important."

While Roberta was able to attend the winter meeting of the Arkansas Press Association in Little Rock the following January, the ANW came into being too late for her to be an active participant in its programs. Even so, the new ANW officers and members found ways to acknowledge her. In February 1950, a notice on the ANW page of the *Arkansas Publisher* reported, "Arkansas newspaper women across the state paid tribute to our Honorary President for Life, Mrs. Roberta Fulbright on her birthday, February 14. Congratulatory messages poured in to the 'Sweetheart' of Newspaper Folk . . . at Fayetteville." The March issue published Roberta's reply. "Thank you for all the wonderful shower of cards on my birthday. It was an 'avalanche' deeply appreciated. Regards always to the ANW and hats off to its ability."

Soon after, she said, "But I can not help holding great hopes and ideals for the press, and I must admit I am pleased that our women are coming in for recognition and organization."

She was also honored that February by members of the *Times* staff with a party in the newsroom for her "77th" birthday. A few days later she commented, ". . . (they) got too generous and gave me an extra year of age! I had not quite given up to being seventy-five years and was straining a point to compass the seventy-six, and they with new deal abandon tossed me an extra year. . . . Then they gave me an extra fine fountain pen and pencil set which seems to say, 'Please write a bit plainer and easier to read.'"

She made another trip in April 1950, flying to Washington with Bill, who had been back home in Fayetteville. She admitted that she approached an airplane trip with some trepidation. It was a far cry from the horse and buggy transportation of her early years. But she always welcomed a chance to accompany Bill, who was gaining a favorable reputation in the Senate for his pronouncements on foreign policy. He was offered—and turned down—the presidency of Columbia University in order to remain in the Congress.

"About the only time I ever had to blush for Bill's shortcomings," she confided, was when ". . . he was asked for a nursery rhyme over the radio one night and could not give one. (Of course it was a temporary lapse.) Too, the switch from peace treaty with Ethiopia to 'Hey diddle diddle' was a bit sudden."

It was about this time that Sen. Joseph R. McCarthy, Republican from Wisconsin, fired his opening salvos in what would become a careless and noisy campaign, charging that communists were controlling American foreign policy. Though Bill Fulbright would later challenge McCarthy's charges and tactics, Roberta did not address McCarthyism in her columns. Her silence—unusual because it was just the sort of demogoguery she loved to challenge—was an indicator that her focus was narrowing and her health declining.

In mid-1950, the appearance of "As I See It" was sporadic. During a two-month period—May and June—Roberta wrote her column only twice. "Unfortunately, I've been sick with a new ailment," she announced, not naming the ailment, "and my thoughts do not wander very far from this old body."

By July she was writing more frequently, although she admitted she was slowing down. "I have to beg the leniency of my readers. I can not get copy off the press as of old, or rather as of young, and I just dilly dally."

Her return coincided with the statewide Democratic primary campaign. She summed up her feelings this way:

> I am about to develop into a "monarchist." The democratic processes get so bedraggled, so trailed in the dust that a body who believes in some human virtue, honestly cries out unwittingly stop, look and listen. Surely we do have candidates for office who do not belong in custody.

She also took time for a point of personal privilege.

> I want to express publicly that I more than appreciate the
> fact that the electorate did not put up an opponent to my
> son, Sen. J. W. Fulbright. Truly I feel the graciousness of it,
> and truly I believe you will be well served, but we desire to
> say "thank you so much."

While Roberta didn't mention it, one of the reasons that Bill
was able to forestall any opposition was the homework he did,
quite literally. A year in advance of the primary, he sent his
Washington aide John Erickson and Erickson's wife, Sarah, to
Little Rock to set up an office, and that, said Erickson, "pre-
empted any strong opposition."

In other races, Roberta continued her newfound reluctance to
endorse candidates, but spoke, in general, of the newspaper's role
when it chose to do so.

> Politically . . . we hope to help in the selection, but we do
> not desire to be autocratic, for we have said before, we always
> think there are more than one running who could fill an
> office.
>
> We think it is our privilege, duty and responsibility to
> have preference, just as it is yours.

Yet she couldn't let the gubernatorial race between former
governor Ben Laney and current governor Sidney McMath pass
without at least some comment.

> It looks now like we are to have an awful governor whether
> or no, from what McMath tells us about Laney and Laney
> informs us relative to Sidney.

Now out and about again, she reported on a dinner she
attended.

"We saw several of our politician friends and we are going to
vote for some of them." Though she didn't indicate whether or
not she provided any tips to these candidates, she did say of herself:
"My desire to give advice outruns my judgement and wisdom,
I know, but these are trying times, and as there is no one to stop
me, I fare forth." After the election she chose only to quote her

now well-known colloquialism. "The primary," she said, "has came and went."

When a new prohibition proposal limiting alcohol possession to one quart per person was placed on the Arkansas ballot in the November 1950 election, she reacted as one who thought that issue had been put to rest many years before. And with the passage of years, her position had softened a bit. "We have thought that our former efforts at prohibition resulted in going into reverse," she asserted. While reaffirming her personal opposition to alcohol, she said, "Liquor is one thing difficult, if not impossible, to control. To prohibit it is impossible. Teaching the evil and the disastrous effects has seemed to us to produce more healthful results than saying 'Thou shalt not.'"

Apparently she carried this mixed philosophy to Fulbright family gatherings. On special occasions, it became a custom among younger family members to enjoy cocktails. This was usually accompanied by a dissertation from Roberta about the dangers of alcohol and how its abuse could ruin people's lives. The lecture was generally concluded with her adding, "I'll take just a thimbleful," and followed by her practice of taking just a sip from everyone's drinks. It seems tasting was not considered a danger, nor a violation of her claim to being a teetotaler.

This new approach did not prevent her from attending a temperance rally at the Baptist Church, an action undoubtedly viewed with some bemusement by those who saw her as the owner of a beer distributorship. "I was brought up on temperance rallies," she stressed. To her they were a sweet remembrance of days gone by when temperance rallies and church revivals were rollicking good occasions.

She also fluctuated between extreme positive and negative positions on growing old. After a wealth of attention on her birthday she would say, "I really believe it's fun to grow old. This is my first time and it isn't half bad." On occasion she would write about friends who were undaunted by growing old. "I am a glowing case of growing old without grace," she confessed. Another time, she said, "Growing old is no fun and really arriving is well-nigh ghastly."

She had not lost her interest in new developments, however, telling her readers in 1950, "Tonight I saw my first television program—a movie in the home. Fantastic." Had she realized the impact that television would have in lessening dependence upon her favorite medium, the printed word, she might not have been so enthusiastic. To her, the newspaper was the sacred purveyor of news and entertainment; hence her habit of capitalizing the word, "Press," in everything she wrote.

Increasingly, it fell her lot to eulogize the citizens of Fayetteville who had been her friends for so long and who were now passing from the scene. When her longtime friend Laura Lighton died, she wrote:

> Seldom have I known a woman more winning. I think of Happy Hollow Farm in the early days when we had always such good times, Mr. Lighton, a newspaperman, novelist and short story writer, with his Billy Fortune stories. . . .

She had begun to take a look back at her own life. When complimenting Walt Lemke on a tribute he had written about a mutual friend, she mused, "What fools we mortals continue to be and vanity is a big ingredient always and forever." She didn't hesitate to add, "You better begin picking up things to say about me 'when.'"

Not content to wait, she would write about herself, "I've lived long. I've loved fighting in the argumentative sense. I abhor war. I believe it must be abolished. I wish I could have done more for humanity." She also pondered an even larger issue: "I really wish I knew the answer to the question of life. I fear I do not, but I get some consolation in the fact I see so many who are in the same boat."

Practicality in Roberta's case always interceded.

> The days of my sojourn seem so much fewer these last months that I can not eliminate the idea of when I'm gone. I do not seem to feel it will make much difference, but I do have a great reluctance to have not helped more with a few projects—City Library on the ground floor and a Boys Club.

While she expressed regret at things undone, she looked with optimism toward the future. "I hope there'll be a crowd in Heaven 'cause I can't take a skimpy crew (now no side remarks) 'cause I know where I'm headed."

Except for her traditional Christmas column, "As I See It" did not appear in the columns of the *Times* during December 1950 and January 1951. In response to an invitation to the 1951 mid-winter meeting of the Arkansas Newspaper Women, Lessie Read sent a telegram expressing her regrets "and those of Mrs. Fulbright for being unable to attend," saying Mrs. Fulbright was ill.

Yet she persevered. And she didn't lose her tart sense of humor. When she returned for a visit to the *Times* office, an employee who was also a justice of the peace, enlisted her as a witness to a wedding—in her office. The couple, she related, had first been married twenty years earlier and divorced five years previous. Roberta was unimpressed by the remarriage. "The clasping of hands was the only touch of sentiment evidenced, a desire for legality the only other emotion in the picture . . . We hope for unrealized and unexpected joy to attend them."

While the *Times* news columns kept the readership up-to-date on Bill Fulbright's activities in the Senate, Roberta did not usually discuss them in her own column. But there were exceptions. When Senator Fulbright and President Truman crossed swords*— as they did from time to time—she had this to say:

> Even our president might be thankful for men of honesty and knowledge instead of blank-blanking them. There is really enough room in the affairs of state for all the honest and efficient and wise ones.

Shortly after, she related that she received a note from her son saying, "We are having a hectic time up here." Roberta asked her readers, "Can you guess where?"

---

*Fulbright and Truman first clashed after the mid-term election in 1946 when Fulbright suggested that Truman should resign after the Republicans gained control of both houses of Congress. In the aftermath of his statement, Fulbright contended he was simply pointing out a flaw in our political and governmental system and a need for its reform. Truman and Fulbright sparred again in 1951 when Fulbright's Senate Banking Subcommittee investigated a Truman staff member on dealings with the Reconstruction Finance Corporation. Roberta's public comments occurred on the latter occasion.

There is some irony to the fact that, even before her son's clashes with him, Roberta's support for President Truman did not approach the level of that for President Roosevelt. After all, she and Harry Truman shared common roots, both growing up in post–Civil War Missouri, raised in hardscrabble farm life, and imbued with the state's show-me attitude. Ever the loyal Democrat, she supported Truman in his 1948 upset victory over Thomas E. Dewey, saying he "has a hard core of tenacity, faith, courage and persistence . . . ," all qualities she consistently equated with her own early life in Missouri. Still, she never really warmed to the plain-spoken Missourian. Surely, the Truman-Fulbright disagreements later had something to do with it, her loyalty to her son surpassing her fondness for anything connected to her native state.

She was well enough by spring to travel to St. Louis to visit the Teasdales and to Omaha to see the Swansons. While she was away, Helen surprised her by writing an "As I See It" column on a local school concert.

> I feel I must take Mother's place this morning and I know if she were here and had heard the concert last night she would have her pencil in hand. I know now how she feels when she just must write to tell how grand something is.

Roberta reported her pride in Helen's initiative when she returned home. And she was back writing again on her usual broad range of subjects: her admiration for Abraham Lincoln and Mahatma Gandhi; the need for cutting weeds and beautifying the local area; the need for prayer; her concern that all the human race had learned was war; her insistence that a local trustee be appointed to the university board and her opinion that ". . . we women seem to stand the strain beyond our men." Some months later Betty Fulbright wrote two guest columns for her on the refurbishing of the White House. This, too, gave her a great deal of pleasure.

She had earlier given her support to editor Ted Wylie's editorial encouraging the appointment of women to city boards and commissions. "I want to put my o.k. on Ted's editorial regarding women on our boards. We have a reserve force of fine women who lack only the *habit* of serving the public." Although she continued to have other suggestions for civic fairness and improvement, she remained proud of her hometown and its growth, its population having reached more than seventeen thousand by 1950.

In late 1951 and early 1952 she made two more trips—to see the Bill Fulbrights in Washington, D.C., and the Jack Fulbrights in Pine Bluff (where Jack had gone to join a lumber operation, the C. C. Fulbright Company—no relation). Upon her return from Pine Bluff she was honored by the *Times* staff on her seventy-eighth birthday with a party at the Washington Hotel. She was pictured in the *Times* the following day cutting a three-tiered cake inscribed "Our Valentine 1913–1952," marking her years of association with the newspaper. She was wearing her usual dark dress, her face now looking gaunt. ". . . I'm thankful I have lived; thankful for the ideals of those who are fit and worthy to govern," she said.

In April 1952, she and Lessie ventured forth to the university to hear a panel discussion on the subject of creation. Once there, they discovered the meeting would be held on an upper floor of the building, necessitating that they walk upstairs. They made the climb. Soon after, Roberta attended a banquet for exchange students at the university, an event which gave her pride because of her son's sponsorship of the successful Fulbright exchange program.

She wrote only three more columns after that. In May and June she was hospitalized for several days. Following her return home, family members including Bill Fulbright, the Swansons, and the Teasdales came to check on her.

At the national Democratic convention in July, Bill was nominated by the Arkansas delegation as a "favorite son" candidate for the presidency. There was talk of Fulbright as a vice presidential running mate for Adlai Stevenson, the Democratic presidential nominee, though that distinction went to Sen. John Sparkman of Alabama. These momentous events passed without Roberta's public comment, the most outward evidence that her health was indeed failing her.

She did not write a farewell column, perhaps believing that she would return to "As I See It," as she had always done in the past. In what proved to be her last column, May 21, 1952, written while she was a patient in the local hospital, she quoted Confucius:

> One must above all things be careful to pass muster at the bar of his own judgement rather than that of others.

Fittingly, these would be her last public words.

Some months before, on the death of nationally syndicated advice columnist Dorothy Dix, Roberta wrote, ". . . I am told she left in her estate copy for three months ahead." As her own writing days came to a close, Roberta regarded that with wonder, not stopping to consider the estimated two million words she had written during her own career.

Roberta believed in the power of the press and in the power of women. Her pioneering path at the *Northwest Arkansas Times* and her leadership in the founding of the Arkansas Newspaper Women made that belief manifest.

CHAPTER XIV

The Passing of the Torch

On Sunday, January 11, 1953, Roberta's stalwart heart finally failed her. She was at home at her beloved Mont Nord. At nine o'clock that morning she lost consciousness. Son-in-law Dr. Allan Gilbert, one of those at her bedside, reported that she died peacefully at 2 P.M. Also with her were Helen and Hal Douglas and a special nurse, Mrs. Harry Jackson. She was seventy-eight, just a little more than a month short of her seventy-ninth birthday.

Her obituary, carried on the front page of the *Arkansas Gazette*, reported that she had been ill with a heart ailment for several months and had been hospitalized three times since the previous August. The *Gazette* took note of her years of writing "As I See It," saying, "The column only appeared when she had something to say on a wide variety of subjects. She was usually MOVED to comment two or three times weekly."

The *Gazette* outlined the circumstances of Bill Fulbright's removal as president of the University of Arkansas by Gov. Homer Adkins and his subsequent defeat of Adkins in the Senate race. "An editorial comment by Mrs. Fulbright is generally credited with helping start her son in politics." said the *Gazette*. "Mrs. Fulbright," noted the *Gazette,* "demanded that her newspaper take a lively interest in public affairs and voice its editorial opinion on major civic issues. Under her direction the paper successfully battled a county political machine and municipal inefficiency."

In an editorial, the *Gazette* printed this tribute:

> At 78, Roberta Fulbright is dead—and despite her long illness it is hard to believe—hard to believe a woman of such vigor could pass from this earth.
>
> Many millions around the world knew her as the mother of a distinguished son. But those who had had the good fortune to live in the hill country of Arkansas knew her in her own right—a tireless, strong woman who had created for herself the role of matriarch in the town of Fayetteville.

Because she had strong opinions on everything from Huey Long to the placement of underarm zippers in women's clothes and expressed them freely in the *Northwest Arkansas Times* of which she stubbornly remained the proprietor in the old fashioned sense of the word, she earned her share of enemies—so did she tilt at her share of windmills.

But no one could quarrel with the verdict of W. J. Lemke, of the University of Arkansas Department of Journalism, who recently read through the two million words she wrote in her daily "As I See It" column and concluded "They were sincere words and put together honestly."

Her own *Northwest Arkansas Times,* in a front-page story, reported although she had not been in good health for some time, she had until her last illness remained constantly interested and active in community affairs. Of her son, Senator Fulbright, the newspaper said:

> She played an important part in his career and the story of Mrs. Fulbright is entwined with that of "Bill" Fulbright.
>
> It was a column Mrs. Fulbright wrote that led, indirectly to Fulbright turning from the life of educator to politics. Mrs. Fulbright encouraged her son to run for public office and followed his activities with close interest though she took no active part in his campaigns.

The *Times* noted that upon her death:

> Western Union reported the receipt of more than 150 telegrams and cablegrams including messages from President Harry Truman, Director of the Federal Bureau of Investigation J. Edgar Hoover,[*] Maj. Gen. Bryan Milburn,[**] stationed in Tokyo, and many other prominent figures.

---

[*]Roberta had long been an admirer of Hoover, and he always went by Mont Nord to see her when he was in Arkansas. John Erickson of Bill Fulbright's staff said, "I'm not sure whether he did it because of the Senator, or because one of 'his boys' (Hal Douglas, a former FBI agent) was her son-in-law." In any case, it pleased her.

[**]Major General Milburn was from Fayetteville.

The *Times* also reported that Arkansas governor Francis Cherry was expected to attend the funeral. The Arkansas legislature, in a joint session of the Senate and House of Representatives, paid tribute to Roberta with the passage of a memorial resolution. Committees from each house were named to represent the legislature at her funeral service. Heading the delegation was Lt. Gov. Nathan Gordon of Morrilton. Joining him were Senate President Pro Tempore Russell Elrod of Siloam Springs; Senators Ellis Fagan of Little Rock and Marvin Melton of Jonesboro; Representatives Clifton Wade and J. W. Murphy of Washington County; L. H. Autry and E. C. Fleeman of Mississippi County; Talbot Feild Jr. of Hempstead County; and Rev. Julian F. Anders, chaplain of the House of Representatives.

Her funeral service was conducted at 2 P.M., January 14, at Fayetteville's First Christian Church where she had been a faithful member and Sunday School teacher for so many years. Prior to the service her body lay in state at the church from noon until 2 P.M.

More than four hundred persons crowded into the church for the funeral, some standing. With the church filled, other mourners had to remain outside. Along with Governor Cherry and the legislative delegation, other prominent Arkansans were present, including Harry S. Ashmore, executive editor of the *Arkansas Gazette*. Pallbearers were Roy Wood, Virgil Blossom, Herbert Lewis Sr., Donald Trumbo Sr., Jerome McRoy, Herman Tuck, Rep. Clifton Wade, and Ted Wylie.

Granddaughter Patty Smith would remember years later the large crowd, filled with dignitaries and led by the governor, who came to pay tribute to the power and influence of Roberta Fulbright. "I had never thought of my grandmother in that way," marveled Smith. To her grandchildren, she would always be remembered as the head of the family, the one who was continually teaching them and treating them as equals.

The church pastor, Rev. J. Robert Moffett, conducted the service assisted by Rev. D. L. Dykes Jr., pastor of Fayetteville's Central Methodist Church, and Rev. John M. Asbell, minister of the First Christian Church from 1924 to 1933. Theme of the service was "triumph and immortality."

"The high point in human relations is the power to love and respect," Roberta once wrote. "The high point in achievement is to be loved and respected. . . ." She had achieved that and more, declared Reverend Moffett.

At the time of her death, she was survived by her five remaining children: Anna, Jack, Bill, Helen, and Bo; two brothers, Jim and Charles Waugh of Rothville; thirteen grandchildren; and two great-grandchildren.

In honor of its longtime president and publisher, the *Times* published an early edition and closed the office during the afternoon of the funeral.

The January 1953 edition of the *Arkansas Publisher*, the monthly magazine of the Arkansas Press Association, reprinted the front-page editorial that editor Ted R. Wylie wrote for the January 12 edition of the *Times*.

> Fayetteville and Northwest Arkansas have lost their greatest friend and most spirited booster. The death of Mrs. Roberta Fulbright will be felt much more widely than just through this Northwest Arkansas section; but it was the home region she loved most dearly. She believed with all her heart in this section and in the state [as] a whole, and spared nothing in aiding in the development of both.
>
> Words telling of her sentiments for her homeland lack the luster necessary to describe how she really felt. We who knew her so well realize the intensity of her fervor—she loved the trees and the hills and the flowers that grow wild in the countryside and in the tended gardens of the communities. She believed in the people; she was confident of their loyalty and their ability; and she never ceased to predict enthusiastically great progress.
>
> She liked people—she loved to talk with them, to hear their views, to discuss with them the issues of the day. She believed that every man and woman should take an interest in public life, in state and national affairs and in the international situation. She had no patience with those who live for themselves without regard to their fellow men—that sort of thing was against her creed.
>
> Her church claimed her attention; not only her church,

but those congregations which represent the faith of other people. To her, the Church meant many churches.

She was particularly interested in and fond of the rural communities—their home demonstration and 4-H clubs, their community meetings, their part in the County Fair. She never turned down an invitation to a gathering in one of the outlying sections if she were able at all to be there. She never failed after returning home to speak highly of those she had met, or what they were doing, of her best wishes for their success.

Her appetite for reading was great and varied. She read newspapers, magazines and books by the score. Of late years the life of Gandhi particularly attracted her attention, and she looked on the late Indian leader as one of the great men of history.

It was her custom in recent years, when she was unable to sleep at night to get up and read and write. It was during the calm hours of early mornings that she put down many of the thoughts which found their way into her popular newspaper column.

Mrs. Fulbright never before her last illness lost for one minute her curiosity about the human race, nor her intense interest in what folks were doing. Whether she agreed with them or not, she welcomed their ideas. The only folks who tried her spirit were those who went out of their way to achieve selfish ends without thought for their fellow men— these she was quick to spot.

Our loss is grievous, deep. Those who knew her best will miss her most but her passing will be more widely felt, for it was of the community of people as a whole that she had thought, and whom she served. A true friend has gone.

In another tribute, Prof. J. A. Thalheimer of the journalism department at the University of Arkansas, announced that a memorial bookshelf honoring Roberta's memory would be placed in Hill Hall, the department's campus home. The bookshelf would be administered by her longtime friend Prof. Walt Lemke.

The analysis of her character and passionate personality would continue long after her death as biographers of Bill Fulbright attempted to assess her influence. As one writer said, she "was the kind of woman who makes the local Rotarians wonder how far she might've gone if she'd ever been a man—only they wonder right out loud and proudly . . ."

The Fulbright family matriarch was gone, but the wide-ranging family interests remained. Son-in-law Hal Douglas became the publisher of the *Northwest Arkansas Times* and her grandson Allan Gilbert, the managing editor. Both worked at the newspaper prior to Roberta's death. Like his grandmother before him, Gilbert wrote a column for the paper.

Douglas also continued his responsibilities for operating other Fulbright interests, a duty Roberta had turned over to him some years before. Like Jay before her, she left no will. She passed on her properties and assets to her family prior to her death. Hal and Helen continued to live at Mont Nord until they sold it in 1962 to build a new home.

As is so often the case when the family leader is gone, the family members gradually moved on to other interests, other places. The *Northwest Arkansas Times* was sold in the 1970s to the Thomson Newspaper Group, a nationwide newspaper chain. The Fulbright family heirs divested themselves of the family holdings. The last holdings were sold May 2, 1985. With the death of Bill Fulbright in 1995, the last of her children was gone.

Still, Roberta Fulbright's legacy remains. Her lifelong love of the printed word and her continuing campaign for a new library is reflected in the naming of the Fayetteville public library building in her honor. In 1959, with the passage of a one-mill tax, the possibility of a new library building became more likely. With this development, Gilbert Swanson offered to donate two lots at 21 East Dickson Street if the library board agreed to name the building for his mother-in-law and for his wife, Bo. The board quickly agreed. The new building was dedicated June 4, 1962; Bill Fulbright spoke briefly.

Roberta's influence on the life and progress of the University of Arkansas was evidenced by the dedication in 1959 of Roberta Fulbright Hall, a women's residence hall located in a complex of buildings on the site formerly known as University Farm.

The Arkansas Newspaper Women, which she founded, became the Arkansas Press Women, still an active organization devoted to supporting and recognizing the talents of Arkansas newspaperwomen.

In 1976, she was one of thirteen mothers featured in *Mothers of Achievement in American History, 1776–1976*, a book compiled by the American Mothers Committee.

Bill Fulbright went on to a distinguished thirty-year career in the United States Senate. "I had no idea I'd ever be in politics," he once mused. "I sometimes wonder what would have happened if Mother hadn't written that editorial."

Without question her most cherished accolade would be one from Bill, who looked back on her life and said simply, "She had more spirit for living than almost anyone."

EPILOGUE

Roberta Fulbright is buried in the family plot alongside her husband, Jay, in the secluded northwest corner of Evergreen Cemetery in Fayetteville. Fittingly, the cemetery is located only yards from the southern boundary of the University of Arkansas campus.

Writing in the Washington County Historical Society's *Flashback* in 1983, William W. Hughes said:

> The plot is one where a number of the members of the Fulbright family, including the redoubtable Roberta Fulbright are buried . . . she who challenged a governor and the state's political establishment, setting up a chain reaction which led to the election of her son, J. William, to Congress. As you stand in the secret corner of Evergreen and gaze at Roberta Fulbright's marker you realize, almost with physical shock, that if it hadn't been for her, there might never have been a Fulbright resolution and the creation of the United Nations. And there never would have been a Fulbright student exchange program with its "greatest movement of scholars across the face of the earth since the fall of Constantinople."

There is no epitaph on her headstone, although many could appropriately be written about the energy and enthusiasm she had for life. Once, in "As I See It," she deemed to write her own.

> I was born in arrears; I've remained in arrears through a long heavy lifetime—striving always to catch up but never quite making the grade. No matter what I do, or give, or stand for, I'm still in arrears. So I've about decided to let the matter stand "in arrears" and let it be graven on my tombstone.

As she did of others, Roberta expected much of herself. In no respect could her life be judged in arrears. Her influence was strongly felt in Fayetteville for many years. Her legacy still lives in the institutions of the community.

Hers was a singular journey. She believed in the good life offered by the beautiful Ozark hills and in the potential of the people who inhabited that region. Despite her successes and disappointments, the occasional anger, and the more frequent praise, she never lost her fervor for life as she saw it. From the harsh early farm life to the lovely hilltop view on Mont Nord, she never lost sight of the progress she thought possible for both people and place.

She suffered her share of personal tragedies; but those aside, the tragedy is that her life has been so little noted in the annals of Arkansas history. Here was a woman who moved confidently in the world of business, who rescued the network of enterprises her husband created and made them prosper, and the businessmen of her community never quite forgave her for it. Further, she forced them to look squarely at the political corruption in their midst, and when they failed to act, she spoke up forcefully to take the lead—sometimes almost too forcefully, but always effectively.

She became her community's voice, its conscience, sometimes even its soul. Her power was such that the state's politicians came calling at her door, hats in hands, like suitors seeking *her* hand. A state university felt her power and presence and experienced her support. Governors, too, benefited from her support and felt the sting of her wrath. Few persons could match her in either oral or writing skills and generations of Arkansas women journalists owe their opportunities to the pioneering trail she blazed. Yet mention of her name today sometimes evokes looks of puzzlement, another acknowledgment of our state's failure to recognize properly the contributions women have made. But as Roberta, herself, was wont to say, "All these things are simply things to know. Not things to discourage one from doing."

Although her grave is marked only by a simple stone, her life was marked by achievement despite personal pain, by admiration despite controversy, and by meaning despite heartache. Life, as she saw it, was much like the gardens she loved. There were thorns and weeds to be dealt with, but the faithful gardener always prevails.

—NAN SNOW

NOTES

ABBREVIATIONS USED IN NOTES

FDD   *Fayetteville Daily Democrat*
NAT   *Northwest Arkansas Times*

ACKNOWLEDGMENTS

ix   "The worst you can say . . .": *NAT*, "As I See It," May 26, 1938, p. 7.

CHAPTER 1: A STARTING PLACE

4   "Not alone . . .": Lucy Waugh, *Twilight Memories* (1903), p. 29, reprinted in Allan Gilbert, *A Fulbright Chronicle* (1980).

5   "It was almost . . .": Ralph R. Rea, *Sterling Price, the Lee of the West* (1959), p. vii.

5   "We had a rough . . .": Waugh, *Twilight Memories*, p. 33.

6   Also of English extraction: Gilbert, *Fulbright Chronicle*, p. 7.

6   John and Julia: T. Berry Smith and Pearl Sims Gehrig, *History of Chariton and Howard Counties* (1923), p. 585.

6   The Chariton County: letter, The Friends of Keytesville, Inc., May 16, 1994.

6   "If that won't do . . .": Waugh, *Twilight Memories*, p. 32.

7   Two years after: St. Louis National Historical Company, *History of Howard and Chariton Counties* (1883), p. 503.

7   "was two miles . . .": Waugh, *Twilight Memories*, p. 36.

7   Most of the township: Donald Zochert, *Laura, The Life of Laura Ingalls Wilder* (1976), p. 24.

7   "Like all . . .": Waugh, *Twilight Memories*, p. 35.

8   "this great forgotten class . . .": Rea, *Sterling Price*, p. vii.

8   In 1864: letter, The Friends of Keytesville, Inc., May 16, 1994.

9   "Who is there? . . .": Waugh, *Twilight Memories*, p. 42.

10   "Are you a widow? . . .": Ibid., p. 43.

10   Peter was wounded: Smith and Gehrig, *History of Chariton and Howard Counties*, p. 585.

11   There they found: letter, The Friends of Keytesville, Inc., May 16, 1994.

11   The first business: St. Louis National Historical Company, *History of Howard and Chariton Counties*, p. 644.

11   "injudicious:" Waugh, *Twilight Memories*, p. 63.

11   Have you heard: Western Historical Manuscript Collection, Columbia, Mo., Beneke Family, Papers, letter dated Jan. 12, 1873.

11   "Pay-day came . . .": Waugh, *Twilight Memories*, p. 63.

11   Another family: Zochert, *Laura*, p. 24.

12   no houses: Ibid., p. 25.

12   "sort of place . . .": *NAT*, "As I See It," Nov. 11, 1948, p. 9.

12   "had a good many . . .": Roberta Fulbright, *As I See It*, compiled by W. J. Lemke (1952), column dated Apr. 4, 1935, page unnumbered.

13   "had been poor . . .": Ibid.

13 "came from Virginia . . .": *NAT,* "As I See It," Dec. 27, 1946, p. 4.

13 "altogether . . .": R. Fulbright, Lemke, *As I See It,* column dated Apr. 14, 1935, page unnumbered.

13 "We used to . . .": Ibid.

13 "It seems . . .": R. Fulbright, Lemke, *As I See It,* column dated Apr. 2, 1935, page unnumbered.

13 The January editions: *Chariton Courier,* June 7, 1878, to December 21, 1883, compiled by May Bartee Couch, Marceline, Mo.

14 "the pleasantest . . .": R. Fulbright, Lemke, *As I See It,* column dated Feb. 1, 1936, page unnumbered.

14 "We waited . . .": *NAT,* "As I See It," Nov. 11, 1948, p. 9.

14 "It was considered . . .": Ibid., Oct. 22, 1943, p. 4.

14 "By the time . . .": Ibid., June 24, 1949, p. 4.

14 "manufactured . . .": R. Fulbright, Lemke, *As I See It,* column dated Nov. 17, 1938, page unnumbered.

14 "One of my . . .": *NAT,* "As I See It," June 24, 1949, p. 4.

15 "that was a step . . .": Ibid., Jan. 18, 1950, p. 4.

15 "Washing . . .": Ibid., May 30, 1949, p. 4.

15 "What a scarcity . . .": Ibid., Aug. 15, 1947, p. 4.

15 "We at our house . . .": Ibid., Aug. 19, 1949, p. 4.

15 "Summer . . .": Ibid., May 21, 1946, p. 2.

15 "So we . . .": Ibid.

15 "Outings . . .": Ibid., June 23, 1947, p. 4.

15 "We usually . . .": Ibid., Aug. 28, 1951, p. 4.

16 "the precepts . . .": R. Fulbright, Lemke, *As I See It,* column dated Nov. 17, 1938, page unnumbered.

16 "My mother . . .": *NAT,* "As I See It," Mar. 15, 1947, p. 4.

16 "But there were . . .": R. Fulbright, Lemke, *As I See It,* column dated Nov. 17, 1938, page unnumbered.

16 "Children . . .": Ibid., Feb. 9, 1938, page unnumbered.

16 "My earliest . . .": *NAT,* "As I See It," Aug. 8, 1950, p. 4.

16 "but I do not . . .": Ibid., Apr. 21, 1947, p. 4.

17 "Since I was . . .": Ibid., May 30, 1949, p. 4.

17 "We grew . . .": Ibid., Sept. 29, 1949, p. 9.

17 "I bet I could . . .": R. Fulbright, Lemke, *As I See It,* column dated Feb. 4, 1939, page unnumbered.

18 "Somehow I think . . .": Ibid., Jan. 14, 1938, page unnumbered.

18 "This vehicle . . .": Ibid.

18 "I grew up . . .": *NAT,* "As I See It," Mar. 19, 1949, p. 4.

18 "had the Englishman's . . .": R. Fulbright, Lemke, *As I See It,* column dated May 13, 1935, page unnumbered.

18 "Her eyes . . .": *NAT,* "As I See It," May 12, 1949, p. 9.

19 "never caught a gleam . . .": R. Fulbright, Lemke, *As I See It,* column dated May 8, 1942, page unnumbered.

19 "I used to hold . . .": *NAT,* "As I See It," Dec. 20, 1944, p. 4.

19 "Gifts . . .": Ibid.

19 "had the passion . . .": Ibid., Jan. 5, 1948, p. 4.

19 "We did have . . .": Ibid., June 17, 1949, p. 4.

19 "nicest Virginia . . .": Ibid., Dec. 16, 1944, p. 3.

19 "I remember . . .": *FDD,* "As I See It," Mar. 27, 1933, p. 2.

19 "I loved . . .": *NAT,* "As I See It," June 24, 1949, p. 4.

19 "We played tennis . . .": Ibid., June 17, 1949, p. 4.

20 "I also recall . . .": Ibid., Mar. 15, 1947, p. 4.

20 "I went . . .": Ibid., June 14, 1946, p. 4.

20 "I tried my . . .": Ibid., Sept. 6, 1944, p. 4.

20 "I was really scared . . .": Ibid.

20 "I remember freezing . . .": Ibid., Dec. 16, 1944, p. 3.

21 "Always . . .": Ibid., June 2, 1948, p. 4.

21 "I had never seen . . .": Ibid., Mar. 23, 1946, p. 4.

21 "I was from . . .": Ibid., Sept. 29, 1947, p. 4.

21 It was small . . . : Ibid.

21 "I've never . . .": Ibid., Aug. 30, 1946, p. 4.

22 "ritzy . . .": Ibid., Sept. 6, 1944, p. 4.

22 "The same old nag . . .": Ibid.

22 "in two of . . .": Ibid., Mar. 21, 1945, p. 4.

CHAPTER II: THE FARMER TAKES A WIFE

23 William Fulbright eagerly: Gilbert, *Fulbright Chronicle,* pp. 22–30.

24 Old Bill traced: Ibid., p. 24.

24 Old Bill's patriotism: Western Historical Manuscript Collection, Columbia, Mo., military papers of William Fulbright.

24 Some family charts: Gilbert, *Fulbright Chronicle,* p. 28.

25 "He sent into the audience . . .": FDD, "As I See It," Oct. 17, 1933, p. 2.

25 "If you did not . . .": Ibid.

25 "She and her love . . .": R. Fulbright, Lemke, *As I See It,* column dated Jan. 14, 1938, page unnumbered.

26 "One thing . . .": Ibid., Feb. 22, 1947, page unnumbered.

26 "His mind . . .": Tristram Coffin, *Senator Fulbright: Portrait of a Public Philosopher* (1966), p. 36.

26 "in a tweed . . .": R. Fulbright, Lemke, *As I See It,* column dated Jan. 14, 1938, page unnumbered.

26 "he always . . .": Ibid., Jan. 22, 1947, page unnumbered.

26 "had the old-fashioned . . .": FDD, "As I See It," Jan. 12, 1934, p. 2.

27 "The biggest pick . . .": NAT, "As I See It," May 27, 1948, p. 4.

27 "While Jay . . .": R. Fulbright, Lemke, *As I See It,* column dated Feb. 22, 1947, page unnumbered.

27 "When I first . . .": NAT, "As I See It," Feb. 24, 1949, p. 9.

27 "was a farmer . . .": Ibid., Dec. 11, 1948, p. 4.

27 "We didn't even drink . . .": Ibid., Feb. 22, 1947, p. 4.

28 "Old woman . . .": Ibid.

28 "I cried . . .": Ibid.

28 "Jay said . . .": R. Fulbright, Lemke, *As I See It,* column dated Feb. 9, 1938, page unnumbered.

28 "At last . . .": Ibid.

28 "working as a regular hand . . .": NAT, "As I See It," Feb. 22, 1947, p. 4.

29 (We) sat up . . . : FDD, "As I See It," Nov. 9, 1934, p. 2.

29 We finally found . . . : Ibid.

30 "We mustered . . .": NAT, "As I See It," Oct. 8, 1946, p. 4.

30 "bought a little . . .": Ibid., Nov. 11, 1948, p. 9.

30 I had put up . . . : Ibid., Oct. 8, 1946, p. 4.

31 "In truth . . .": Ibid., Jan. 28, 1949, p. 4.

32 "It was strawberry . . .": Ibid., Nov. 11, 1948, p. 9.

32 "My father-in-law . . .": Ibid., May 3, 1946, p. 4.

32 "I think a political seed . . .": Ibid., Nov. 11, 1948, p. 9.

CHAPTER III: THE MOUNTAINTOP

34 "whirled and swirled . . .": *NAT*, "As I See It," Sept. 30, 1946, p. 4.

35 Built in 1915: Shiloh Museum, *History of Washington County* (1989), p. 664.

36 "delicacy of flavor . . .": *FDD*, June 20, 1921, p. 6.

36 ". . . we have struggled . . .": *NAT*, "As I See It," Nov. 3, 1949, p. 13.

36 "pushed the Fulbright's . . .": Brock Brower, "The Roots of an Arkansas Questioner," *Life*, May 13, 1966, p. 96.

36 He was one of five: M. L. Price, "Start of Poultry Industry in Northwest Arkansas," *Flashback* 18 (Jan. 1965), pp. 12–15.

37 "My husband built . . .": *NAT*, "As I See It," June 9, 1951, p. 4.

37 "paid a huge sum . . .": Ibid., Aug. 8, 1950, p. 4.

37 We were in on . . . : Ibid., Feb. 26, 1947, p. 4.

37 "had a hand . . .": Judge Thomas Butt, interview, Mar. 24, 1993.

38 "he reaped . . .": Gilbert, *Fulbright Chronicle*, p. ii.

38 "I tell you . . .": *NAT*, "As I See It," July 23, 1946, p. 4.

38 The City water system . . . : Ibid., Apr. 18, 1949, p. 4.

39 (Today it still stands . . .): Ray Adams, interview, Mar. 23, 1993.

39 "I was brought up . . .": *NAT*, "As I See It," Mar. 15, 1947, p. 4.

39 "To him . . .": Ibid.

39 "used to often say . . .": *FDD*, "As I See It," Jan. 13, 1934, p. 2.

39 Jay, sympathetic to: Suzanne Teasdale Zorn, telephone interview, Feb. 22, 1995.

39 "Roberta's pattern . . .": Gilbert, *Fulbright Chronicle*, p. 43.

40 "I don't want one . . .": *NAT*, "As I See It," Oct. 8, 1945, p. 4.

40 At the university: J. W. Fulbright, *Against the Arrogance of Power* (1991), p. 17.

40 the influenza epidemic: *Arkansas Times*, June 1986, p. 73.

41 "It was kind of . . .": J. W. Fulbright, *Against the Arrogance of Power*, p. 14.

41 "good literature . . .": Gilbert, *Fulbright Chronicle*, p. 61.

41 The house: Fayetteville, Arkansas Historic District Commission for the National Register of Historic Places Inventory, U.S. Department of Labor, "Mt. Nord and Washington-Willow Historic Districts," undated, unnumbered.

42 The house later . . . : Rowena McCord Gallaway, "Two Stirman Brothers," *Flashback* 7 (Mar. 1957), p. 35.

42 "tough times . . .": Anna Fulbright Teasdale, quoted by Allan Gilbert, interview, Sept. 21, 1992.

42 Once Anna and cousin: Margaret Waugh Crittenden, interview, Mar. 17, 1993.

43 "a lovesome thing . . .": R. Fulbright, Lemke, *As I See It,* column dated Jan. 21, 1935, page unnumbered.

43 "Plant a tree . . .": *FDD*, "As I See It," May 11, 1935, p. 2.

43 death of her beloved mother: *The Mendon Constitution*, Mendon, Mo., June 30, 1933. Also, Margaret Waugh Crittenden, interview, Mar. 17, 1993.

43 "bequeathed to me . . .": R. Fulbright, Lemke, *As I See It,* column dated May 13, 1935, page unnumbered.

43 For a long time: Sen. J. W. (Bill) Fulbright, interview, June 9, 1992.

43 "Our biggest escapade . . .": *NAT*, "As I See It," Apr. 18, 1949, p. 4.

44 "We used to struggle . . .": Ibid., Jan. 3, 1945, p. 2.

44 Once Lucile: Sen. J. W. (Bill) Fulbright, interview, June 8, 1992.

44 "It was . . .": *FDD,* June 7, 1920, p. 4.

44 When it came time: Margaret Waugh Crittenden, interview, Mar. 17, 1993.

45 At Anna's wedding: Dick Waugh, telephone interview, Mar. 9, 1993.

45 "his teammates . . .": J. W. Fulbright, *Against the Arrogance of Power,* p. 16.

46 Jack was: Anna Fulbright Teasdale, quoted by Allan Gilbert, interview, Sept. 21, 1992.

CHAPTER IV: "ME AND MEN"

47 "We came in . . .": *NAT,* "As I See It," Aug. 4, 1950, p. 4.

47 In 1919: *Arkansas Times,* June 1986, p. 168.

47 On the heels: Gilbert, *Fulbright Chronicle,* p. 123.

48 The university assigned: Robert Leflar, *The First 100 Years: Centennial History of the University of Arkansas* (1972), p. 122.

49 Morris Collier recalled: Morris Collier, interview, Mar. 23, 1993.

50 In Mr. Fulbright's . . . : *FDD,* July 23, 1923, p. 3.

51 "was one of the largest . . .": Ibid., July 25, 1923, p. 1.

51 "Throughout the day . . .": Ibid.

51 "I recall . . .": *NAT,* "As I See It," June 1, 1946, p. 4.

51 On the day: *FDD,* July 23, 1923, p. 1.

52 The *Democrat* is . . . : Ibid., July 24, 1923, p. 2.

53 Jay Fulbright . . . : William S. Campbell, *One Hundred Years of Fayetteville, 1828–1928* (1928), p. 105.

53 He had little . . . : R. Fulbright, Lemke, *As I See It,* column dated Feb. 22, 1947, page unnumbered.

54 "silky smooth . . .": Allan Gilbert, interview, Sept. 21, 1992.

54 "She got burned . . .": Ibid.

54 "the first encouraging . . .": *NAT,* "As I See It," Apr. 17, 1948, p. 4.

54 "Old Lady, . . .": Gilbert, *Fulbright Chronicle,* p. 63.

55 "I thought . . .": Sen. J. W. (Bill) Fulbright, interview, June 8, 1992.

56 ". . . Mrs. Fulbright . . .": Campbell, *One Hundred Years of Fayetteville,* p. 105.

57 "Everyone in town . . .": Floyd Carl Jr., interview, Feb. 20, 1995.

57 "Although menfolk . . .": Gilbert, *Fulbright Chronicle,* pp. 64–65.

57 "Considering her . . .": Lessie Stringfellow Read, *Arkansas Democrat* Sunday Magazine, "Arkansas' Most Noted Woman Publisher," Feb. 2, 1947, p. 3.

57 "This was designed . . .": Gilbert, *Fulbright Chronicle,* p. 65.

58 Men take it . . . : R. Fulbright, Lemke, *As I See It,* column dated Sept. 12, 1934, page unnumbered.

59 Her illness: *FDD,* Apr. 9, 1925, p. 1.

59 "The family": Ibid., Apr. 8, 1925, p. 1.

60 "It takes . . .": *NAT,* "As I See It," Apr. 16, 1948, p. 4.

60 ". . . going of an older . . .": Ibid., June 26, 1946, p. 4.

60 ". . . it is he . . .": Ibid., June 1, 1946, p. 4.

61 "This is to me . . .": *FDD,* June 27, 1928, p. 6.

61 "The hawthorne . . .": Ibid., Aug. 8, 1928, p. 3.

61 "I hear . . .": Ibid.

61 ". . . I am beginning . . .": Ibid., Aug. 21, 1928, p. 1.

61 "and had cocktails . . .": Ibid., Aug. 27, 1928, p. 3.

61 "addict . . .": Ibid., Aug. 30, 1928, p. 2.

62 "I thought when . . .": R. Fulbright, Lemke, *As I See It,* column dated Mar. 4, 1936, page unnumbered.

62 "I always . . .": R. Fulbright to Anna Fulbright Teasdale, quoted by Suzanne Teasdale Zorn, telephone interview, Feb. 22, 1995.

63 "While keeping in touch . . .": Read, "Arkansas' Most Noted Woman Publisher," p. 3.

CHAPTER V: AS I SEE IT

65 "the fellow . . .": Gilbert, *Fulbright Chronicle,* p. 43.

66 Lessie Stringfellow Read: Thomas Rothrock, "A History of the Washington County Press," *Flashback* 16 (Feb. 1966), p. 2.

66 Her journalistic fervor: Gilbert, *Fulbright Chronicle,* pp. 108–9.

67 "Mrs. Read . . .": FDD, "As I See It," Aug. 14, 1935, p. 2.

67 I can only . . . : Ibid.

67 "The letters . . .": FDD, July 27, 1928, p. 6.

68 "It was just after . . .": Ibid., Mar. 8, 1933, p. 2.

68 In a compilation: R. Fulbright, Lemke, *As I See It,* foreword, page unnumbered.

68 It's just plain . . . : Ibid., Feb. 24, 1938, page unnumbered.

69 "Maude . . .": FDD, "As I See It," Aug. 15, 1935, p. 2.

69 "I knew . . .": Maude Hawn, interview, Sept. 22, 1992.

69 "That's how . . .": Floyd Carl Jr., interview, Feb. 20, 1995.

69 "he considered . . .": Gilbert, *Fulbright Chronicle,* p. 91.

70 "The Fayetteville . . .": Rothrock, "A History of the Washington County Press," p. 1.

70 "Northwest Arkansas . . .": NAT, Mar. 29, 1992, p. 81.

71 On Mondays: Sam Harris, interview, Aug. 26, 1992.

71 University historian: Dr. Robert Leflar, interview, Sept. 21, 1992.

71 "I have been thrust . . .": R. Fulbright, Lemke, *As I See It,* Aug. 14, 1935, page unnumbered.

71 "What with . . .": Ibid.

72 "Who was the . . .": Floyd Carl Jr., interview, Feb. 20, 1995.

72 Once she came: Maude Hawn, interview, Sept. 22, 1992.

72 "She wasn't all . . .": R. Fulbright, Lemke, *As I See It,* foreword, page unnumbered.

72 "on any topic . . .": *Time,* Jan. 22, 1965, p. 17.

73 "The heartstrings . . .": NAT, "As I See It," Nov. 15, 1949, p. 4.

73 A town . . . : NAT, "As I See It," June 7, 1941, p. 2.

73 "We think Fayetteville . . .": Ibid.

73 ". . . even a cat . . .": FDD, "As I See It," Mar. 16, 1933, p. 2.

73 "She's not here . . .": Ray Adams, interview, Mar. 23, 1993.

74 "But the word . . .": R. Fulbright, Lemke, *As I See It,* foreword, page unnumbered.

74 "she was pretty sincere . . .": Sam Schwieger, telephone interview, Mar. 22, 1993.

74 "It would be . . .": Floyd Carl Jr., interview, Feb. 20, 1995.

74 "I never write . . .": R. Fulbright, Lemke, *As I See It,* column dated May 8, 1935, page unnumbered.

74 "you cannot imagine . . .": Ibid., Jan. 30, 1940, page unnumbered.

74 "I wrote . . .": Ibid., July 31, 1934, page unnumbered.

74 "In my story . . .": Ibid., Feb. 14, 1947, page unnumbered.

74 "In my going-on . . .": FDD, "As I See It," Mar. 7, 1933, p. 2.

75 "I'm liable . . .": NAT, "As I See It," Apr. 4, 1945, p. 4.

75 "She used . . .": Allan Gilbert, interview, Sept. 21, 1992.

75 "although we . . .": R. Fulbright, Lemke, *As I See It,* column dated Aug. 14, 1935, page unnumbered.

75 The other night . . . : *NAT,* "As I See It," Mar. 18, 1949, p. 4.

75 "We made it . . .": Ibid.

75 ". . . I believe I am . . .": Ibid., Feb. 18, 1938, p. 7.

76 "If she thought . . .": Floyd Carl Jr., interview, Feb. 20, 1995.

76 (From) Bob Wimberly . . . (to) . . . of the story: Bob Wimberly, interview, May 26, 1993.

76 (From) "Before we get started" (to) "those businesses": Ibid.

77 "She was her own . . .": Floyd Carl Jr., interview, Feb. 20, 1995.

77 At the newspaper: Gilbert, *Fulbright Chronicle,* p. 35.

77 "forthright . . .": Sam Schwieger, telephone interview, Mar. 22, 1993.

77 "I wish Nelly Don . . .": R. Fulbright, Lemke, *As I See It,* column dated May 31, 1938, page unnumbered.

77 "Marriage . . .": *NAT,* "As I See It," July 23, 1938, p. 2.

77 "You have often . . .": R. Fulbright, Lemke, *As I See It,* column dated Feb. 29, 1944, page unnumbered.

77 "There's a naivete . . .": Ibid., foreword, page unnumbered.

77 "I've either heard . . .": *FDD,* "As I See It," Jan. 11, 1936, p. 2.

78 I went . . . : *NAT,* "As I See It," July 16, 1938, p. 2.

78 Our politics . . . : R. Fulbright, Lemke, *As I See It,* column dated Apr. 25, 1941, page unnumbered.

78 "A Republican . . .": *FDD,* "As I See It," Jan. 8, 1936, p. 2.

78 The democratic mode . . . : R. Fulbright, Lemke, *As I See It,* column dated Feb. 19, 1938, page unnumbered.

79 When Dr. J. W. Workman . . . : *NAT,* "As I See It," Feb. 17, 1938, p. 7.

80 Expecting only . . . : Ibid.

80 "I asked . . .": Ibid., Feb. 18, 1938, p. 7.

80 "Gardening . . .": Ibid., Oct. 4, 1951, p. 4.

80 I recall . . . : Ibid., May 21, 1938, p. 2.

80 . . . if I owned . . . : Ibid.

81 "She used . . .": Betty Lighton, interview, Feb. 20, 1995.

81 "Everytime . . .": *NAT,* "As I See It," Nov. 7, 1945, p. 4.

81 "It is a fallacious . . .": R. Fulbright, Lemke, *As I See It,* column dated Feb. 28, 1935, page unnumbered.

81 "Some of her . . .": Ibid., foreword, page unnumbered.

CHAPTER VI: THE PUBLISHER AND POLITICS

82 "This control . . .": Harry Lee Williams, *Behind the Scenes in Arkansas Politics* (1934), page unnumbered.

83 "very corrupt . . .": Maude Hawn, interview, Sept. 22, 1992.

83 "Dee McConnell . . .": Maupin Cummings, interview, Mar. 24, 1993.

83 According to: Judge Thomas Butt, interview, Mar. 24, 1993.

84 We believe in . . . : *FDD,* "As I See It," Mar. 6, 1933, p. 2.

84 Today we will . . . : Ibid., Mar. 9, 1933, p. 2.

85 "I'm getting . . .": Ibid., Oct. 18, 1933, p. 2.

86 (From) Seven days (to) before the primary. Diane D. Kincaid, editor, *Silent Hattie Speaks, the Personal Journal of Senator Hattie Caraway* (1979), pp. 6–10.

87 Hattie Caraway . . . : *FDD,* Oct. 24, 1932, p. 2.

88 "the vote . . .": Ibid., Aug. 23, 1932, p. 1.

88 The "Democrat . . .": Ibid., Dec. 8, 1932, p. 1.

89 "Mrs. Fulbright . . .": Ibid., May 6, 1934, p. 1.

89   A week later . . . : Ibid., May 14, 1934, p. 1.

89   My name . . . : R. Fulbright, Lemke, *As I See It,* column dated May 17, 1934, page unnumbered.

90   "aiding and . . .": *FDD,* June 10, 1933, p. 1.

90   "dirty, filthy . . .": Ibid., June 17, 1933, p. 1.

90   "$45,366 . . .": Ibid., Oct. 23, 1933, p. 1.

90   "The Fayetteville fiasco . . .": Ibid., Apr. 28, 1934, p. 1.

90   "adverse publicity . . .": Ibid., May 2, 1934, p. 2.

91   Several organizations . . . : Ibid., May 4, 1934, p. 1.

91   "county committeemen . . .": Ibid., June 9, 1934, p. 1.

91   I looked over . . . : Ibid., "As I See It," July 21, 1934, p. 2.

92   "I can't perceive . . .": Ibid., Aug. 13, 1934, p. 2.

92   "feather . . .": Ibid., Aug. 16, 1934, p. 2.

92   The Democratic Primary . . . : Ibid., Aug. 17, 1934, p. 2.

94   Two days: *FDD,* Nov. 8, 1934, p. 2.

94   The telephone . . . : Ibid., Nov. 9, 1934, p. 2.

95   Do you know . . . : Ibid., "As I See It," Feb. 6, 1935, p. 2.

95   "Clean Sweep . . .": *FDD,* Mar. 7, 1935, p. 1.

95   "people will . . .": Ibid., "As I See It," Mar. 7, 1935, p. 2.

96   We are almost . . . : Ibid., Oct. 10, 1935, p. 4.

96   "Gover removal . . .": *FDD,* Oct. 28, 1935, p. 1.

97   So there is . . . : Ibid., "As I See It," Nov. 23, 1935, p. 2.

97   The middle . . . : Ibid., Jan. 25, 1936, p. 2.

98   I am afraid . . . : *FDD,* Feb. 8, 1936, p. 2.

98   "the shame . . .": Ibid., "As I See It," Feb. 10, 1936, p. 2.

98   Here is the tragedy . . . : *Arkansas Democrat,* Feb. 8, 1936, p. 3.

99   The *Democrat* . . . : *FDD,* Feb. 24, 1936, p. 1.

99   "the city attorney . . .": Ibid., Feb. 21, 1936, p. 2.

99   ". . . of the recent . . .": Ibid., "As I See It," Feb. 27, 1936, p. 2.

100   "through childish . . .": *FDD,* Mar. 28, 1936, p. 6.

100   The lawsuit . . . : Ibid., "As I See It," Mar. 19, 1936, p. 4.

100   As you may . . . : Ibid., Apr. 2, 1936, p. 4.

100   In a dramatic . . . : *FDD,* Apr. 27, 1936, p. 1.

101   Combs would: Ibid., June 30, 1936, p. 1.

101   "Of course there is . . .": Ibid., "As I See It," July 3, 1936, p. 2.

102   "anonymous phone calls . . .": Gilbert, *Fulbright Chronicle,* p. 105.

102   In keeping with . . . : Ibid.

102   During the tenure . . . : *FDD,* "As I See It," July 29, 1936, p. 2.

102   Henry says . . . : Ibid., Aug. 7, 1936, p. 2.

103   There is one thing . . . : Ibid., Aug. 3, 1936, p. 2.

103   (From) "every man" (to) "the bribe": Ibid.

103   I felt in . . . : Ibid.

105   "crooks are trying . . .": *FDD,* Aug. 10–11, 1936, pp. 1–2.

105   In the beginning . . . : Gilbert, *Fulbright Chronicle,* pp. 105–6.

105   Friends . . . : *FDD,* "As I See It," Aug. 7, 1936, p. 2.

105   Lessie Read may . . . : Ibid., Aug. 11, 1936, p. 2.

106   Cummings recalled: Maupin Cummings, interview, Mar. 24, 1993.

106   "those people . . .": *Springdale News,* Aug. 6, 1936, p. 14.

106   We are proud . . . : *FDD,* "As I See It," Aug. 13, 1936, p. 4.

106   "So long as . . .": *FDD,* Sept. 10, 1936, p. 2.

107   I can't believe . . . : *NAT,* "As I See It," Sept. 22, 1938, p. 2.

108   In the absence . . . : Ibid., Aug. 6, 1938, p. 2.

108 "I prophesy . . .": Ibid., Feb. 21, 1938, p. 4.

108 It sort of seems . . . : Ibid., June 28, 1938, p. 2.

108 The best efforts . . . : Ibid., July 29, 1938, p. 2.

108 I fancy . . . : Ibid., Aug. 8, 1938, p. 2.

CHAPTER VII: OF OTHER THINGS

110 At the Red Cross: Morris Collier, interview, Mar. 23, 1993.

110 We are turning . . . : *FDD*, "As I See It," Mar. 6, 1933, p. 2.

111 A moratorium . . . : Ibid., Mar. 7, 1933, p. 2.

111 "That Roberta . . .": Lin H. Wright, "Arkansas' Largest Little Bank," *Flashback* 22 (Nov. 1972), p. 2.

112 Secretary of Agriculture . . . : *FDD*, "As I See It," Sept. 11, 1934, p. 2.

112 A phenomenon . . . : Gilbert, *Fulbright Chronicle*, p. 155.

113 A university city . . . : R. Fulbright, Lemke, *As I See it,* column dated Sept. 20, 1934, page unnumbered.

113 I never considered . . . : *FDD*, "As I See It," Sept. 9, 1935, p. 2.

114 "I was brought up a rank . . .": *NAT*, "As I See It," July 30, 1947, p. 4.

114 In the newspaper's: Kent R. Brown, *Fayetteville. A Pictorial History, A Timeless Epoch* (1982), p. 110.

114 I was brought up on prohibition . . . : R. Fulbright, Lemke, *As I See It,* column dated Nov. 26, 1934, page unnumbered.

114 The absence of . . . : *FDD*, "As I See It," June 10, 1933, p. 2.

115 (From) "are distressed . . ." (to) "of this community": Gilbert, *Fulbright Chronicle,* pp. 100–101.

115 "It is pretty well . . .": *FDD*, "As I See It," Oct. 17, 1933, p. 2.

116 A few things . . . : R. Fulbright, Lemke, *As I See It,* column dated Mar. 4, 1936, page unnumbered.

116 "My mother gave me . . .": J. W. Fulbright, *Against the Arrogance of Power,* p. 31.

117 "My mother . . . was very happy . . .": Ibid., p. 34.

117 "take a course . . .": *FDD*, June 12, 1933, p. 3.

117 "the finest . . .": Ibid., "As I See It," June 15, 1933, p. 2.

117 (From) James Waugh (to) "acute": Dick Waugh, telephone interview, Mar. 9, 1993.

118 (From) Roberta was fond (to) Mont Nord: John Wallace, letter, Apr. 16, 1993.

119 "They are truly . . .": R. Fulbright, Lemke, *As I See It,* column dated Jan. 18, 1935, page unnumbered.

120 "This is how . . .": Allan Gilbert, interview, Sept. 21, 1992.

120 "the essentials . . .": R. Fulbright, Lemke, *As I See It,* column dated Nov. 17, 1938, page unnumbered.

120 "generally enjoyed . . .": Allan Gilbert, interview, Sept. 21, 1992.

120 "just as plain . . .": Brower, "The Roots of an Arkansas Questioner," p. 93.

120 "come north . . .": Ibid., p. 94.

121 Later: Ibid.

121 (From) When Betty's (to) Roberta's cabin . . . : Betsey Fulbright Winnacker, telephone interview, Dec. 4, 1992.

121 "huge snake . . .": Patty Fulbright Smith, interview, Jan. 12, 1995.

121 "fried chicken parties . . .": Suzanne Teasdale Zorn, telephone interview, Feb. 22, 1995.

122 Betty Lighton: Betty Lighton, interview, Feb. 20, 1995.

123 "The thrills . . .": R. Fulbright, Lemke, *As I See It,* column dated Jan. 18, 1935, page unnumbered.

123 "A hundred years . . .": *NAT*, "As I See It," May 24, 1938, p. 2.

CHAPTER VIII: ON CAMPUS

124   "she scared me . . .": Willie Oates, interview, Aug. 25, 1992.

124   (From) "The sorority . . ." to "power of women.": Ibid.

125   Men always . . . : R. Fulbright, Lemke, *As I See It,* column dated Nov. 9, 1935, page unnumbered.

126   Sometimes we . . . : Ibid., Nov. 10, 1936, page unnumbered.

126   "If I am thankful . . .": Ibid., Apr. 10, 1937, page unnumbered.

127   . . . I said . . . : *NAT,* "As I See It," Oct. 3, 1949, p. 4.

127   "I am attached . . .": Ibid.

127   (From) "She was a . . ." (to) failure: Dr. Robert Leflar, interview, Sept. 21, 1992.

127   "It is our crowning . . .": *NAT,* "As I See It," July 22, 1940, p. 2.

127   "the baccalaureate . . .": Ibid., June 7, 1938, p. 4.

127   "She (the university) . . .": Ibid., Apr. 25, 1947, p. 4.

128   I sat . . . : Ibid., Aug. 30, 1949, p. 4.

128   The 1933 legislature . . . : *FDD,* "As I See It," Mar. 13, 1933, p. 2.

128   Little Rock never . . . : Ibid., Feb. 12, 1936, p. 2.

129   "In my recent . . .": *NAT,* "As I See It," Mar. 1, 1949, p. 4.

129   "wise and expedient . . .": Ibid.

129   It is our heart . . . : Ibid., Mar. 24, 1949, p. 12.

129   We see Little Rock . . . : Ibid., July 26, 1946, p. 4.

129   "A university is . . .": Coffin, *Senator Fulbright,* p. 39.

130   "The Arkansas-SMU game . . .": *NAT,* "As I See It," Oct. 25, 1937, p. 2.

130   "Lively, vibrant . . .": Gilbert, *Fulbright Chronicle,* p. 102.

130   We who are blest . . . : *NAT,* "As I See It," Nov. 13, 1948, p. 4.

130   "I do wish . . .": Ibid.

130   The Homecoming game . . . : R. Fulbright, Lemke, *As I See It,* column dated Nov. 10, 1936, page unnumbered.

131   Football . . . : *NAT,* "As I See It," Dec. 5, 1949, p. 4.

131   As Barnhill . . . : Ibid., Oct. 23, 1946, p. 4.

CHAPTER IX: THE UNIVERSITY PRESIDENCY

132   (From) On September (to) seriously.: *Arkansas Democrat,* Sept. 13, 1939, pp. 1–2.

132   newspaper accounts: *Arkansas Gazette,* Sept. 13, 1939, p. 1.

132   "During his tenure . . .": *NAT,* "As I See It," Sept. 13, 1939, p. 2.

132   "domineering . . .": Leflar, *The First One Hundred Years,* p. 97.

133   Giles E. Ripley . . . : Ibid., p. 100.

133   "Governor Bailey . . .": Dr. Robert Leflar, interview, Sept. 21, 1992.

134   "I'm in favor . . .": Ibid.

134   "Whereupon . . .": Ibid.

134   "A quick campaign . . .": Leflar, *The First One Hundred Years,* p. 174.

134   Bailey's friendship . . . : Gilbert, *Fulbright Chronicle,* p. 137.

135   His election: *Arkansas Democrat,* Sept. 18, 1939, p. 12; *Arkansas Gazette,* Sept. 16, 1939, p. 2.

135   The board: Harrison Hale, *University of Arkansas 1871–1948* (1948), p. 125.

135   Bailey's plucking . . . : Gilbert, *Fulbright Chronicle,* p. 137.

136   "the dominant force . . .": Bill Penix, interview, Jan. 24, 1995.

136   "I do not think . . .": Ibid.

136   "tarred with . . .": Leflar, *The First One Hundred Years,* p. 175.

136   "It seems like . . .": *Arkansas Democrat,* Sept. 19, 1939, p. 8.

136   "join a landslide . . .": *FDD,* "As I See It," Aug. 1, 1936, p. 2.

136 Governor J. M. Futrell: Boyce Drummond, "Arkansas Politics: A Study of a One Party System," doctoral dissertation, University of Chicago (1957), pp. 196–97.

137 August 5 . . . : *FDD*, "As I See It," Aug. 10, 1936, p. 9.

137 Our Governor-elect . . . : Ibid., Sept. 25, 1936, p. 2.

138 The Bailey-Miller . . . : *NAT*, "As I See It," Oct. 6, 1937, p. 9.

138 We concur . . . : Ibid., Oct. 20, 1937, p. 2.

139 Some say . . . : Ibid., July 20, 1938, p. 2.

139 These last two . . . : Ibid., July 26, 1938, p. 4.

139 In the "Cook Book" . . . : Ibid., Aug. 8, 1938, p. 2.

139 "was in his element . . .": Ibid., Oct. 25, 1948, p. 4.

140 "He recommended me . . .": J. W. Fulbright, *Against the Arrogance of Power*, p. 37.

140 "give it a try . . .": Ibid.

140 "The old guard . . .": Bill Penix, interview, Jan. 24, 1995.

140 "Arthur Harding . . .": Sen. J. W. (Bill) Fulbright, interview, June 8, 1992.

140 "Many remarks . . .": Sen. J. W. (Bill) Fulbright, speech, Fort Smith, Ark., Dec. 10, 1939. Cited by Mary Lynn Kennedy, "Politics in Academe: Roberta Fulbright's Role in Her Son's University Presidency," unpublished graduate essay, University of Arkansas, Department of History (1975), p. 10.

140 "The president's . . .": J. W. Fulbright, *Against the Arrogance of Power*, p. 37.

140 He was regarded: Haynes Johnson and Bernard M. Gwertzman, *Fulbright the Dissenter* (1968), p. 48.

140 You can't impress . . . : R. Fulbright, Lemke, *As I See It*, column dated Mar. 22, 1940, page unnumbered.

141 "There went . . .": Eloise King, interview, Feb. 20, 1995.

141 "I probably . . .": Bill Penix, interview, Jan. 24, 1995.

141 "I was seen . . .": J. W. Fulbright, *Against the Arrogance of Power*, p. 39.

142 America . . . : R. Fulbright, Lemke, *As I See It*, column dated Mar. 5, 1941, page unnumbered.

142 Here's a little . . . : Ibid., Mar. 2, 1939, page unnumbered.

143 What worries . . . : Ibid., June 30, 1939, page unnumbered.

CHAPTER X: THE LAST WORD

144 "anti-thesis . . .": Drummond, "Arkansas Politics: A Study of a One Party System," p. 189.

144 Adkins has . . . : Ibid.

145 "he stumped . . .": Ibid., p. 205.

145 "interference . . .": *Arkansas Democrat*, July 12, 1940, p. 2.

145 "Adkins Talks . . .": *NAT*, Aug. 5, 1940, p. 8.

145 Declaring that . . . : Ibid.

145 Well, Mr. Homer Adkins . . . : Ibid., "As I See It," Aug. 5, 1940, p. 9.

146 I can hear . . . : Ibid., Aug. 6, 1940, p. 2.

146 So the old . . . : Ibid., Aug. 9, 1940, p. 2.

147 The next day: *NAT*, Aug. 10, 1940, p. 1.

147 "We still believe . . .": Ibid., "As I See It," Aug. 12, 1940, p. 4.

147 Governor Bailey's record . . . : Ibid.

147 The *Northwest*: *NAT*, Aug. 14, 1940, p. 1.

147 Adkins carried: Stephen Dew, "The New Deal and Fayetteville, Arkansas 1933–1941," master's thesis, University of Arkansas (1987), p. 245.

148 Arkansas voters . . . : *NAT*, "As I See It," Aug. 14, 1940, p. 2.

148 "One of Adkins . . .": Leflar, *The First One Hundred Years*, p. 175.

148   "It is possible . . .": Ibid., p. 196.

149   "How soon . . .": Bill Penix, interview, Jan. 24, 1995.

149   "efficient . . .": *Arkansas Gazette,* Oct. 20, 1940, p. 13.

149   (From) Rather than (to) three appointments: Maupin Cummings, interview, Mar. 24, 1993.

150   The *Northwest: NAT,* June 4, 1941, p. 1.

150   At this initial: Kennedy, "Politics in Academe: Roberta Fulbright's Role in Her Son's University Presidency," p. 15.

150   However, Sen. Maupin Cummings: Maupin Cummings, interview, Mar. 24, 1993.

150   "no matter . . .": *NAT,* "As I See It," June 4, 1941, p. 2.

151   "But I didn't . . .": J. W. Fulbright, *Against the Arrogance of Power,* p. 40.

151   "In order . . .": Sen. J. W. (Bill) Fulbright, interview, June 8, 1992.

152   "Soon," accused Park: *Van Buren Press Argus,* July 20, 1940, p. 1.

152   "there has been ample . . .": Ibid., June 13, 1941, p. 1.

152   "A tree cannot . . .": *NAT,* June 10, 1941, p. 1.

153   Several changes . . . : Ibid., June 9, 1941, p. 1.

153   It is high . . . : Ibid., June 10, 1941, p. 2.

155   I would like . . . : Ibid., "As I See It," June 10, 1941, p. 2.

155   Needless to say . . . : Leflar, *The First One Hundred Years,* p. 181.

155   "got his story . . .": *NAT,* June 11, 1941, p. 2.

156   "one of Adkins' . . .": Leflar, *The First One Hundred Years,* p. 175.

156   Hers weren't . . . : Gilbert, *Fulbright Chronicle,* p. 138.

156   "The firing . . .": Sen. J. W. (Bill) Fulbright, interview, June 8, 1992.

157   In so far as . . . : Kennedy, "Politics in Academe," p. 1, quoted from untitled, undated handwritten statement, J. W. Fulbright papers, Special Collections Division, University of Arkansas Libraries, Fayetteville.

157   "Bailey was . . .": Sen. J. W. (Bill) Fulbright, interview, Jan. 21, 1993.

157   "Gov. Adkins . . .": Ibid.

158   (From) "The consensus (to) "Mama, I don't know.": Donald Murray, letter, Mar. 22, 1993.

158   "I had never thought . . .": J. W. Fulbright, *Against the Arrogance of Power,* p. 41.

158   "My mother . . .": Ibid.

158   "If she hadn't . . .": Sen. J. W. (Bill) Fulbright, interview, June 8, 1992.

159   We of Northwest Arkansas . . . : *NAT,* Aug. 6, 1942, p. 2.

160   Even being compelled . . . : Ibid., "As I See It," Aug. 27, 1942, p. 4.

160   "It was well-known . . .": J. W. Fulbright, *Against the Arrogance of Power,* p. 45.

160   "Fulbright polled . . .": *NAT,* July 30, 1942, p. 1.

160   "very interesting . . .": John Erickson, telephone interview, Mar. 23, 1995.

160   "We were so glad . . .": Roberta Fulbright to J. W. Fulbright, Jan. 19, 1943, J. W. Fulbright papers, BCN 5, F 31, Miscellaneous Correspondence, Special Collections Division, University of Arkansas Libraries, Fayetteville.

161   "There is a very great urge . . .": Ibid., letter, dated Jan. 21, 1943.

161   "Your mother and I . . .": Ibid., Sam Gearhart to J. W. Fulbright, Sept. 4, 1944.

161   "Men and women . . .": Irene Carlisle, "J. W. Fulbright, Minister from Arkansas," *Flashback* 16 (May 1966), p. 3.

161   "Bill's mother . . .": Ibid.

161   Few people . . . : Ibid.

162   "For Bailey and me . . .": J. W. Fulbright, *Against the Arrogance of Power,* p. 52.

163   . . . And Fulbright . . . : *NAT,* "Round About Town," June 24, 1944, p. 4.

163   "It is from my bed . . .": Ibid., "As I See It," June 28, 1944, p. 2.

163   "We entertain . . .": Ibid.

163   "Thank God . . .": Ibid., July 6, 1944, p. 2.

163 "a mean race.": Sen. J. W. (Bill) Fulbright, interview, June 8, 1992.

163 Adkins promoted: Carol Griffee, *Arkansas Gazette,* Feb. 9, 1986, p. 2J.

164 A political campaign . . . : *NAT,* "As I See It," July 19, 1944, p. 4.

164 "Paths of . . ." *NAT,* Jan. 27, 1944, p. 1.

165 Just as quickly: *Arkansas Gazette,* July 27, 1944, p. 1.

165 In almost every community: Sen. J. W. (Bill) Fulbright, interview, June 8, 1992.

165 "she believed she would . . .": *NAT,* July 29, 1944, p. 1.

165 My children tell . . . : Ibid., "As I See It," Aug. 3, 1944, p. 4.

165 My "thank you" list . . . : Ibid., Aug. 11, 1944, p. 4.

166 The *Times: NAT,* Aug. 9, 1944, p. 1.

166 The next day: Ibid., Aug. 10, 1944, p. 1.

166 We've had a Senate . . . : Ibid., "As I See It," Aug. 16, 1944, p. 4.

167 "There is no doubt . . .": John Erickson, telephone interview, Mar. 23, 1995.

167 "I think . . .": Ibid.

167 "The largest single . . .": Leflar, *The First One Hundred Years,* p. 181.

167 "It was in a measure . . .": *Arkansas Gazette,* Jan. 12, 1953, p. 1.

167 "In a political . . .": Sam Harris, interview, Aug. 26, 1992.

167 It just doesn't . . . : *NAT,* "As I See It," Aug. 16, 1944, p. 4.

167 I suppose I . . . : Ibid., Aug. 19, 1944, p. 3.

168 "But Mrs. Fulbright . . .": Read, "Arkansas' Most Noted Woman Publisher," p. 3.

168 "the people . . .": Ibid.

CHAPTER XI: THE VIEW FROM MONT NORD

170 "You could see . . .": Kenneth Teasdale, interview, June 29, 1992.

170 "Everybody . . .": Ibid.

170 "going down . . .": Suzanne Teasdale Zorn, telephone interview, Feb. 22, 1995.

170 "There was lots . . .": Patty Fulbright Smith, interview, Jan. 12, 1995.

170 "If she were sitting . . .": Kenneth Teasdale, interview, June 29, 1992.

170 "Wings make you . . .": Patty Fulbright Smith, interview, Jan. 12, 1995.

171 Even her cousin . . . : Martha Twichell, interview, Nov. 3, 1995.

171 "Wonderful place . . .": Dick Waugh, telephone interview, Mar. 9, 1993.

171 "Give me . . .": Margaret Waugh Crittenden, interview, Mar. 17, 1993.

171 "She was a wonderful . . .": Betsey Fulbright Winnacker, telephone interview, Dec. 4, 1992.

171 "There was no sense . . .": Kenneth Teasdale, interview, June 29, 1992.

172 "You dreaded it . . .": Patty Fulbright Smith, interview, Jan. 12, 1995.

172 Suzanne Zorn remembered: Suzanne Teasdale Zorn, telephone interview, Feb. 22, 1995.

172 "If the discussion . . .": Betsey Fulbright Winnacker, telephone interview, Dec. 4, 1992.

172 "Grandmother included . . .": Patty Fulbright Smith, interview, Jan. 12, 1995.

172 Because he lived: Doug Douglas, telephone interview, Mar. 20, 1993.

172 "Rained . . .": *NAT,* "As I See It," Oct. 8, 1946, p. 4.

172 "I respected her . . .": Doug Douglas, telephone interview, Mar. 20, 1993.

172 "Grandmother gets cross . . .": *NAT,* "As I See It," June 9, 1949, p. 9.

173 "Those were wonderful . . .": Doug Douglas, telephone interview, Mar. 20, 1993.

173 Patty Smith: Patty Fulbright Smith, interview, Jan. 12, 1995.

173 Smith recalled: Ibid.

173 "and as an old . . .": *NAT,* "As I See It," Dec. 20, 1947, p. 4.

173 "By the way . . .": Ibid., "As I See It," Dec. 16, 1944, p. 3.

173 Christmas gatherings: Betsey Fulbright Winnacker, telephone interview, Dec. 4, 1992.

173 "O Little Town . . .": Bosey Fulbright Foote, telephone interview, Dec. 12, 1992.

174 "She had a latent . . .": Betsey Fulbright Winnacker, telephone interview, Dec. 4, 1992.

174 Author Tristram Coffin: Coffin, *Senator Fulbright,* p. 39.

174 "Life never . . .": *NAT,* "As I See It," Nov. 21, 1945, p. 4.

174 "Pride in . . .": Ibid., June 7, 1951, p. 4.

174 "I was taking . . .": Ibid., Apr. 21, 1951, p. 4.

174 "a blood . . .": Kenneth Teasdale, interview, June 29, 1992.

175 "Go ahead . . .": Suzanne Teasdale Zorn, telephone interview, Feb. 22, 1995.

175 "I was inspired . . .": Ibid.

175 When Zorn: Ibid.

175 Robert Louis Stevenson . . . : R. Fulbright, Lemke, *As I See It,* column dated Oct. 23, 1935, page unnumbered.

175 "grind me . . .": Ibid., Jan. 30, 1940, page unnumbered.

175 (From) A former editor (to) rarity in those years: Robert S. McCord, letter, Mar. 16, 1993.

176 "I have always hoped . . .": *NAT,* "As I See It," June 9, 1949, p. 9.

177 "She was not domineering . . .": Morris Collier, interview, Mar. 23, 1993.

177 "There was always . . .": Coffin, *Senator Fulbright,* p. 38.

177 "I was very much . . .": Betty Lighton, interview, Feb. 20, 1995.

177 "marvelously warm . . .": Dick Waugh, telephone interview, Mar. 9, 1993.

177 I went to . . . : *Arkansas Traveler,* Apr. 1, 1941, p. 2.

178 "she laughed . . .": Bill Penix, interview, Jan. 24, 1995.

178 (From) Another time (to) "any woman in the state.": Ibid.

178 "You can't be down . . .": Read, "Arkansas' Most Noted Woman Publisher," p. 3.

179 "There was always . . .": Allan Gilbert, interview, Sept. 21, 1992.

179 "He was probably . . .": Suzanne Teasdale Zorn, telephone interview, Feb. 22, 1995.

179 The Fulbrights gave . . . : Mrs. Brooks Hays, "From the Political Diary of an Unpolitical Person," *Arkansas Historical Quarterly,* 36, Summer 1977, p. 177.

179 "very pleasant . . .": Marion Hays, telephone interview, Apr. 19, 1994.

180 While Mahan enjoyed: Suzanne Teasdale Zorn, telephone interview, Feb. 22, 1995.

180 "She loved . . .": Brower, "The Roots of an Arkansas Questioner," p. 96.

180 "big talker . . .": Martha Twichell, interview, Nov. 3, 1995.

180 "Every time I . . .": Dick Waugh, telephone interview, Mar. 9, 1993.

180 "The gift . . .": Suzanne Teasdale Zorn, telephone interview, Feb. 22, 1995.

180 "Mother . . .": Margaret Waugh Crittenden, interview, Mar. 17, 1993.

180 "Mother and . . .": Ruby Thomas, interview, May 28, 1992.

180 "Her head . . .": Ibid.

181 "She had a wonderful . . .": Henryetta Peck, interview, May 28, 1992.

181 "They were fascinated . . .": Ibid.

181 "She wasn't in accord . . .": Sen. J. W. (Bill) Fulbright, interview, June 8, 1992.

181 "Grandmother loved . . .": Patty Fulbright Smith, interview, Jan. 12, 1995.

181 "She was insouciant . . .": Suzanne Teasdale Zorn, telephone interview, Feb. 22, 1995.

181 "the telephone . . .": *NAT,* "As I See It," May 6, 1947, p. 4.

182 "You'd go . . .": Suzanne Teasdale Zorn, telephone interview, Feb. 22, 1995.

182 "It is always . . .": *NAT,* "As I See It," Aug. 8, 1950, p. 4.

182 "I'm a terribly . . .": Ibid., Apr. 23, 1947, p. 4.

182 "I might . . .": Read, "Arkansas' Most Noted Woman Publisher," p. 3.

182 "did not have . . .": *NAT,* "As I See It," Apr. 23, 1947, p. 4.

182 "She was won over . . .": Allan Gilbert, interview, Sept. 21, 1992.

183 "Mother, I don't care . . .": *NAT,* "As I See It," Feb. 20, 1946, p. 4.

183 When the twins: Suzanne Teasdale Zorn, telephone interview, Feb. 22, 1995.

183 "everyone should have . . .": Margaret Waugh Crittenden, interview, Mar. 17, 1993.

183 "Friends . . .": R. Fulbright, Lemke, *As I See It,* column dated June 15, 1935, page unnumbered.

183 "When I become . . .": Ibid., Jan. 21, 1935, page unnumbered.

183 "They do not talk . . .": Ibid.

184 "If anyone doubts . . .": *NAT,* "As I See It," Apr. 15, 1949, p. 4.

184 (From) "No one . . ." (to) "no end.": Ibid., June 23, 1947, p. 4.

184 I am about . . . : Roberta Fulbright to J. W. Fulbright, Jan. 19, 1943, J. W. Fulbright papers, BCN 5, F 31, Miscellaneous Correspondence, Special Collections Division, University of Arkansas Libraries, Fayetteville.

184 We are having . . . : Ibid.

184 "As I See It" . . . : R. Fulbright, Lemke, *As I See It,* column dated Apr. 7, 1941, page unnumbered.

185 One thing about . . . : Ibid., Feb. 10, 1944, page unnumbered.

186 Dresses: *NAT,* June 20, 1944, p. 3.

186 It is a gloomy . . . : Ibid., "As I See It," May 7, 1941, p. 2.

186 "There is rank . . .": Ibid., Dec. 13, 1944, p. 4.

186 Strasbourg . . . : Ibid., Sept. 8, 1944, p. 4.

187 "She was one . . .": Betsey Fulbright Winnacker, telephone interview, Dec. 4, 1992.

187 "She grew up . . .": Patty Fulbright Smith, interview, Jan. 12, 1995.

187 "I was born . . .": *NAT,* "As I See It," Mar. 21, 1945, p. 4.

187 "visited . . .": Ibid., Dec. 2, 1948, p. 8.

187 "I myself . . .": *FDD,* "As I See It," Mar. 18, 1933, p. 2.

CHAPTER XII: THE PASSING YEARS

188 "The height . . .": R. Fulbright, Lemke, *As I See It,* column dated Oct. 26, 1934, page unnumbered.

188 "There is much . . .": Coffin, *Senator Fulbright,* p. 37.

188 She was bothered: Allan Gilbert, interview, Sept. 21, 1992.

188 "She was the only . . .": Bosey Fulbright Foote, telephone interview, Dec. 12, 1992.

188 "Well, here I am . . .": *NAT,* "As I See It," Jan. 10, 1945, p. 4.

189 "That seems typical . . .": Ibid., Jan. 12, 1945, p. 4.

189 "Washington doesn't . . .": Ibid., Feb. 2, 1945, p. 4.

189 "like a balloon . . .": Ibid., Jan. 12, 1945, p. 4.

189 "You would go . . .": Ibid., Jan. 26, 1945, p. 4.

189 "I really should . . .": Ibid., Jan. 15, 1945, p. 2.

189 "She, though . . .": Ibid., Jan. 19, 1945, p. 4.

189 "Folks, my age . . .": Ibid.

190 "Hats seem . . .": Ibid., Apr. 27, 1951, p. 4.

190 "I, with my . . .": Ibid., Jan. 19, 1945, p. 4.

190 "Columnists are . . .": Ibid., Jan. 22, 1945, p. 2.

190 If Mr. Dewey . . . : Ibid., Aug. 19, 1944, p. 3.

190 "The occasion . . .": Ibid., Jan. 27, 1945, p. 2.

190 "I will say . . .": Ibid., Feb. 2, 1945, p. 4.

190 "HOME . . .": Ibid., Feb. 14, 1945, p. 4.

191 "I am enjoying . . .": Roberta Fulbright to W. J. Lemke, Jan. 5, 1945, W. J. Lemke papers, Series 2, BCN 1, F 10, Special Collections Division, University of Arkansas Libraries, Fayetteville.

191   "It's a city . . .": R. Fulbright, Lemke, *As I See It,* column dated Mar. 28, 1935, page unnumbered.

191   "to stand . . .": Ibid.

191   ". . . I think . . .": Ibid., Apr. 10, 1935, page unnumbered.

191   "It's forever . . .": Roberta Fulbright to J. W. Fulbright, Dec. 1, 1944, J. W. Fulbright papers, BCN 5, F 31, Miscellaneous Correspondence, Special Collections Division, University of Arkansas Libraries, Fayetteville.

191   "You are on . . .": Ibid., Dec. 7, no year given.

191   "I have a dreadful . . .": Ibid.

192   "His mother especially . . .": Kurt Karl Tweraser, "Advice and Consent of Senator Fulbright. A Longitudinal Analysis of His Images of International Politics and His Political Role Conceptions," doctoral dissertation, American University (1971), p. 7.

192   "an imposing woman . . .": Karl E. Meyer, editor, *Fulbright of Arkansas, The Public Positions of a Private Thinker* (1963), p. xxii.

192   "of course as a rule . . .": *NAT,* "As I See It," Nov. 11, 1947, p. 4.

192   "As we older . . .": Roberta Fulbright to J. W. Fulbright, Dec. 1, 1944, J. W. Fulbright papers, BCN 5, F 31, Miscellaneous Correspondence, Special Collections Division, University of Arkansas Libraries, Fayetteville.

192   "Gone is . . .": *NAT,* Apr. 12, 1945, p. 1.

193   "that my baby . . .": Ibid., "As I See It," Feb. 16, 1946, p. 4.

193   Also while she was away: *NAT,* Jan. 15, 1945, p. 1.

194   "When I get . . .": Ibid., "As I See It," Mar. 21, 1945, p. 4.

194   "Someone said . . .": Ibid.

194   "Doctor . . .": Ibid., June 20, 1945, p. 4.

194   Recently I was . . . : Ibid.

195   "The University . . .": Ibid., Aug. 15, 1945, p. 4.

195   "What can we . . .": Ibid., Aug. 3, 1945, p. 4.

195   Our own self-righteousness . . . : Ibid., Nov. 21, 1945, p. 4.

195   "About the only . . .": Ibid., Oct. 17, 1945, p. 4.

196   He pointed out . . . : *NAT,* Dec. 24, 1945, p. 1.

196   One neighbor: Suzanne Teasdale Zorn, telephone interview, Feb. 22, 1995.

196   We may not be . . . : Ibid., "As I See It," Jan. 29, 1946, p. 4.

196   "When God . . .": R. Fulbright, Lemke, *As I See It,* column dated Feb. 17, 1939, page unnumbered.

197   Man's life . . . : *NAT,* "As I See It," Mar. 7, 1947, p. 4.

197   "not one . . .": Ibid., Nov. 11, 1947, p. 4.

197   "I realize . . .": Ibid., Mar. 19, 1949, p. 4.

197   "What will I do . . .": Gilbert, *Fulbright Chronicle,* p. 150.

197   In my column . . . : *NAT,* "As I See It," Mar. 19, 1949, p. 4.

197   "He and I . . .": Ibid., Jan. 25, 1947, p. 4.

198   "I take it . . .": Ibid., Apr. 12, 1949, p. 4.

198   "Jack refuses . . .": Ibid., Oct. 5, 1945, p. 4.

198   "Jack treated . . .": Ibid., Nov. 7, 1945, p. 4.

198   "but that's . . .": Ibid., Apr. 12, 1949, p. 4.

198   "Those who live . . .": Ibid., Aug. 30, 1946, p. 4.

198   "A bit of . . .": Ibid.

199   Just for a . . . : Ibid., Sept. 13, 1946, p. 2.

199   "The only thing . . .": Ibid., Sept. 20, 1946, p. 2.

199   "I didn't . . .": *NAT,* Sept. 27, 1946, p. 1.

199   A first grader . . . : Ibid., "As I See It," Oct. 8, 1946, p. 4.

200   ". . . my time . . .": Ibid., Mar. 6, 1947, p. 4.

200   "I just got . . .": Ibid., Apr. 4, 1947, p. 4.

200 ". . . we will try . . .": Ibid., Apr. 11, 1947, p. 3.

200 He was born . . . : Ibid.

201 "Up to now . . .": Ibid., June 6, 1947, p. 3.

201 "Under pressure . . .": Ibid., Apr. 25, 1947, p. 4.

201 We also desire . . . : Ibid.

201 We accept . . . : Ibid., Apr. 30, 1947, p. 4.

202 I am reminded . . . : Ibid., May 16, 1947, p. 4.

202 I so often . . . : Ibid., June 16, 1947, p. 4.

202 "A Free Press . . .": Ibid., Oct. 8, 1946, p. 4.

202 "I am old-fashioned . . .": Ibid., Apr. 17, 1946, p. 4.

202 "Governor Laney strikes . . .": Ibid., July 20, 1946, p. 4.

202 "I missed . . .": Ibid., Sept. 3, 1946, p. 4.

203 The governor . . . : Ibid., Feb. 28, 1947, p. 4.

203 "Governor Laney is always . . .": Ibid., June 14, 1947, p. 4.

203 "There were about eight . . .": Ibid., July 8, 1947, p. 4.

204 "engaging . . .": Roberta Fulbright to W. J. Lemke, letter dated Nov. 15, 1949, authors' files.

204 "young life . . .": *NAT,* "As I See It," Sept. 27, 1946, p. 1.

204 "Senator Byrd . . .": Ibid., Dec. 7, 1951, p. 4.

204 For some unknown . . . : Ibid., May 3, 1947, p. 4.

204 At least one . . . : Cone Magie, telephone interview, Jan. 3, 1995.

205 Up in the visitor's . . . : *NAT,* "As I See It," Mar. 25, 1948, p. 4.

205 I told Bill . . . : Ibid., Mar. 29, 1948, p. 4.

205 (From) "Ma only" (to) "my own column . . .": Ibid., May 10, 1948, p. 4.

205 (From) "Mother" (to) "follow.": Ibid., Apr. 17, 1948, p. 4.

205 She and daughter-in-law: Marion Hays, telephone interview, Apr. 19, 1994.

206 "Sounds nearly . . .": *NAT,* "As I See It," Apr. 13, 1948, p. 4.

206 He was one . . . : Ibid., Oct. 25, 1948, p. 4.

206 I declare . . . : Ibid., July 26, 1948, p. 4.

206 "I am just saying . . .": Ibid., Oct. 26, 1948, p. 4.

206 "because he . . .": Ibid., Nov. 1, 1948, p. 4.

207 "A rare treat . . .": Ibid., Nov. 1, 1948, p. 4.

207 "Truman says . . .": Ibid., Nov. 4, 1948, p. 9.

207 "She would have . . .": John Erickson, telephone interview, Mar. 23, 1995.

207 "I just believe . . .": *NAT,* "As I See It," Jan. 12, 1949, p. 4.

208 "has the talent . . .": Ibid., July 30, 1948, p. 4.

208 "Her one . . .": Brower, "The Roots of an Arkansas Questioner," p. 96.

208 "I keep saying . . .": *NAT,* "As I See It," Apr. 29, 1949, p. 4.

208 "As I . . .": Ibid., May 3, 1949, p. 4.

209 "Why in heaven's . . .": Ibid., Dec. 6, 1949, p. 9.

209 "the wedding party . . .": Ibid., July 1, 1949, p. 4.

209 "to improve . . .": *NAT,* June 19, 1949, p. 1.

209 "so I figured . . .": Ibid., "As I See It," Jan. 25, 1949, p. 5.

210 "Let's be careful . . .": Ibid., Aug. 8, 1950, p. 4.

210 "My two . . .": Ibid., Mar. 2, 1951, p. 2.

210 "I plead . . .": Ibid., Oct. 7, 1950, p. 4.

210 "One thing . . .": Ibid., Mar. 7, 1949, p. 4.

210 "a sort of . . .": Ibid., Feb. 28, 1946, p. 4.

210 "To tell . . .": Roberta Fulbright to W. J. Lemke, Dec. 8, 1949, W. J. Lemke papers, Series 2, BCN 2, F 25, Special Collections Division, University of Arkansas Libraries, Fayetteville.

210 "She is so . . .": Anna Teasdale to W. J. Lemke, Dec. 20, 1949, ibid.

210 "This little . . .": *NAT*, "As I See It," Nov. 7, 1950, p. 4.

211 ". . . believes strongly . . .": Read, "Arkansas' Most Noted Woman Publisher," p. 3.

211 ". . . altogether we hate . . .": *NAT*, "As I See It," May 10, 1949, p. 4.

211 "more Southern . . .": Ibid., May 6, 1947, p. 4.

211 "I have a friend . . .": Ibid., Dec. 16, 1948, p. 10.

212 "Chocolate and Lace": Roberta Fulbright, *Sea (See) Foam and Dashes of Spray* (1949), page unnumbered.

212 "Real and Ethereal": Ibid.

213 "Women": Ibid.

214 "Do Not Be Old": *NAT,* "As I See It," Dec. 17, 1951, p. 4.

214 "I have spread . . .": Ibid., June 28, 1949, p. 4.

CHAPTER XIII: THE WOMEN ORGANIZE

215 "There is a peculiar . . .": *NAT,* "As I See It," June 23, 1949, p. 4.

216 As you know . . . : Roberta Fulbright to Arkansas newspaper women, undated, W. J. Lemke papers, Series 2, BCN 2, F 21, Special Collections Division, University of Arkansas Libraries, Fayetteville.

217 I quite agree . . . : Aline Murray to Roberta Fulbright, ibid., June 4, 1949.

218 Indeed, I think . . . : Mary Louise Wright to Roberta Fulbright, ibid., no date.

218 I'm fully . . . : Esther Bindursky to Roberta Fulbright, ibid., May 31, 1949.

218 Your proposal . . . : Margaret Woolfolk to Roberta Fulbright, ibid., May 30, 1949.

218 "I am so delighted . . .": Maude Duncan to Roberta Fulbright, ibid., June 9, 1949.

218 "a tiny piece . . .": *NAT*, "As I See It," July 27, 1945, p. 4.

219 "Other organizations . . .": Arkansas Press Association, *Arkansas Publisher* (June 1949), p. 4.

219 "Under the leadership . . .": Ibid.

219 "I have great . . .": *NAT,* "As I See It," June 28, 1949, p. 4.

219 . . . The Arkansas newspaper . . . : Ibid., June 23, 1949, p. 4.

220 "Women have . . .": Ibid., Oct. 5, 1949, p. 4.

220 "Arkansas newspaper women . . .": Arkansas Press Association, *Arkansas Publisher* (Feb. 1950), p. 7.

220 "Thank you . . .": Ibid., (Mar. 1950), p. 6.

220 "But I . . .": *NAT,* "As I See It," Mar. 21, 1950, p. 4.

220 ". . . (they) got . . .": Ibid., Feb. 21, 1950, p. 4.

221 "About the only . . .": Ibid., Sept. 13, 1950, p. 4.

221 "Unfortunately . . .": Ibid., June 14, 1950, p. 4.

221 "I have to beg . . .": Ibid., July 1, 1950, p. 4.

221 I am about . . . : Ibid., July 12, 1950, p. 4.

222 I want to express . . . : Ibid., July 21, 1950, p. 4.

222 "pre-empted . . .": John Erickson, telephone interview, Mar. 23, 1995.

222 Politically . . . : *NAT,* "As I See It," July 24, 1950, p. 4.

222 It looks now . . . : Ibid.

222 "We saw several . . .": Ibid., Aug. 8, 1950, p. 4.

223 "The primary . . .": Ibid., Aug. 3, 1950, p. 9.

223 "We have thought . . .": Ibid., Oct. 21, 1950, p. 4.

223 "I'll take just . . .": Patty Fulbright Smith, interview, Jan. 12, 1995.

223 "I was brought up . . .": *NAT,* "As I See It," Nov. 1, 1950, p. 4.

223 "I really believe . . .": Ibid., Feb. 17, 1947, p. 4.

223 "I am a glowing . . .": Ibid., Jan. 4, 1949, p. 4.

223 "Growing old . . .": Ibid., Mar. 19, 1949, p. 4.

224 "Tonight I saw . . .": Ibid., Aug. 22, 1950, p. 4.

224 Seldom have I . . . : Ibid., Sept. 8, 1949, p. 4.

224 "What fools . . .": Roberta Fulbright to W. J. Lemke, Jan. 5, 1945, W. J. Lemke papers, Series 2, BCN 1, F 10, Special Collections Division, University of Arkansas Libraries, Fayetteville.

224 "I've lived long . . .": Coffin, *Senator Fulbright,* p. 38.

224 The days of my . . . : *NAT,* "As I See It," Feb. 24, 1951, p. 4.

225 "I hope . . .": Ibid., Apr. 17, 1951, p. 4.

225 "and those of . . .": Arkansas Press Association, *Arkansas Publisher* (Jan. 1951), p. 8.

225 "The clasping . . .": *NAT,* "As I See It," Feb. 24, 1951, p. 4.

225 Even our president . . . : Ibid., Mar. 2, 1951, p. 2.

225 "We are having . . .": Ibid., Apr. 21, 1951, p. 4.

226 "has a hard core . . .": Ibid., Nov. 4, 1948, p. 9.

226 "I feel I must . . .": Ibid., May 23, 1951, p. 4.

226 ". . . we women . . .": Ibid., Aug. 24, 1951, p. 4.

226 "I want to put . . .": Ibid., Apr. 25, 1950, p. 13.

227 She was pictured: *NAT,* Feb. 15, 1952, p. 2.

227 ". . . I'm thankful . . .": Ibid., "As I See It," Feb. 19, 1952, p. 2.

228 One must above all . . . : Ibid., May 21, 1952, p. 4.

228 ". . . I am told . . .": Ibid., Dec. 29, 1951, p. 4.

CHAPTER XIV: THE PASSING OF THE TORCH

229 "The column . . .": *Arkansas Gazette,* Jan. 12, 1953, p. 1.

229 "An editorial . . .": Ibid.

229 "Mrs. Fulbright . . .": Ibid.

229 At 78 . . . : Ibid., p. 4A.

230 She played . . . : *NAT,* Jan. 12, 1953, p. 1.

230 Western Union . . . : Ibid.

230 "I'm not sure . . .": John Erickson, telephone interview, Mar. 23, 1995.

231 "I had never . . .": Patty Fulbright Smith, interview, Jan. 12, 1995.

232 "The high point . . .": Gilbert, *Fulbright Chronicle,* p. 153.

232 Fayetteville and . . . : Arkansas Press Association, *Arkansas Publisher* (Jan. 1953), p. 7.

234 "was the kind . . .": Brower, "The Roots of an Arkansas Questioner," p. 96.

235 "I had no idea . . .": Ibid.

235 "She had more spirit . . .": Sen. J. W. (Bill) Fulbright, interview, June 8, 1992.

EPILOGUE

237 The plot . . . : William W. Hughes, "Evergreen Cemetery," *Flashback* 33 (Nov. 1983), p. 5.

237 I was born . . . : R. Fulbright, Lemke, *As I See It,* column dated Feb. 22, 1936, page unnumbered.

238 "All these things . . .": *FDD,* "As I See It," Mar. 24, 1936, p. 2.

BIBLIOGRAPHY

PRIMARY SOURCES

Interviews

All interviews are personal interviews conducted by the authors, unless otherwise indicated.

Ray Adams, Fayetteville, Arkansas, March 23, 1993.
Harry S. Ashmore (by telephone), Santa Barbara, California, June 24, 1993.
Judge Thomas Butt, Fayetteville, Arkansas, March 24, 1993.
Floyd Carl Jr., Fayetteville, Arkansas, February 20, 1995.
Morris Collier, Fayetteville, Arkansas, March 23, 1993.
Margaret Waugh Crittenden, North Little Rock, Arkansas, March 17, 1993.
Judge Maupin Cummings, Fayetteville, Arkansas, March 24, 1993.
Doug Douglas (by telephone), Fayetteville, Arkansas, March 22, 1993.
Bill Dunklin (by telephone), Pine Bluff, Arkansas, February 12, 1995.
John Erickson (by telephone), Atlanta, Georgia, March 23, 1995.
Roberta Fulbright Foote (by telephone), Miami, Florida, December 12, 1992.
Lucy Freeman, Newport, Arkansas, March 18, 1993.
Sen. J. W. (Bill) Fulbright, Washington, D.C., June 8–9, 1992, January 21, 1993.
Allan Gilbert, Fayetteville, Arkansas, September 21, 1992.
Sam Harris, Little Rock, Arkansas, August 26, 1992.
Maude Gold Hawn, Fayetteville, Arkansas, September 22, 1992.
Marion Hays (by telephone), Bethesda, Maryland, April 19, 1994.
Sam Hodges (by telephone), Little Rock, Arkansas, March 31, 1993.
Eloise King, Fayetteville, Arkansas, February 20, 1995.
Dr. Robert Leflar, Fayetteville, Arkansas, September 21, 1992.
Betty Lighton, Fayetteville, Arkansas, February 20, 1995.
Cone Magie (by telephone), Cabot, Arkansas, January 3, 1995.
Willie Oates, Little Rock, Arkansas, August 25, 1992.
Henryetta Peck, Little Rock, Arkansas, June 3, 1992.
Bill Penix, Jonesboro, Arkansas, January 24, 1995.
Sam Schwieger (by telephone), Fayetteville, Arkansas, March 22, 1993.
Patty Fulbright Smith, Little Rock, Arkansas, January 12, 1995.
Ed and Liz Summers, Fayetteville, Arkansas, March 23, 1993.
Kenneth Teasdale, St. Louis, Missouri, June 29, 1992.
Ruby Thomas, Little Rock, Arkansas, May 28, 1992.
Martha Twichell, Rothville, Missouri, November 3, 1995.
Richard Waugh (by telephone), Los Altos, California, March 9, 1993.
Bob Wimberly, Little Rock, Arkansas, May 26, 1993.
Betsey Fulbright Winnacker (by telephone), Columbia, Missouri, December 4, 1992.
Jamie Jones Young (by telephone), Searcy, Arkansas, March 31, 1993.
Suzanne Teasdale Zorn (by telephone), Minneapolis, Minnesota, February 22, 1995.

Letters

Jean Gordon, Little Rock, Arkansas, May 29, 1992.
Robert S. McCord, North Little Rock, Arkansas, March 16, 1993.
Donald Murray, Fulton, Illinois, March 22, 1993.
Connie Stuck, Tucson, Arizona, June 22, 1992.
John M. Wallace, St. Augustine, Florida, April 16, 1993.

Newspapers

ARKANSAS

Arkansas Democrat
Arkansas Gazette
Arkansas Traveler
Fayetteville Daily Democrat
Northwest Arkansas Times
Springdale News
Van Buren Press Argus

MISSOURI

Chariton Courier
Mendon Constitution

Special Collections Consulted at the Special Collections Division, University of Arkansas Libraries, Fayetteville, Arkansas

Papers of Senator J. W. Fulbright
Papers of W. J. Lemke

Public Document

Mont Nord and Washington-Willow Historic Districts. Prepared by the Fayetteville, Arkansas, Historic District Commission, for the National Register of Historic Places Inventory, U.S. Department of the Interior, undated.

Other Library and Archival Sources Consulted

ARKANSAS

Arkansas History Commission, Little Rock
Fayetteville Public Library
Little Rock Public Library
Washington County Historical Society

MISSOURI

The Friends of Keytesville, Inc., Keytesville
Missouri State Archives, Office of the Secretary of State of Missouri
State Historical Society of Missouri, Columbia
Western Historical Manuscript Collection, Ellis Library, University of Missouri,
    Columbia, Benecke Family, Papers; Military Papers of William Fulbright
May Bartee Couch, MBC Genealogy Publishing, Marceline

SECONDARY SOURCES

Books

Allsopp, Fred W. *History of the Arkansas Press for a Hundred Years and More.* Little Rock, Arkansas: Parke-Harper Publishing Company, 1922.

Brown, Kent R. *Fayetteville, A Pictorial History, A Timeless Epoch.* Norfolk, Virginia Beach, Virginia: Donning Company, Publishers, 1982.

Campbell, William S. *One Hundred Years of Fayetteville, 1828–1928.* Jefferson City, Missouri: n.p., 1928.

Coffin, Tristram. *Senator Fulbright: Portrait of a Public Philosopher.* New York: E. P. Dutton & Co., 1966.

Donovan, Timothy D., and Willard B. Gatewood, editors. *The Governors of Arkansas, Essays in Political Biography.* Fayetteville, Arkansas: University of Arkansas Press, 1981.

Fulbright, J. W. *Against the Arrogance of Power.* Tokyo: Nihon Keizai Shimbun, 1991.

Fulbright, Roberta. *As I See It,* compiled by W. J. Lemke. Fayetteville, Arkansas: n.p., 1952.

——. *Sea (See) Foam and Dashes of Spray.* Siloam Springs, Arkansas: John Brown University Press, 1949.

Gilbert, Allan. *A Fulbright Chronicle.* Fayetteville, Arkansas: Fulbright Investment Co., 1980.

Hale, Harrison. *University of Arkansas, 1871–1948.* Fayetteville: University of Arkansas Alumni Association, commissioned by Board of Trustees, 1948.

Herndon, Dallas T., editor. *Annals of Arkansas, 1947.* Hopkinsville, Kentucky; Little Rock, Arkansas: n.p., n.d.

History of Howard and Chariton Counties. St. Louis, Missouri: National Historical Company, 1883.

History of Washington County, Arkansas. Springdale, Arkansas: Shiloh Museum, 1989.

Johnson, Haynes, and Bernard M. Gwertzman. *Fulbright: The Dissenter.* Garden City, New Jersey: Doubleday & Co., 1968.

Kincaid, Diane D., editor. *Silent Hattie Speaks: The Personal Journal of Senator Hattie Caraway.* Westport, Connecticut: Greenwood Press, 1979.

Leflar, Robert. *The First One Hundred Years: Centennial History of the University of Arkansas.* Fayetteville, Arkansas: University of Arkansas Foundation, 1972.

Meyer, Karl E., editor. *Fulbright of Arkansas: The Public Positions of a Private Thinker.* Washington, D.C.: Robert B. Luce, 1963.

Rea, Ralph R. *Sterling Price, the Lee of the West.* Little Rock, Arkansas: Arkansas Pioneer Press, 1959.

Smith, T. Berry, and Pearl Sims Gehrig. *History of Chariton and Howard Counties, Missouri.* Topeka, Kansas: Historical Publishing Company, 1923.

Waugh, Lucy. *Twilight Memories,* reprinted in *A Fulbright Chronicle* by Allan Gilbert. Fayetteville, Arkansas: Fulbright Investment Co., 1980.

Williams, Harry Lee. *Behind the Scenes in Arkansas Politics.* N.p., 1934.

Zochert, Donald. *Laura, The Life of Laura Ingalls Wilder.* New York: Avon Books, 1976.

Dissertations, Theses, and Other Academic Papers

Dew, Stephen. "The New Deal and Fayetteville, Arkansas, 1933–1941." M.A. thesis, University of Arkansas at Fayetteville, 1987.

Drummond, Boyce. "Arkansas Politics: A Study of a One-Party System." Doctoral dissertation, University of Chicago, 1957.

Kennedy, Mary Lynn. "Politics in Academe: Roberta Fulbright's Role in Her Son's University Presidency." Unpublished graduate essay, University of Arkansas at Fayetteville, n.d.

Tweraser, Kurt Karl. "Advice and Consent of Senator Fulbright. A Longitudinal Analysis of His Images of International Politics and His Political Role Conceptions." Doctoral dissertation, American University, 1971.

Published Sources

Arkansas Historical Association, *Arkansas Historical Quarterly,* Fayetteville
Arkansas Press Association, *Arkansas Publisher,* Little Rock
Washington County Historical Society, *Flashback,* Fayetteville

Periodicals

Arkansas Times. June 1986.
Life. "The Roots of an Arkansas Questioner." Brock Brower. May 13, 1966.
Time. January 22, 1965.

Photographs

Arkansas History Commission
Special Collections Division, University of Arkansas Libraries, Fayetteville
Washington County Historical Society
Harriet Fulbright
Nan Snow
Kenneth M. Snow
Suzanne Teasdale Zorn
Joel's Photography, Little Rock

INDEX